NINE
LIVES

MAKING THE
IMPOSSIBLE POSSIBLE

NINE LIVES

LIVES

MAKING THE
IMPOSSIBLE POSSIBLE

Peter Braaksma

Nine Lives: Making the Impossible Possible

First published in the UK by
New Internationalist™ Publications Ltd
Oxford OX4 1BW, UK
www.newint.org
New Internationalist is a registered trade mark.

First published in 2009.

Series editors: Troth Wells and Chris Brazier
Designed by Alan Hughes

 Printed on recycled paper by TJ International, Cornwall, UK, who hold
environmental accreditation ISO 14001.

British Library Cataloguing-in-Publication Data.
A catalogue record for this book is available from the British Library.

Library of Congress Cataloguing-in-Publication Data.
A catalogue record for this book is available from the Library of Congress.

ISBN: 978-1-906523-26-8

Dedication

Life may not be fair, but it is crucial we try to make it so.

This book is dedicated to those who did not get a fair deal – and to those that may still get exactly that, perhaps aided by the efforts of the contributors to this book.

About the author

Peter Braaksma (born in 1960) has worked as an editor, communication adviser and corporate journalist in the Netherlands and Britain. From Asian countries he contributed to various public and corporate magazines. This caused him to focus on human rights, the environment and (corporate) social responsibility, and to create *Nine Lives*. These stories reflect the endeavors of people who embody Gandhi's notion 'you must be the change you wish to see in the world'.

Acknowledgements

This book could not have been realized without the support of many people around the world. Naturally, the contributors come first, as the book is essentially theirs.

Rami Elhanan, thank you for that cup of coffee (or two) and pointing out the many things I didn't know. May your nation of peace-seekers continue to grow.

Bassam Aramin, thank you for your double efforts to see justice done. May peace prevail in every Palestinian and Israeli household.

Youk Chhang, thank you for your humility and understanding. May the mothers, fathers and children of Cambodia enjoy a prosperous future.

Chaeli Mycroft, thank you for your indomitable spirit. May your example remind differently-abled people everywhere to believe in themselves.

Harry Wu, thank you for your extra time and Chinese tea. May your work, and the Laogai Museum, contribute to greater respect for human rights in China.

Oscar Arias Sánchez, thank you for being a peacemaker. May the Arms Trade Treaty help towards a safer and more honorable world.

Sompop Jantraka, thank you for your generosity. May your unstoppable work for girls, boys and families succeed throughout the Mekong region.

Malalai Joya, thank you for your time and above all your courage. May the people of Afghanistan overcome the 'enemies of happiness'.

Monireh Baradaran, thank you for your hospitality – and the Iranian meal. May the people of Iran find their way to reconciliation and civil rights.

Second, in alphabetical order by country, I would like to thank all staff at the supporting or sympathizing organizations and all those who have helped as – appointed or unappointed – proofreaders, critics and providers of advice and suggestions.

Afghanistan / Spain: Eugenia Garcia Raya of the Spanish Commission for Aid to Refugees (CEAR), the Association for Human Rights of Spain (APDHE) and the Revolutionary Association of the Women of Afghanistan (RAWA).

Cambodia: Staff at the Documentation Center of Cambodia and the Tuol Sleng Museum; Lisa Som (Royal Secretariat of Cambodia).

China / United States: Kirk Donahue and staff at the Laogai Research Foundation and the China Information Center.

Costa Rica: Katherine Stanley of the Presidential Office and staff members Alejandra Valderrama, Ana Yancy Espinoza and Felicia Ramírez Agüero of the Arias Foundation for Peace and Human Progress.

Iran / Germany: The One Million Signatures Campaign.

Israel and the Palestinian National Authority: The Parents Circle and Combatants for Peace, with special thanks to the Palestinian NGO Wi'am, and Search for Common Ground (United States).

South Africa / The Netherlands: The Mycroft and Terry families and all staff at The Chaeli Campaign, Jesse Randelhoff, Lezanne de la Rey and staff at the Ocean View and Sinethemba Special Care Centers, with special thanks to Jessy Lipperts (South Africa) and the CSR Chicks (The Netherlands).

Thailand: Staff members Alinda Suya, Somporn Khempetch of the Development and Education Program for Daughters and Communities (DEPDC); volunteers Sarah Tilford, Jaymi Holt, and Graziella Ramponi; Rebecca Perham (United States).

Zimbabwe / South Africa: Never and Sibongile Chanengeta and Hope in Motion.

International: in alphabetical order of last names, I would like to thank Leonardo Alfonso (Colombia), Hannah Asomaning (Ghana), Pia Boonstra (The Netherlands), Dusan Gamser (Serbia), Indeevari Illangasinghe (Sri Lanka), Desi Indrimayutri (Indonesia), Elvira Helena Mendoza (Colombia), Mazdak Mirramezani (Iran), Intong Eric Monchu (Cameroon), Michael Sarcauga (The Philippines), Emma Tilquin of the Unrepresented Peoples Organization (UNPO, The Netherlands), Janine Tijhoff (The Netherlands), as well as those who chose to remain anonymous. Special thanks to Marjon van Opijnen (The Netherlands), who provided invaluable help on various aspects of the project. As the inclusion of various chapters depends on time and circumstance, some of the help from the people and countries mentioned may manifest in later editions. Thanks also to all at New Internationalist, especially Chris Brazier, Alan Hughes, Jo Lateu, Dan Raymond-Barker and Troth Wells.

Photo credits
Page **21**: Rami Elhanan © Circle of Bereaved Parents, Israel. Page **49**: Bassam Aramin © Combatants for Peace, Palestinian National Authority. Page **77**: Youk Chhang © Documentation Center of Cambodia, Cambodia. Page **105**: Chaeli Mycroft © AP Braaksma, The Netherlands. Page **129**: Harry Wu © Laogai Research Foundation, United States. Page **165**: Oscar Arias Sánchez © Casa Presidencial, Costa Rica. Page **183**: Sompop Jantraka © Development and Education Program for Daughters and Communities, Thailand. Page **215**: Malalai Joya © Defense Committee for Malalai Joya, Afghanistan. Page **245**: Monireh Baradaran © AP Braaksma, The Netherlands.

'It always seems impossible, until it's done.'
Nelson Mandela

Contents

Introduction
What if?

ANYTHING IS POSSIBLE! But who would think so in times of recession and depression? Half a century ago, writer JK Galbraith passed a bookshop on his way to New York's La Guardia airport. Not revealing who he was, he asked the bookseller about a book with a bright red jacket, his own 'disaster study' *The Great Crash*. 'That's certainly not a title you could sell in an airport,' the woman replied.

Even though the last few years are reminiscent of previous crashes and crises, let's hope that *Nine Lives* fares better. And not just in airports. This book presents the life stories of people who were confronted with insurmountable obstacles, opposition and oppression. Yet they make the impossible possible. Reading this book, you might think more lightly about the barriers in your path. As contributor Rami Elhanan says: 'If we can, *anyone* can.'

'Sorry, your call cannot be connected'
Snapshot 1.

'Can I speak to any of the human rights activists we talked about?'
Silence. But the woman at the other end of the phone hasn't hung up.
'No,' she says after a sigh. 'That won't be possible.'
'Why not?'
'They're all in jail.'

Compiling these personal narratives led me into some very unexpected encounters – and to anticipated meetings that never took place. 'Don't come,' someone said. 'If they find the two of us in one room, it will be too tempting to destroy us.' But arranging these meetings with remarkable men and women was not always so hard or risky. Most of them were able and willing to share their stories. However different, they each represent a cause that rises above them and the region they represent.

If there was only one *raison d'être* for this book, it would be that these stories deserve to be heard. Amidst today's information anxiety, the sheer speed and volume of news that snowballs from every corner of the globe, it is difficult to get any depth. Our mental and emotional disk space runs out, leaving us little time to uncover the underlying stories that gave birth to the news, the *why* and *how* of it – let alone take up a well-informed stance on each of them. Does it matter? Well, entire wars are being waged based on 'misrepresentations', to use a friendly term, so I think it does.

It helps us to understand more deeply if we learn about people's intimate personal experience. If you don't *feel* it, both the talking and the listening become meaningless. This is why these stories are told in the first person. It gives them a sense of intimacy, as if you were sitting across the kitchen table – which in fact is the way some of them came into being. They have not been summarized to meet the needs of fast-track information, as shortcuts often misinform. You get, as much as possible, an unadulterated experience. Consequently, paraphrasing a famous beer commercial, these stories refresh the parts that other stories cannot reach.

The phrases you will remember from the book will not be headlines – 'War in Gaza'; 'Arms Trade Treaty Postponed'. Instead, they might be memorable lines in which important messages are embedded: 'There is no future without making peace with the past'; 'Opportunity is there all the time, but often we don't see it'; 'Our global military expenditure is simply immoral'; 'You can cut the flower, but you cannot stop the coming of spring.' But now we're returning to soundbites again, when actually these statements gain in power when read in context.

So, why these nine individuals? Well, I was searching for people that matched three criteria. Are they *authentic*, is their cause *constructive*, and is their work of (global) *significance?* I was seeking out lives that embody Gandhi's famous phrase 'you must *be* the change you wish to see in the world'. Of course, it must be possible to have thousands of such encounters, and I have had the privilege of meeting many more than the nine lives reflected here. There were some that did not warrant inclusion, while other stories were set aside for a future book. While I gained access to some people quickly, in other cases it took seven months to fix a date – or multiple dates. It changed my agenda into a stand-by button. Impressed as I was by the odysseys of the contributors, their stories became my odyssey in turn, and may become yours.

The stories, though, are worth it. They are captivating,

'This way, please'
Snapshot 2.

At Phnom Chisor, in southern Cambodia, a young girl guides me to an ancient Angkorian temple. Her friends join us on the climb to the hill top that offers a panoramic view of the surroundings. But does she know where she is going? Why does she keep stumbling over rocks and bumping into branches? She knows the site well, as she grew up here, and she can almost find her way by memory and by touch. And that's exactly what she is doing. She speaks about the site from memory, as she is being blinded by a tick that has infected her eye. In developed countries, this condition is easy to cure at little cost. But, despite the changes that are taking place in her country, in Cambodia she will simply become blind.

---

confronting and uplifting. They demonstrate self-effacing honesty, resilience, courage, ingenuity. They show some people staying true to their beliefs, and others leaving cherished views behind forever to embrace entirely new ones. When it comes down to it, people from every corner of the globe have a similar decency and dignity. In their darkest hour, every person hopes to survive, to return to normal life, or to rise again like a phoenix. Ordinary people can accomplish extraordinary things. There is hope for the unrecognized, the suppressed, the underprivileged. Sometimes, that hope or last straw turns out to be... *yourself.*

The book functions as a platform for views that would otherwise go unreported. As Nelson Mandela says, 'it always seems impossible, until it's done'. It *can* be done and it *is* possible. Each of these nine voices was confronted with an urgent and inescapable need to dig deep, either to rescue themselves or to forge a fresh way forward for others. Cats are said to have nine lives; perhaps some of these contributors do too. In several cases, the only way out was by teaming up with former adversaries. Despite their trials and tribulations, they built bridges across their predicaments to a different future. Not only that, they made their cause public, as is evident from their activities and websites.

You may be familiar with a few of these names, some of whom I could only meet abroad or in exile. I spoke with Malalai Joya, Harry Wu and Monireh Baradaran in Madrid, Washington and Frankfurt respectively instead of Kabul, Beijing and Tehran. The other six chapters were created in the places where the interviewees live. Some simply call for recognition of their cause, others speak truth to power. As such, they reflect the challenge of *homo sapiens* to live up to its noble name, or claim the rights as enshrined in the UN Universal Declaration of Human Rights. *Their* rights are *everybody's* rights; *our* rights.

What they did and still do presents us with a mirror and makes you wonder: what if I had been in their shoes? How would I deal with questions without answers, problems without solutions? Where to begin, for example, when confronted with the question: What should be done with the former Khmer Rouge leaders? Youk Chhang of the Documentation Center for Cambodia feels it is impossible truly to punish them. 'How would they pay back two million lives? Should they die two million times? Live in hell for two million years? The crimes they committed are so grave that I don't know what punishment would be fair.'

Efforts to improve one's lot and that of others reflect a universal, innate and irrepressible urge towards human fulfillment that exists before laws, text books or permits. Together, these *Nine Lives* represent a microcosm of such efforts, and the resistance they encounter. It shows what the human race is capable of – its best and its worst.

Questions remain. *What if* poverty was an epidemic and could grab you this afternoon, drain your bank account and force you to live in a cardboard box tomorrow? *What if* trafficking and rape suddenly became contagious and you found yourself systematically abused, and crying out for help from a windowless cellar? *What if* freedom of speech was suddenly abolished and

---

Have-nots and will-nots?
Snapshot 3.

Landing in Kathmandu, Nepal, in 2004 as a volunteer teacher of English to a Buddhist monastery in Bodhinath and Little Angels Primary School, I notice something awkward. It is possible to run my shower for an entire day at no additional cost. But it represents a stark contrast to my immediate environment. Leaning against the outer wall of the guesthouse is a man that cannot even afford one bottle of clean drinking water – he is exhausted and ailing. Why is this life-saver in short supply in a country that has it in superabundance?

---

for an innocent remark the 'thought police' dragged you out of your home? Plausible? Possible? A person's greatest fear may be a knock on the door by a man in a three-piece suit; their greatest joy making friends with the enemy.

The snapshots above and the chapters that follow demonstrate that human rights are not abstract – and neither are missions impossible that are made possible. They're hands-on affairs. Born under a different constellation, I might well have been the subject of any of these stories. But on which side? It caused me to look into the mirror and ask: What if I had been in their shoes?

Any shortcomings of the book are my own.

Peter Braaksma

1

Cracks in the Wall

Introduction

LEADERS GATHER, SUMMITS are held and, time and again, people hope that peace negotiations will finally result in the handshakes that deliver the long-awaited settlement for both Israelis and Palestinians. But even in 2005, after Ariel Sharon and Mahmud Abbas got together and Israel withdrew from the Gaza Strip, tension and fighting continued, followed in 2006 by the Second Lebanon War and the bombardments of the Gaza Strip in 2008-9. There seems to be no way to end the conflict.

Many Israelis feel threatened by the fact that their country is surrounded by an overpowering majority of Arab nations that do not support its policies or its very existence on the map. Ever since 1948 this has meant that military and defense issues have played a major role in Israeli politics. The country's air force is the world's fourth largest after the United States, Russia and China. Foreign policy therefore weighs heavily even on decisions that simply concern internal affairs.

A state of siege and continuous mobilization has had a strong influence throughout Israel's history. Although the roots of this go back to the Ottoman Empire and the British Mandate periods of Palestine, the turning point was 1948, the year of Israel's independence. David Ben-Gurion, the country's first Prime Minister, has always claimed that in establishing independence 'Israel did not expel a single Arab'. But most historians now see clear evidence of the disaster that befell the Palestinians and the less glorious role Israeli troops played in causing this. Only about 150,000 Palestinians remained where previously 940,000 had lived, in a land that their people had called home for centuries.

Even today, 50 per cent of Palestinians are still listed by the UN as refugees and in the West Bank, the Gaza Strip and East Jerusalem together there are 20 refugee camps – not to mention the Diaspora of millions of Palestinians in the region and the world at large. A third of the population of Jordan, for example, consists of Palestinian refugees and their descendants (1.7 million people). Naturally, over the past six decades most have integrated with Jordanian society. But where do they belong *by right* if not in the country they were expelled from?

Aware of the demographic consequences – will there still be a majority of Jewish people in our state? – Israel is most concerned about the Palestinian demand for the Right of Return, preferring to consider it non-negotiable. In international law, the Geneva Convention and UN charters however, this demand is normal and legitimate. Fears and hopes on both sides remain. After 60 years there is still no solution and thus frustration, clashes, intimidations and wars are almost unavoidable.

Over time there have been more and more people on both sides of the conflict who feel that solutions can no longer be expected from the Government or the policy-brokering of Americans, Norwegians or others. This has led to some unusual initiatives in which ordinary citizens have sought peace or come face to face with their 'opponents'. Despite the conflict and its obstacles, there are Israeli and Palestinian citizens who build friendships and lasting relationships. In some cases, this even occurs when they know that in the past they have fired at each other, perhaps even killing neighbors or family members.

On both sides of the conflict, many people grieve for lost loved ones and in the entire region there is hardly a family that has not been affected. All families share loss, bereavement, pains, stress and anxieties about the future. One of these is the family of Rami Elhanan, an Israeli man who lost his daughter in a suicide bombing in 1997.

Tormented with anger and grief, Rami initially wanted revenge, to get even. But he asked himself whether killing someone else would release his pain. It wouldn't. It was clear to him and his wife Nurit that the blame rested with the occupation.

'Just like my daughter, the suicide bomber was a victim, grown crazy out of anger and shame. I don't forgive and I don't forget, but when this happened to my daughter I had to ask myself whether I had contributed in any way. The answer was that I had – my people had, by ruling, dominating and oppressing 3.5 million Palestinians for 35 years. It is a sin – and you pay for sins.'

A year later, Rami met with and joined the Circle of Bereaved Families, a joint Israeli-Palestinian organization. In March 2002, 19 members traveled to New York City en route to Washington DC and Boston. They came with a ceremony for peace and a plea to the world for help, calling upon the United States, the European Union and the United Nations to take concrete steps to end the violence by pressuring the parties to return to the negotiating table.

At times, the bereaved parents are considered 'unpatriotic'. But they would counter by saying that this is the most patriotic thing they can do. The Circle of Bereaved Families bears a message of dialogue and coexistence. Part of Rami's argument relates to the words of former Prime Minister Ehud Barak. 'He said: "There is no-one to talk to," when returning from talks at Camp David. And so, there is nothing to talk about, and we don't have to give up anything. Most Israelis agreed, and most Israelis never saw the other side. They never understood the anger of the Palestinians, not the pain… not the story… not the narrative… nothing.'

When, after 37 years of humiliation without any democratic rights, Palestinians started to bite back in the First Intifada, most Israelis were overwhelmed and shocked. Suicide bombers took people completely by surprise. Many could not understand how someone could kill himself and little children.

'There was no explanation. From this fear came the anger. From the anger came a very strong public demand for a wall to hide behind.' And thus the Separation Wall was designed and erected. Rami opposes the Separation Wall but, more importantly, he is also trying to change the psychological wall of beliefs. An Arab proverb says: 'May the coffee always run in your house'. In Rami's Jewish household and office it runs like this: 'Help yourself to some coffee. I'll be with you in a moment.'

Rami Elhanan
Israel

'I am a Jew as my eyes are green... but the Zionist idea of "a land without people for people without a land" was terribly wrong and totally blind.'

Rami Elhanan (born in 1949) is a graphic designer from Jerusalem and is part of the Israeli-Palestinian Circle of Bereaved Parents. His 14-year-old daughter Smadar was the victim of a suicide bombing in 1997.

MY FATHER IS a Holocaust survivor from Auschwitz, who came to Palestine from a little town in Hungary called Kish Warde in 1946. He came from a family with nine children, but when he left after the Second World War, only two of his sisters had survived.

When my father came to Israel he joined the British Mandate police in the Old City of Jerusalem. During one of the early battles over the Old City in 1948 he was severely wounded, and when he was in the hospital the nurse that was taking care of him was my mother. She was from a traditional, highly orthodox Jewish family that had been living in Palestine for six generations. I was born in Jerusalem, and have four kids with my wife Nurit, who is a lecturer at Jerusalem's Hebrew University. This is my origin.

Our family embraced the ideals of Zionism. Not in the sense that we woke up to that every morning, but it was certainly the reason why my father came here after the Second World War. But my mother came from an ultra-orthodox family, and for them Zionism is not really something that they appreciate. But since she met my father, she left her religion behind and became very much like him. It was more like an ideology in the background, but not something to raise the flag about every morning. It was more a reason for being in Israel in the first place.

But yes, basically I am a Zionist. I am a Zionist in the sense that I deeply believe that the Jewish people, like any other people in the world, deserve their right to self-determination in their ancient homeland. Being Jewish is part of me. I'm a Jew as my eyes are green. It's a destiny and an identity that I cannot escape. It's because of my own history, my forefathers, my roots, and because of the fact that I feel a deep emotional connection to this people that was murdered and persecuted and victimized throughout history. Nevertheless, I believe that this huge and successful revolution of the Jewish people in the form of its national liberation organization, the Zionist movement, was accompanied by some great mistakes. The idea of 'a land without people for people without a land' was terribly wrong and totally blind.

Zionism: for a Jewish national home

'To secure the establishment of the Jewish national home, as laid down in the preamble and the development of self-governing institutions, and also for safeguarding the civil and religious rights of all the inhabitants of Palestine, irrespective of race and religion.'

This was the mandate the League of Nations gave Britain in 1922, based on the Balfour Declaration.

The international political movement of Zionism supported the re-establishment of a homeland for the Jewish people in Palestine. The movement was started by the Austro-Hungarian journalist Theodore Herzl in the late 19th century and was eventually successful in establishing Israel in 1948, as the world's first and only modern Jewish state.

Zionism is in part based upon religious tradition linking the Jewish people to 'Zion', a mountain near Jerusalem that came to represent the Land of Israel. According to Judaism, Zion is a land promised to the Jews by God. The modern movement was mainly secular, beginning as a response to antisemitism across Europe. In 1897, Herzl organized the First Congress of the World Zionist Organization in Basel, Switzerland, aiming at a political agreement with the ruler of Palestine. Up to 1917

Today, I feel a bit ashamed of being a Zionist. But to cut a long story short: Zionism was one of the greatest, most influential, most significant, and most amazing revolutions in the history of humankind. This is what I think, because it turned a religion into a nation. It didn't only change the destiny of just one nation, but of the whole Middle East. It swapped and moved the destinies of people in a way that only very few revolutionary movements have ever been able to do. And it created something out of almost nothing with a passion, a vision, and a success that was almost unprecedented.

The bad part of it was that the price was very, very high. The

---

this was the Ottoman Empire, and until 1948 it was Britain on behalf of the League of Nations.

In the 19th century, the idea of a return of the Jews from the Diaspora grew in popularity. Jewish immigration to Palestine started in 1882 with the arrival of about 30,000 Jews, mostly from Russia, where antisemitism was rampant. This continued, especially following the Nazi persecution in the 1930s. Palestinian Arabs resisted Zionist migration. There were riots in the 1920s, sometimes accompanied by massacres of Jews. Subsequent migration led to the 1936-39 Arab revolt.

The British were unable to resolve the conflict and referred the issue to the newly created United Nations. In 1947, the UN recommended the partition of Palestine into a Jewish state, an Arab state and a UN-controlled territory around Jerusalem. The Arab states rejected this, demanding a single state with an Arab majority. On 14 May 1948, at the end of the British mandate, the Jewish Agency led by Ben-Gurion declared the creation of the State of Israel. The same day, the armies of four Arab countries invaded Palestine. Israeli forces defended the proposed Jewish territory and conquered parts of the proposed Arab territory, leading to an exodus of Arab Palestinians. The war ended with the 1949 Armistice Agreements, which included ceasefire lines along the so-called Green Line (see box *The West Bank Barrier* below).

---

price was almost unbearable, both for Israelis and for Palestinians. The price of Jewish nationalism, ignoring the fact that there were other people living here, was due to a combination of ignorance, blindness – sometimes on purpose, sometimes due to naivety – colonialism, and patronizing European attitudes to this region. That was very common at the time, but the view of a 'land without people for a people without a land' was the essence of everything. I really believe that at that time they did not see that there were other people living here, and that when they bought the land – very legally – from the *effendis* in Beirut, they truly felt they were doing the right thing: saving their own people by buying land that was empty for the rescue of a dying nation. But the moment the first peasant was evacuated from the land that their families had been living on for hundreds of years, the armed conflict began. And we're still paying the price for that today.

There were only a few people that saw it, but there was a huge struggle between Zionism and the Bund, the Jewish socialist party. What is a Jew? How do you look at these extraordinary phenomena? Is it a religion, a culture, a nation or is it a political entity? All these things were so complicated. But still I believe that, given the history of the Jewish people, given the problems of these 2,000 years of Diaspora, pogroms and the Holocaust and everything, that the Zionist solution for the Jewish people was a necessity. It was vital for the rescue of the Jewish people and for the creation of the self-determination of the Jewish people in the form of an independent state. And not just any place; you couldn't do it in Uganda or anywhere else. There is a direct connection between my name Rami [short for Abraham], and the Abraham of 4,000 years ago. There is a reason why we are here – it's not out of the blue.

But at the same time a feeling of deep shame has arisen in me about what has happened since that time. And that shame relates to the price of the emergence of two national movements, the Jewish national movement in the form of Zionism and the

Palestinian national movement arising at the same time. They grew up together, so conflict was inevitable. We were doomed to clash! And the price of this clash is unbearable for both nations. I think that today, after 150 years of this clash, there is a way out. Not a way out that can give justice to everyone, for there is no such thing. But there is a possibility of opening some kind of chance of being able to live together without the political aspect of one state, two states, a hundred states... That really doesn't matter. The very first thing that should be done to get out of this cycle of violence is: stopping the occupation. That is the first thing and it is a necessity, stopping this reality of one nation dominating the other, one nation ruling the other and one nation oppressing the other. It is not Jewish, it is not moral and it must be stopped – the sooner the better. Theodore Herzl, the father of Zionism, said that 'oppression naturally creates hostility against the oppressors'. People in Jerusalem generally get on fine with each other. But the problems arise mainly in the Occupied Territories, where the oppression is felt most strongly.

A spartan society

I have fought in three different wars. In the first two – the War of Attrition between 1967 and 1970, and the Yom Kippur War in 1973 – I genuinely felt I was defending my country. But things changed during the third, the Lebanon War in 1982. You have to understand the process of growing up in Israel. It is different now, but it is still something that gets under your skin, something that you're not able to talk to yourself about and that only very few people can stand against. Being brought up as a young person in Israel, the army socializes you and prepares you for society; you live with the idea that it is an honor to join the army. It's an honor like it was in the military society of ancient Sparta. When the Jewish state of Israel began, it was a society that had to stand together very firmly and very strongly.

In 1967, when I went into the army, I was only 18, but I was anxious to go. It was right after the Six Day War. The army was sacred and the whole atmosphere was: if I don't go now, I'll miss the action! And it was something that was totally irrational, it was entirely behavioral. And when you came back from the army on Friday nights with the 'gang', people would talk about what happened to them in the army last week and what operations they were involved in. And when you were not able to participate, you were 'out'. And to be 'out' was the most horrible thing to be. It takes time to understand that sometimes 'out' is better than 'in', simply because that is the way in which you have grown up since you were 18. And there is a reason why they take 18-year-old kids to the army. The social thing, the gang, the group, is so vital, so important, that you are unable to give yourself any answers and you do not ask questions about anything.

There was a feeling that we were on the verge of destruction and needed to gather all forces in order to cope with it. In 1967, from my personal experience I can tell you that in May of that year I genuinely felt I was going to be thrown into the sea. Today I know it was not true, but at the time that was what I really felt. I still remember the sight of children digging ditches in the streets and putting rubber on the windows preparing themselves for war, and all the civilians disappearing from work to be at war. We were a *fully* mobilized society and it's something that gets under your skin. You cannot wipe it off and pretend it didn't happen. It did. It was a genuine feeling and a genuine fear.

The second war I fought in was the Yom Kippur War of 1973. It caused me to become completely detached from any kind of commitment and any kind of involvement. That war was a turning point for me – the first crack if you like – in the sense that I didn't get a uniform until the tenth day of the war, and as a reserve soldier I didn't even have a gun, whereas the normal standard is that you are equipped right away and you go to battle. But the tanks were not ready; there was no ammunition, no guns, no uniforms, and no food. There was nothing. We were driving by the 'chains of our tanks', the caterpillar of the tanks, and we drove all the way for 480 kilometers. But normally you don't ever do this: the tanks are transported to the battle on trucks. So going all that distance by tank told me something was definitely wrong in terms of preparing the army.

We were a company of 11 tanks and came out of the war with only 3. It really was a horrible war. And it was the first time I felt something was wrong. Not with the ideology, for that was still very much intact. But the people 'upstairs' were not as wise as I used to think they were. Leaders are not angels. This was my first understanding that leaders can not only be wrong, but sometimes they are stupid. And the outcome was that, when I came out of the army, I completely erased all my political commitments. I was determined to look only after myself and no longer had any interest in participating in elections whatsoever. This was the time of leaders like Golda Meir and Moshe Dayan. It was really a period of total disillusion.

Historically, it was also part of nation building and the necessary solidarity. But if you look at the history of the Israeli army, and the creation of the State of Israel, it was a terrible war and the price was unendurable. The price that was paid amounted to the lives of one per cent of the entire population. It meant that, from a population of 600,000 people, 6,000 were dead. Every house had lost someone! The role of the army was determined by a feeling that if we don't win this war, then we will be pushed into the sea, there will be another Holocaust. I didn't really know whether that was true, but you have to understand that that was the actual feeling, the narrative. We *genuinely* believed that if we didn't win, we would all die. It was the most basic of things and we were brought up with those slogans: we are one state, fighting for our lives after the Holocaust against the whole world. And in this way we were 'socialized' and it is still going on today. Today there are many more questions asked, but in my time no one asked any questions.

But during the Lebanon War in 1982 I began to feel that something was completely wrong. In 1967 the feeling still was that we were fighting for our lives. And in 1973 too, because we were definitely attacked. The main feeling then was that these were wars in which I was defending my family, no questions asked. But the Lebanon War was different in many ways. It was not a war against an attacker, it was not a war against an outside threat or imminent danger. It was a war to achieve political victories. I remember that when I was drafted on a Sunday night as a reserve soldier, my wife stood in the door saying: 'If you go, you won't come back.' She didn't say that because I would be dead, but because she would not *allow* me to come back. She felt it was irresponsible and that I should not go. I remember thinking to myself: 'What will the guys say, what will my fellow soldiers say about me if I don't come?' That was unthinkable. So I went on my way to the north. I was on a crew of armored vehicles and it was a very long drive until we got to Beirut, giving me a lot of time to think. This was one part of the equation. The other part was that this time I had two kids, which I did not have before. Therefore, in moments of danger I would think about that. And there were lots of moments of great danger out there. While before I had the feeling that I had to see, to touch, to do and dare and be part of it all, this time while on the move I felt smaller and smaller, because at home there was something to get back to.

The wall of beliefs
During the first leave from my time in Beirut, I looked around me in Israel and saw how everyday life was going on and people were having fun and sitting in coffee houses. It was like two completely different worlds altogether. And for the first time in Israeli society there was a huge debate about this war, about the whole necessity of it. The sacred ring of not asking questions was broken, the sacred ring of doing what you are told without hesitation. You ask yourself: What is it for? What will be the

outcome? What is the price to be paid and what are the limits of it? So when I got back from Beirut I saw things in a very different light. In Beirut itself it was another matter of agony and despair and the poverty of the Muslim side against the happily-going-on everyday life of the Christian side. The gap was enormous. So from that time onwards I began to feel different. It created the first major crack in my wall of beliefs.

At the time I was a graphic designer with my own office and it was the beginning of my professional life. I was so occupied with it that I couldn't look any other way. The Occupied Territories were not really a problem yet and the atmosphere was quite good. Although there were sporadic terror attacks, you could still go into the Arab villages, Palestinians were still working in Israel and the occupation of that time was not the same as the one we have now. It was quiet, things seemed to be normal and there was nothing to be alarmed about. The questions we asked, however, were big ones. 'Do we need the territories? How long will we have to live by our swords? Can we make peace with the Arab world?' The Palestinians were not the issue. That is, until 1987, when the First Intifada started. Then things began to fall down; the full price of the occupation began to emerge. And ever since the problem has remained.

The cracks in my wall of beliefs that started during the Yom Kippur and Lebanon Wars were followed by more cracks. But it is more like a slow erosion of everything that was once sacred to me. I started asking myself questions about Zionism, about the idea of 'peace for land', about the *kibbutzim*, about socialism – in short, about all the myths that I had grown up with. For the first time in my life I rejected these things. For the first time in my life, when I was 32 years old, I was asking myself basic questions about life. 'What is it to be a Jew? What is the meaning of a Jew? What is the meaning of freedom and democracy?' Things that people usually do not question. But it was an academic debate between me and myself. I considered myself to be an anarchist, totally outside of the system. The Yom Kippur period had caused a personal psychological crack; the Lebanon War created a political crack.

The loss of my daughter

In 1997, my 14-year-old daughter Smadar got killed during a suicide bomb attack. It was an intensely dramatic moment for my entire family. I was on my way to the airport when my wife called and told me she was missing. When something like this happens, a cold hand grabs your heart. You rush between friends' houses and hospitals, then eventually you find yourself in the morgue and you see a sight you'll never forget for the rest of your life. From that moment you are a new person. Everything is different. It didn't immediately influence my thinking; that was something that took time. It was an ongoing process, the move from total cynicism and anarchism, indifference and contempt for the political system to the kind of views that I have today – that took almost a year. It's not simple, because of who we were and the personal story and background of my family. When Smadar died, it was an earthquake. Not just because of the bombing itself, but because Smadar was the granddaughter of Matti Peled, the father of my wife. Matti Peled was a general, a war hero in 1948, a company commander who got badly wounded and was considered to be a hero. Then he stayed on in the army and he was one of the general staff of the 1967 war as head of logistics. He was considered to be a military genius, a very able person.

When Matti Peled got out of the army in 1969, he left everything and started an academic career from scratch. He became a professor in Arab literature at Tel Aviv University. His PhD was about the great Egyptian writer Naguib Mahfouz and he became very prominent. But he was also one of the first Israelis that raised the flag of two states and argued that we should come to understand each other – not to continue living by fighting, tanks, airplanes and military power, but by our ability to create connections with our neighbors. That is why he became a professor of Arabic, and that is why he became a political activist. He became the first Israeli chair of a joint Jewish-Arab party in the Knesset (the Israeli parliament), the Progressive Party for Peace, which no longer exists today. In any event, a joint Jewish-Arab party is very uncommon. But Matti Peled was a much-admired figure, because he was as straight as an arrow. He said what he felt, and he said what he believed. He was from the inner circle of Israeli nobility. His personal friends included Yitzhak Rabin and Ezer Weizmann, Arik Sharon and this was his milieu, the world in which he grew up. But he turned his back on them, after which he was considered by many Israelis to be a traitor. He was one of the first Israelis that met with Yasser Arafat in Tunis back in 1983, this famous meeting.

But when Matti Peled died in 1995, his funeral was an outstanding event. The coffin was carried by six generals of the Israeli army. Behind the coffin were Prime Minister Yitzhak Rabin, President Ezer Weizmann, and all his friends, including his Palestinian friends, all the unbelievable colors of the rainbow of this land, even people who before had turned their backs on him. It was a huge event, with thousands and thousands of people upon the hill. Similarly, it was an earthquake when the granddaughter of this man – my daughter Smadar – died. Her funeral was like his funeral, as she was buried beside him, with the same presence of people from both sides, Israelis, Palestinians, Muslims, Christians. It generated a huge public interest, especially as we publicly announced that we blamed the Government of Israel. This was unprecedented, it had never happened before. It created a lot of noise. Of course, the suicide bomber did do it, but we blame the occupation and oppression that creates such misery.

Another part of the interest that was generated was the fact that my wife Nurit, daughter of Matti Peled and Smadar's mother, was a personal friend of Bibi Netanyahu at that time. They had studied in the same class at school. He called us and I didn't want to speak to him, but Nurit asked him: 'What have you done?!' And this question 'what have you done?!' made the front page of every newspaper. So all this started a long journey that took almost a year, a journey that changed my indifference. I couldn't go back any more to my life as if nothing had happened. I could no longer pretend that I was still the same person. I had completely changed, while I was dragging myself to work every morning.

Matti Peled

'The Palestinian People will hold in the highest respect the memory of Matti Peled, for his effective role in extending bridges of understanding and coexistence between the two Peoples.'
Yasser Arafat, President of the Palestinian National Authority,
in a message read at Peled's funeral

The life of Mattiyahu ('Matti') Peled (1923-1995) is symbolic of the Israeli-Palestinian conflict. Having been a Major-General in the Israeli Defense Forces and a scholar of Arabic Language and Literature, Peled became a leading proponent of dialogue with the Palestine Liberation Organization (PLO) and of withdrawal from the Occupied Territories.

Together with Yitzhak Rabin, the young Peled was among the militia officers who became the backbone of the newly founded Israeli Defense Forces in 1948. The two were to maintain a lifelong contact. As the military commander of the Jerusalem region following the 1948 war, Peled participated in a single project of resettling Palestinian refugees, a marked exception to the Government policy of rejecting outright the return of Palestinian refugees.

During the half-year-long Israeli occupation of the Gaza Strip following the 1956 Sinai War, Peled served as the military commander of Gaza. It was a turning point in his life. Peled found himself 'lord and

Even today I still have moments of hatred and revenge. This is something that is very essential to understand: it's an ongoing process of making choices. Every morning you get up, after a long and sleepless night, and you choose. You choose to overcome your anger, to go this way and not the other. And this choosing process is not easy. I fully understand the people who are angry. I can understand where it comes from, and I can understand it from both sides. The only question is: what do you do with this anger? So after about a year, Nurit joined

---

master' over hundreds of thousands of Palestinians – all without his knowing their language, culture or way of life. It led him to decide to study Arabic and to the idea that Jews and Arabs sharing a single country should know each other's language.

In 1975, Peled was one of the founders of the Israeli Council for Israeli-Palestinian Peace, which called for Israeli withdrawal and the creation of an independent Palestinian state in the Occupied Territories, Jerusalem being shared between them. Peled took a leading role in meeting with PLO leaders. He and other Israelis first met with PLO senior official Issam Sartawi in 1976. Peled kept his comrade-in-arms Rabin informed. Rabin, however, would never send a return message. 'That would be negotiating with the PLO and I will never do that.'

In 1984, Peled was also one of the founding members of the Jewish-Arab Progressive List for Peace. With his 'academic lectures' in the Knesset (the Israeli parliament), he sought to advance a dialogue of mutual recognition and respect between Israelis and Palestinians. In 1993, he took part in forming Gush Shalom, the Israeli Peace Bloc. At first sharply critical of Rabin for severe human rights violations, he later warmly congratulated him for his handshake with Arafat on the White House lawn. Peled's funeral brought together peace activists and former generals. Messages of condolence were read from both the Israeli Government and PLO Chair Arafat.

---

a group of mothers that was united against the presence of the Israeli forces in southern Lebanon. They held demonstrations in front of the President's House to put pressure on Israel to withdraw from Lebanon. And while I was continuing my work as a graphic designer, in the evening I brought them some food, but also to support and protect them, for the drivers passing them were calling them 'whores' and other bad names. And every night, like clockwork, there was a man standing there, a big man with a 'kippah', the traditional head cover honoring God. And I immediately stereotyped him as a fascist and someone who eats Arabs for breakfast. His name was Yitzhak Frankenthal.

We started talking and he told me a story of how he had lost his son, who had been kidnapped by Hamas and was killed in 1984. And I suddenly remembered he was one of the people that had come to my house during the seven days of mourning for my daughter Smadar. I went crazy, asking him: 'How could you do it? Step in someone's house that has just lost their daughter and talk about peace and forgiveness? How dare you?' He then invited me to come over to meet with this group called the Circle of Bereaved Parents. Although I thought this group of people was crazy, at the same time I was a little bit curious. So I went to see them at a meeting in the house of President Ezer Weizman, who was in support of these gatherings. This was about nine years ago. I was standing aside, very detached, very reluctant and very cynical.

But as I watched these people coming down from the buses, I realized that there were many people that I knew, people that I used to read about in the newspapers, many people that I looked up to, heroes that I admired as an Israeli patriot. I had never thought that some day I might meet them or be part of them. They were political heroes, such as Yakov Guterman, who had lost his son in the First Lebanon War. He was one of the first Israeli bereaved parents who dared to stand in front of Begin's house [Menachem Begin, Israeli prime minister 1977-83] with a sign saying 'murderer'. He must have been a very courageous person to do so. Then there was Roni Hirshenzon, who was a very close and dear friend of mine. He lost two sons, but remained very active in the peace movement. They were there, very determined, and it was something incredibly moving, this whole movement of Israeli people who had paid the highest price possible, but still believed in peace. It was not a common thing to see. Together, Yitzhak and Roni, both of whom had lost their sons, had founded the Circle of Bereaved Parents in 1995. They decided that bereavement is a power that they can use to prevent more bereavement. From that day on, slowly but surely, the number of member families has grown to about 300 Israeli bereaved families and about 200 Palestinian bereaved families today.

Brothers and sisters in grief

During those first meetings of the Circle of Bereaved Families I saw something that was completely new to me. I was 47 and had never met a Palestinian before. And they were coming from the buses, people who had lost loved ones. They were shaking my hands; we were hugging and crying, and it was a very emotional moment. I remember seeing an old Arab lady coming down from the bus in a long black dress. And she had a picture of a six-year-old child on her chest. They lit some candles for the dead and then we sang both Israeli and Arab songs. I don't know how to put it, but it was like lightning hitting my brain. I am not a religious person, so I don't know how else to explain what exactly happened. But I wanted to be part of them and became part of them. It gave me a reason to get out of bed in the morning. This was the exact moment. And ever since it has been the most important thing for me. Sometimes it clashes with my work, because it takes so much time, effort and energy, which is a problem, because it consumes you. It has a price.

The Circle of Bereaved Parents has great potential and it is a very powerful thing, because no-one can deny the grief that happened to them. But our basic premise is that we are decidedly non-political. That is essential for us, for it allows us to talk to as many people as possible. Because the moment you are political, you are put aside or categorized into one rubric or the other. And we are also determined to be non-political because we don't want to tell the politicians where to draw the lines on the map or how to phrase the articles of the peace negotiations. We are focused on the common denominators between us and our Palestinian brothers and sisters. We won't tell how the occupation needs to stop. We want there to be a solution, but we understand that the only way out of this endless cycle of violence is stopping the oppression and stopping the occupation. This is the essential thing. We give lectures at high schools, we meet with so many people, and I think we are the only organization today in the spectrum of the peace movement that meets with so many people. Last year, for example, we gave more than a thousand lectures.

This ticket, to go into people's houses and to talk to people, is something that is unprecedented. The respect it generates opens many doors and enables us to do many things. It creates an argument and this debate is essential. For most of the people – Israelis or Palestinians – it is the first time in their lives that they see an Israeli person calling a Palestinian person 'brother' or 'sister'. It carries an enormous power.

And this is really the message: If we – Israelis and Palestinians who lost our loved ones – if we can still talk to one another, then anyone can. Meeting these people, listening to their message of forgiveness and healing, touched me deep inside. From that moment on, I devoted my life to conveying this very simple message: We are not doomed! It is not our destiny to keep on dying here in this Holy Land forever! We must break down this wall of hatred and fear that divides our two nations. We must turn our pain into hope. Because if we can persuade only one person, we might be able to save one drop of blood. And that's a lot! Since then my work with the Parents' Circle has become the center of my life, a sacred mission. There is a high wall between our two nations, a wall of hate and fear. Someone needs to put cracks in the wall in order for it to fall down.

The problem begins when you ask yourself: what is the next step? The doors begin to open, and we are talking, so now what? There are many people in the forum who feel that meeting, hugging and kissing is absolutely wonderful, but that it is not enough. And therefore there is a debate about the question: what is the next step after the hugging and kissing? What is the political stance that the forum should take, for example, in issues like Bil'in, where villagers protesting the Separation Wall can no longer reach their fields and orchards, and the Israeli Supreme Court even had to order the state to redraw the route. Bil'in has come to symbolize opposition to the Wall, in which the villagers have been supported by Israeli and foreign supporters every Friday for the past two-and-a-half years. Will we go there as an organization or as individuals? If possible, I would like to go there every Friday.

But I cannot tell the father of a dead pilot, who is a 100-percent Zionist and believes with all his heart that his son has died while defending our nation, that something is basically wrong with his beliefs. It is a very long road to take, from the place where he is to the place where I am. And yet, I fully understand it, because I have been there too. But I am not impatient about people who are not there yet. They will be one day. It is a process. Everybody will be there one day.

The meetings and lectures are also held in the Occupied Territories, always by Israelis and Palestinians together. It's essential to always be together; otherwise we cannot set an example. The Circle of Bereaved Families doesn't have a specific agenda; we don't even say that the occupation needs to end; we're only talking about a process of reconciliation. That enables a lot of people from different political camps to participate together. Most people are good people, but often ignorance is the main obstacle. I'll give you an example. One of the most important projects of the Circle of Bereaved Families is the Narrative Project. It is a huge project designed to allow people to tell their personal stories, their backgrounds, and their experience in their own villages. And getting to know and understand these stories is an essential part of the process of reconciliation. The highlight of it was an organized visit of the Circle of Bereaved Families to Yad Vashem, the Holocaust memorial, which was – I don't know how to tell you – unbelievable. I brought my own father over there and he said: 'If I hadn't seen it with my own eyes, I wouldn't have believed it.' There were lots of people going through it crying – it's a very emotional thing.

'This cannot be true!'

The next day we went to the ruins of Kubeiba, an Arab village that was destroyed in 1948. When we were standing there, the father of one of the Palestinians told the story of how the people there had been defeated and how in some cases women had been raped. One person who was listening said: 'This cannot be true! This did not happen!' This man really believed that it hadn't happened. 'There is no evidence of it anywhere, it's not written anywhere.' But he was ignoring the fact that the Palestinians were ashamed of such a thing, so they would not have recorded 'evidence' about that. This shows how big the gap is between the narrative and the belief of this man. He lost his own son in the army and he has to come quite a distance in order to appreciate the narrative of another person that suffered and to accept something that for him is an impossible truth. He can't live with it. The only way for that to happen is an ongoing process of coming to terms and realization.

We share with the Palestinians that we need to be able to live here together, and we need to stop killing each other. We share humanity and basic human rights values, we share basic emotional connections. We can understand how the experience is for each of us, because we have been through the same process. This is a start. And it is also a personal thing. One day I stepped into a classroom with a Palestinian friend and he said: 'I lost two brothers, but I gained a new one.' To me, that was an enormous compliment. It's a very personal experience. I don't divide people along Palestinian, Jewish, Muslim or Christian lines; I look at whether they are willing to pay the price of peace. These are 'my' two nations: the peace-seekers and the war-mongers. The nation of people who are willing to pay the price of establishing peace, and all the others, the nation of war-mongers.

This was also part of our message when we visited New York and Washington in 2002 with the Circle of Bereaved Parents. We had with us 1,200 coffins, representing the exact number of casualties on both sides. Our statement was: 'Better have pains of peace than the agonies of war', a phrase from a speech of Yitzhak Rabin. One of the problems is that there are so many people who have an interest in not stopping this conflict, and who have something to gain from it. And they range from peace organizations and peace activists to war criminals and arms dealers, including entire nations such as the United States. There simply are so many people who have a vital interest in the continuation of the conflict and who will even inflame it.

The United States is the only nation with the ability to coerce and influence Israeli policy. But it doesn't. And right now I don't even think that Mahmud Abbas and Ehud Olmert will get very far. I am pessimistic and optimistic at the same time. In the short run I am very pessimistic. I think we're on the verge of a third Intifada and I think the pressure on the

Palestinian people is unbearable, due to the ongoing state of siege. I am afraid that the outcome of the current situation will be another outburst of violence. The ability of the Israelis to understand the situation is failing, because we're still trying to conquer something that we cannot conquer. This is the short term; I don't know about the long term. For the long term I always say: there is an agreement lying on the table. It can be signed; everyone knows exactly what should be done to stop this war tomorrow morning. Inside our hearts we all know, each in his own way, what is the one and only solution, and we have never been as close... And this agreement has many names: UN Resolution 242, the Beilin-Abu Mazen Understandings, the Camp David Draft and the Taba Draft, the Clinton Proposals and the Saudi Plan, The Nusseibeh-Ayalon Document and the Geneva Accords.

It may not be the best and ultimate solution, but it is the only one that is acceptable to more than 70 per cent of the Palestinians, the Arab League, and more than 70 per cent of the Israelis and most of the nations of the world. It has the widest acceptance of all. Of course there are parties that claim that it is not enough, that we need justice and this and that. Yes, in the end justice must prevail and equality must be achieved, including freedom for all and living together in peace. But the thing that needs to be done now, immediately, is stopping the occupation. I cannot make any prophesies about whether then everything will be OK. But if you go to a doctor and you have cancer in your leg, you ask: 'If I take off this leg, will I be OK?' He says: 'I don't know. I cannot make any promises. But if we don't, you'll die.'

We *must* stop the occupation. Not because of the Palestinians, but because of ourselves, because of our core values, because of our humanity. As I say in my lectures: every Israeli family, without any exception, including my own, has a son outside. There is a reason for it. The best people in the country are finishing their military service and leaving the country – you can call it the wandering Jew, you can call it many names, but they won't be able to live here. For how long?

The Wall of Shame

Some people claim that the Separation Wall that was started after the beginning of the Second Intifada in 2000 is stopping a lot of violence, a lot of terrorism, a lot of car thefts and so on. But that is complete and utter bullshit. It really is a wall of shame for the Israeli nation. Someone who wants to make an attack, like someone who wants to make peace, will always find a crack in the Wall. There are so many cracks in the Wall – I can take you right now to dozens of places where you can cross it without any problem. I do it every day, so suicide bombers can do that too. The reason why there currently are no attacks is not because of the Wall, but because we're in a very complicated political situation. What we need is not walls. We need bridges. Especially when you build this monstrous creature in the living room of your neighbor – it's not on the accepted border between the two territories.

Now that the Wall is being built, more and more hate and anger is being created. The Wall divides Palestinians from their lands, from their schools, from their doctors, from everything. The anger and rage it creates will make them hit back and there is no wall on earth that can stop the one determined suicide bomber who will go under it, behind it or above it. If they find a crack they will go into it and people who will lose their lives in a vicious suicide bombing will not be comforted by the existence of the Wall. The more we fortify ourselves, the more they will look for this inevitable crack. You confiscate land, you put the Wall in the middle of land for farming, and you hope that people will accept it? They will *never* accept it. It creates hatred, it creates agony, it humiliates people, it takes away their property and it means people who need to go to hospital have to drive so many miles to reach one. This Wall creates hate, and hatred is like water: it will find a way out. If they don't find a crack in the Wall here, they will find it in a kindergarten in Belgium. The short-term advantages of this Wall are nothing compared to the sea of hatred that it creates. I have no doubt in my mind that it will fall down like the Berlin Wall did, and like so many other walls did. For me it is a mission in life to put cracks in the Wall.

Dan Tirza, one of the designers of the Wall, said: 'The main thing the Government told me when giving me the job was to include as many Israelis inside the fence and leave as many Palestinians outside as possible.' The creation of the Wall is so inhumane, so

---

The West Bank Barrier

'It is difficult to overstate the humanitarian impact of the Barrier,' said a UN report in 2005. 'The route inside the West Bank severs communities, people's access to services, livelihoods and religious and cultural amenities.'

The West Bank Barrier is a 703-kilometer-long network of multi-layered fences and eight-meter walls. It is located mainly within the West Bank, partly along the 1949 Armistice Line or Green Line between Israel and Jordan. It may take until 2010 before it is completed. The Barrier follows a complex path, diverging from the Green Line by anywhere from 200 meters to as much as 20 kilometers. As a consequence, many Israeli settlements in the West Bank remain on the Israeli side of the barrier, and some Palestinian towns are nearly encircled by it. Only 20 per cent is on the Green Line.

Supporters argue that it is a necessary tool protecting Israeli civilians from Palestinian terrorism and that the onus is on the Palestinian Authority to fight terrorism. Opponents argue that the barrier is an illegal attempt to annex Palestinian land, with the intention of pre-empting final status negotiations, and that it severely restricts Palestinians who live nearby.

---

vicious and insensitive, and so stupid. There is a wonderful movie about it called *The Wall* by Simone Biton that people should see. In a way, it contains everything you need to know about the Wall. One scene makes people like me shiver. She is doing an interview with Amos Yaron, one of the general managers of the Ministry of Defense. She asks him basic questions: 'How many cubes of cement are required? What are the costs for every meter of the wall?' He answers them all. And when you look at it, you see he is a technocrat, a clerk. He measures the world by inches and by mathematical figures. You look at this and you feel: this is like Eichmann. 'This is the number of trains that should leave the station on time, on schedule, to get to their destination.' He is a clerk, and he doesn't reveal himself. Even while co-operating with her, he cannot feel the purpose of her questions, which are very, very clever. It shows the huge insensitivity related to this project that is supposedly securing my safety. It's all bullshit and it certainly doesn't protect my safety. I feel that it creates so much hatred, that it is so racist, so inhumane, that people will pay the price for it for years to come.

I cannot say I *expect* or *hope* that European countries and the United States will do something. I really *demand* that they do not stand aside. Every lecture that I give, I finish with this very personal note that is painful to me. I am the son of a Holocaust survivor. My father is an Auschwitz survivor and, 60 years ago, when they took my grandparents to the ovens, the world stood aside. And today, while these two crazy nations are massacring each other, with more than 5,000 deaths since the last eruption of violence, massacring each other without any sense of mercy, the civilized world is still standing aside. And not only that, it is also supporting one side almost unconditionally: Israeli policy, Israeli power and Israeli behavior. I am an Israeli and consider myself to be an Israeli patriot. But I hate this policy. I think it has a price and I am one of the people who has paid the price of that Israeli policy.

This ongoing support for Israel is actually damaging Israel. It is against the most basic Israeli interests. It endangers the very existence of the State of Israel. Standing aside when you see a crime being committed? You *must not* stand aside, you *must* have a point of view, you *must* stand up for what is right, you *must* stand up in support of basic human values. You know, there was a very tiny item in the newspaper yesterday about three Palestinian kids that were killed in the Gaza Strip, 10-year-olds. I don't think they ever reported this in any of the international newspapers. The killing of little children is something that is not to be forgiven forever. You cannot forgive the killing of the innocent. It doesn't matter whether they are Jews or Arabs or Christians or whatever. There must be a punishment for killing little children. And the best punishment ever is peace.

Israeli society is a victim society; it harbors victimhood. In one of the Summer Camps of Bereaved Families with Israeli and Palestinian children there is a poignant moment. It shows two children. One is Yigal Elhanan, who is 11 years old, my son. The other is Urud Abu Awad, a 13-year-old Palestinian girl. She says: 'Yigal lost his sister, I only lost my uncle. I cannot even think about his loss.' So he responds: 'I suffered a heavy blow once; they suffer it every day.' Nobody told them what to say. The ability of these two children to touch the essence of each other's experience, that is the heart of the matter. And it gives hope, because instead of growing into the conflict, they grow into the understanding.

I recommend you talk next to someone whom I consider to be a real peace combatant and a soul brother of mine. His name is Bassam Aramin from the village of Anata. Together with my son Elik, Bassam was one of the founders of the organization 'Combatants for Peace'. Bassam lost his 10-year-old daughter Abir in January 2007 (see Chapter 2).

2

The Closest Thing to the Heart

Introduction

'THE 40-YEAR occupation balance sheet: $90 billion wasted, 18,000 houses destroyed, 600,000 Palestinians spent time behind bars – shall we continue?' This was among the messages held up on banners during a protest march by a coalition of peace movements in 2007. Shauki Hatib, chair of the Israeli Arab Monitoring Committee that represents Israel's Arab citizens said: 'The Six Day War has already lasted 40 years – it is time to end it.'

Whether it's Oslo, Sharm el-Sheikh or Annapolis, peace and justice are like a mirage. Moreover, armed struggle in the 1970s, nonviolent resistance at the end of the 1980s, suicide bombings in the 1990s and the occasional Qassam rockets fired now from the Gaza Strip do not bring the Palestinians any closer to a solution. Periods of longing for peace alternate with times of revenge and retribution.

Meanwhile, settlers continue their illegal projects, the Separation Wall increases unrest, and east Jerusalem and its hinterland are being annexed. Palestinians only control 54 per cent of the West Bank; the rest has been taken by Israeli settlements. The remaining Palestinian land is divided into mini-enclaves by 570 closures – concrete blocks, mounds of earth and checkpoints. And opinions run deep, with roots in the past. 'As a child, I was in Buchenwald concentration camp,' says a retired rabbi waiting for bus 947 to Jerusalem. 'But the Muslims are worse than the Germans, because it is their religion to wipe us out. Are there any Jews in your family?'

Everyone seems to have a point of view 'for balance': 'Human rights are for Christians and Jews,' says a Palestinian taxi driver. 'For Muslims they do not exist.' His colleague: 'Why don't you send a letter to our President, Mahmud Abbas? Tell him to put a Nakba Museum next to Yad Vashem. For balance.'

'If you want readers to make up their own mind,' says an Israeli taxi driver, 'do tell them about 1967. We were attacked by three countries at the same time. We won. But what would have happened had *they* won? We would have been wiped out. Do put that in!'

'The story of Cain and Abel is repeating itself,' says a man who has been coming to Israel for the last 29 years. 'The Bible is my reference. The prophets of the Old Testament predicted this state of conflict. The only real solution is the Second Coming of the Messiah. Do you *know* your Bible?'

Several of Israel's 'new historians' are holding their country's past to the light, finding that many of its foundation myths are untrue. Some even claim that the myth of the War of Independence of 1948 is 'sheer fabrication'. Although 1948 was the glorious year of Israel's independence, for Palestinians it was a disaster ('Nakba'). The greatest hero of the Jewish War of Independence and Israel's first Prime Minister, David Ben-Gurion, is now seen by some as the architect of the ethnic cleansing of Palestine and as a war criminal. With a select group of Zionists he oversaw the 'judaization' of Palestine. For Israelis,

1948 was the climax of Jewish aspirations to have a state and fulfill a long dream of returning to a homeland. For Palestinians, it was a disaster whose shock waves still reverberate today. Thus, as historian Ilan Pappe says, 'the most evil and most glorious moment converged into one.'

The actions between 1947 and 1949 resulted in the expulsion of almost 800,000 people, the destruction of more than 500 villages and 11 city districts. The names of these villages have all been changed and their remnants and memory have been systematically erased or covered by nature reserves. In Golda Meir's words, the Zionists did not think of Palestinians as people, but as an 'inconvenient obstacle'. The books on the bookshelves of many Israeli households glorify the Israeli army. But beneath that lies the tragedy of the Palestinians. Israeli textbooks, curricula, media and political discourses have ignored for a long time the expulsion of the Palestinians, the colonization, massacres, rape, executions and the destruction of villages. It was snowed under by heroism, glorious campaigns and stories of moral courage. They speak about the settlement of newcomers, not about the dispossession at gunpoint and the expulsion of the indigenous population from the land.

Under attack from three sides in 1967, Israel occupied the Gaza Strip, the West Bank, Jerusalem and parts of Egyptian and Syrian territories. These became the Occupied Territories, in which Israel has perpetrated war crimes, killed, jailed and expelled thousands of people, assassinated leaders, inflicted physical and psychological torture and bulldozed thousands of houses. The list of human rights violations is long. The United States, Europe and the United Nations have done very little to end the agony, and criticism of Israel's policies is easily silenced as 'antisemitism'.

Reconciliation may be hard, but is there any other way? It requires recognition of the historical injustice that befell the Palestinians and acknowledging their 'Right of Return'. But even a Palestinian radio station wishing to start broadcasting under the name Resolution 194 (the UN resolution about the Right of Return) is denied permission to do so. The generation of displaced Palestinians that still have keys to their former homes, erased or reoccupied by Israelis, is gradually disappearing. But their descendants in the Diaspora – in Egypt, Jordan, Lebanon, and around the world – have grown in number.

Although the existence of Israel is based on a UN resolution, the state hardly acts in keeping with other UN resolutions, the Geneva Convention and the rules of engagement of any other state. Therefore, if today there still is a peace process with the Palestinians, it is arduous, complicated, politicized and seemingly without direction. A similar view is reflected in the telling title of Tanya Reinhart's last book *The Roadmap to Nowhere* and her view that 'saving the Palestinians also means saving Israel.' This is echoed by Usama Nicola, youth co-ordinator at the Bethlehem-based Palestinian NGO Wi'am ('Cordial Relationships'): 'Don't go away becoming pro-Palestinian. That will only add to the conflict. Be pro-*justice*.'

Nobel laureate Albert Einstein was one of Israel's greatest supporters. His position of half a century ago still holds a message for today. He preferred to 'see a reasonable agreement with the Arabs based on living together in peace [rather] than the creation of a Jewish state.' He wrote to Chaim Weizmann, Israel's first President: 'If we do not succeed in finding the path of honest co-operation and coming to terms with the Arabs, we will not have learned anything from our 2,000-year ordeal and will deserve the fate which will beset us.' Prime Minister Ben-Gurion asked Einstein in 1952 whether he would be President of Israel. He declined. 'The most important aspect of Israel's policy must be our ever-present, manifest desire to institute complete equality for the Arab citizens living in our midst. The attitude we adopt toward the Arab minority will provide the real test of our moral standards as a people.' One current member of this Arab minority is Bassam Aramin.

Bassam Aramin
Palestinian National
Authority

'We will double our efforts to work for peace.'

As a young man, Bassam Aramin (born in 1968) served a seven-year prison sentence in Hebron for attacks on Israeli Defense patrols. In 2007, his daughter Abir died when shot by the border police. Ever since, Bassam has been seeking justice. He works at the National Archives and is co-founder of Combatants for Peace.

WHEN I WAS young and still throwing stones, there was no chance even to speak to anyone. But now I can take my children to some places, visit my Israeli friends in Tel Aviv and other cities, so that they can discover that other Israelis exist.

As a little boy, I lived in a village called Saeer near Hebron on the West Bank and I went to school with my friends. I remember myself and most other children struggling against the occupation. But we did not understand what it meant and we had no idea of fighting for a Palestinian state. We only wanted those people who were occupying our area to leave, so that we could play. There were armored vehicles and armed patrols all the time in the area of Hebron and Zakariyya village and we always knew when seeing these patrols that we must escape and run. Because if they caught you, even when you were playing in the streets, they beat you. Why? We didn't know. The moment they saw Palestinians they got crazy.

Then, one day we found a way of making them even crazier. Without our fathers and mothers knowing, we decided to take clothes with red, black, white and green colors and cut them into pieces to sew Palestinian flags. In the middle of the night we looked for the tallest trees and raised the flags on the tree tops. Every night we did this and a game of cat and mouse, like

Tom and Jerry, began. The patrolling soldiers got so angry with us that finally they cut down all the trees around the school. Of course, we soon realized that our flags made no difference whatsoever. The soldiers were still coming.

'Who are these people?' we asked ourselves. 'What do they want?' I asked my parents. They could only say: 'They want to occupy us.' 'Why?' 'We don't know.' At school I did not ask these questions, because we had been warned never to ask about it.

Nakba

The current situation of the Israeli-Palestinian conflict is inextricably bound to the events of 1947-49, a period that most Palestinians refer to as 'Nakba' ('disaster'). The last six months of the British Mandate of Palestine, the founding of the State of Israel and the ensuing Arab-Israeli War led to an exodus of Palestinian Arabs. As historian Benny Morris puts it: 'The refugee problem was caused by attacks by Jewish forces on Arab villages and towns and by the inhabitants' fear of such attacks, compounded by expulsions, atrocities, and rumor of atrocities – and by the crucial Israeli Cabinet decision in June 1948 to bar a refugee return.'

By 1951, the United Nations estimated that 711,000 Palestinian refugees existed outside Israel, with about a quarter of that number remaining in Israel as internal refugees. Today, Palestinian refugees and their descendants number over four million people. For decades, the Israeli Government claimed that the Palestinian Arabs left because they were ordered to by their own leaders, who wanted the field cleared for the 1948 war. But Palestinian Arabs charge that their people were evicted at bayonet point. This view is also upheld by Morris, who feels that Ben-Gurion was correct in expelling the Arab population.

'Without the uprooting of the Palestinians, a Jewish state would not have arisen here.' New historians claim that it was a deliberate plan and, as Edgar O'Ballance puts it: 'Wherever the Israeli troops advanced into Arab country, the Arab population was bulldozed out in front of

No-one ever spoke about the occupation. So the only education we ever had about the occupation was the behavior of the soldiers and patrols themselves. Our education also never included the disaster, the Nakba, that befell the Palestinians in 1948. The Independence of Israel, yes, but never the Nakba.

As we became teenagers, we started throwing stones. It was child's play and I was 13 then. And there were still many things that we did not understand about Israel or about ourselves. But

---

them.' At times, even the Israelis themselves were troubled by this. In his memoirs *Soldier of Peace*, Yitzhak Rabin remembers the civilians of the city of Lydda. What was to be done with them? 'Ben-Gurion waved his hand in a gesture that said: Drive them out!'

Hundreds of villages were destroyed and urban neighborhoods emptied. Yossef Weitz, head of the Settlement Department of the Jewish National Fund (JNF) recorded in his diary on 30 May 1948: 'We have begun the operation of cleansing, removing the rubble and preparing the villages for cultivation and settlement. Some of these will become parks.' In 1949 at the Lausanne conference, Israel proposed allowing 100,000 refugees to return. But the Arab states refused to negotiate, as that would imply they recognized Israel's existence. Morris: 'The "100,000 Offer" was a classic of too little, too late.' After that, Palestinians trying to return home were regarded as 'infiltrators'. By 1954, more than a third of Israel's Jewish population (250,000 people) lived on absentee property or had settled in urban areas abandoned by Arabs.

The term 'Nakba' first appeared in George Antonius' *The Arab Awakening* (1938), focusing on the year 1920, the first armed protests and the effects of the Balfour Declaration which promoted the establishment of an independent Jewish state. The term was given its present meaning by Constantin Zureiq's book *The Meaning of the Disaster* (1948). Perhaps that meaning is best symbolized by the keys to their former homes that many Palestinians still carry. In their calendar, the day after Israel declared independence (15 May) is observed as Nakba Day.

we did know that the soldiers always showed up and disrupted our games. And one time I was clubbed by a soldier during a demonstration in the streets of Saeer. Another time I saw soldiers shoot and kill a Palestinian demonstrator. And once I saw how a soldier of the Israeli Defense Forces fired six bullets into the legs of an elderly Palestinian farmer, even though he was simply working on his land. He fell to the ground and was screaming in pain. All this happened in Saeer and I will never forget it.

One day there was a demonstration with banners and people shouting for 'autonomy'. I asked someone what it meant. 'It means self-control,' he said. 'We don't want the Jews to control us.' And I began to realize that raising flags and throwing stones wouldn't make any difference. So, fortunately or unfortunately, some of us found some weapons that had been left behind in the war of 1967. Two Kalashnikovs, two grenades and a small gun. They had been left behind by the departing Jordanian army. I remember saying to the other boys: 'From tomorrow onwards there will be nothing named Israel any more. We will kill all of them.' At that time I was only 16 and I really believed that. We then brought the guns to Hebron. A few times we fired the Kalashnikovs at Israeli soldiers, but no-one got hurt. After a while, my friends did not allow me to come along, because I have a limp due to a bout of polio when I was young. But the fourth time we tried this, the soldiers came after us. Even though I didn't fire a gun myself, I was arrested with my two friends. I could not run, so they caught me.

The next moment I was in Hebron prison. Life in prison changed me from playing childlike games to an adult and a freedom fighter. But I also started to learn about my own history and that of the Palestinians, the Israelis and the Jews. And why things were the way they were. Still, I was full of anger and hatred toward the Israelis. But I also learned about the Holocaust, which started a process of feeling more sympathetic toward the Jews. In 1986, while in prison, I saw a film about the Holocaust, *Schindler's List*.

Sympathy for oppressors

Watching the film was a defining moment in my life. At the beginning of the film I said to myself: 'Why did this Hitler not kill all the Jews? For then they would not have been here to suppress me!' But after a while I found myself crying when seeing these defenseless people, without clothes. I saw bulldozers, poison gas and executions in which the Jews just stood there, waiting for their death. I saw more films. In some they were buried alive, in others they were going to the gas chambers.

That night, I could not sleep. But I did not want any other prisoner to see me crying, because they said: 'What is the matter with you? Crying for the people who lock you up and hurt you?' But at that moment I didn't think of them as Israelis, but as human beings, even while I was still angry at them. And I also wondered why the people in the film did not do anything, while they knew they were about to die. I felt I wanted to enter the movie and fight back!

While thinking about this, I heard the noise of the keys from the jailer. He said to me: 'Hey, wake up! Don't sympathize with me!' But in spite of that I started to understand why these Jews are such aggressive people. It seems that for every Palestinian child there are two or three hundred troops, curfews... Why? Sometimes there are airplanes, sometimes helicopters... Why? And I realized that the Jewish people were like this because they paid such a price in the Holocaust. But at the same time I asked myself: 'Why us? It is not the Palestinian people that did the Holocaust to them!' And I have also read stories that there were Muslims that gave documents to Jews to protect them from deportation and who refused to persecute them during the time of the Nazis. There are many stories of Muslims in Europe and North African countries that risked their lives to save Jews during the Second World War. And now we are here. It's an incredible paradox. Why?

Part of the answer is that many Israeli politicians learned something from Nazism, because they act the same unto the Palestinians as they experienced under the Nazis. They took it as an example. Instead of saying that it was forbidden to ever do something like that again, they practice it. Most Israeli people know that during the Holocaust six million Jews were killed by Hitler's regime and how they were treated in the ghettos. But when I read about this and look at the suffering of the Palestinians, it's the same! There were many things that I knew about the Holocaust that I later witnessed in the Occupied Territories in real life.

In fact, before I was released from Hebron prison, I experienced something on 1 October 1987. We were waiting for our lunch and suddenly more than one hundred soldiers entered our section, number 120. They were masked and carried clubs. We were only kids of 13 to 19 and they started searching every room. Next, they commanded us to undress and to run past lines of soldiers blindfolded. The soldiers were lined up all the way from our rooms to the courtyard and each of us had to pass through these rows and was beaten again and again. Before it was my turn, I remembered the film. And I thought about my anger about the fact that the Jews in the film did not struggle, while knowing that they were going to die. I was in the last room and the distance in front of me was more than 60 meters. I started to shout: 'Nazis! Animals!' Things like that. And I found that the anger made me very strong. Because of the blindfold I didn't see them. But more important, because of my anger I didn't feel the blows of their sticks.

After it finished and the men had gone, I asked the jailer, a settler from Kiryat Arba: 'Why, just tell me why these men were here?! We are just kids and this is our fate?' The man was known to be harsh toward us prisoners. He said: 'No, no, no. They don't belong to the jail. They're from the army. It was just training.' So you can imagine what kind of training these young recruits are getting! They are only 18, 19 years of age and are being trained in this way.

War of the stones

Then came the First Intifada, from 1987 to 1993, sometimes called the 'war of the stones'. It was a mass uprising against the Israeli military occupation that began in Jabalia refugee camp and spread to Gaza, the West Bank and east Jerusalem. I saw three young people in Salem, a village near Nablus, who were buried alive with a bulldozer. It was filmed and broadcast on TV. I even spoke about it with the Israelis in jail; it is something they all knew about. Some of the people were pulled out of the rubble alive and were saved. Another thing that I remembered from *Schindler's List* is the scene where the camp commander has just been with his girlfriend. He goes out to the veranda and he sees a woman and kills her. She falls down and the people simply continue doing what they are doing. I have seen the same thing happening in Hebron and Jenin. A Palestinian woman fell down and the people did nothing because they were afraid.

About five months ago, Parents Circle invited me to go to Yad Vashem, the Holocaust Museum. I told them that I had already been in 1987 and that I didn't want to go. By this I meant my experience in prison. But it has made things more difficult. I cried for those people in the film, not in the actual situation. And I did not cry for my own daughter, because she is still in my heart and only sleeping. What the Israelis practice is as bad as what their killers did. This was my message at that time. But one day I will go to Yad Vashem.

About the Holocaust some of the Arabs say: 'No, it wasn't six million.' But I don't accept that attitude. I tell them: 'Listen, even if it was only one million or one hundred thousand, we're speaking about people, not chickens.' The German people said it was 'six million' and I said to them it was 'ten million'. When later, after my release from prison, I visited the city of Bremen in Germany to receive an international award for an unknown peace worker, I found myself defending the Jewish people there. I said to the German audience: 'You are the worst people I know and you have good reason to feel guilty. But the young generation cannot be held responsible for what happened in the past. They are just young people.' I got on very well with the Germans. They were good and very warm. But I also told them: 'Because of your unconditional support for Israel, you are actually killing Israelis and Palestinians, for we are fighting them because of the occupation. Support the peace,' I said. 'Don't simply support the Israelis or the Palestinians.' At any time, that is our message: 'Don't be pro any side, but be pro-peace, pro-humanity and pro-justice.'

In fact, I had a unique dialogue with one of my jailers, that settler from Kiryat Arba near Hebron. He was very extremist, as they all are. One day he looked at me and said: 'You look like a quiet man, too refined to be a terrorist. It's not good for you to be a terrorist.' Immediately I said to him: 'I am not a terrorist. *You* are! You are an occupier and I am a freedom fighter.' He responded: 'No, you are settlers, because the land belonged to the Jews. We came here to liberate this land. And despite the fact that we are providing you with food and job opportunities in Israel, you are killing us. Why?' I saw that he really believed that. But I didn't want to make him nervous. So I said to him: 'You know, every time you come here we can talk a little bit about this. Maybe you can convince me; maybe I can convince you, I don't know. We're just talking.' And he said: 'Yes.' For these talks I went to my room, I prepared some questions to ask him, some thoughts to talk about and how to convince him. After that, we talked for seven months. He came to understand the Palestinian situation and why we are fighting. He felt more supportive toward the Palestinians. 'When we don't talk,' he said, 'we can only eliminate each other. And at least you are fighting for your honor.'

He began to accept the idea of having two states in which we could live side by side and accept each other. It was a big success for me that I had been able to change his mind by nothing other than dialogue. At the same time, his colleagues still had the same reaction, continuing the same cycle of violence, bloodshed and conflict. But it made a point in my mind that was worthwhile to remember. Next, I started to talk with some more extremist officers. Some of them really became like friends to such an extent, that other officers warned each other saying: 'Don't speak to that man. He is very dangerous.' I was dangerous because I was able to influence their minds. I spoke many times with one of the most extreme men and surprisingly, we became friends. 'You know, it is very easy to punish any prisoner,' I said. 'What you do, is simply hit them. And for the Palestinian political prisoners it is forbidden to do anything like that.' So after this, if any Palestinian did anything that wasn't good, this Israeli man came to me, believing that I would punish my fellow prisoners. Because of this, we developed trust and understanding.

Today, I still strongly believe in dialogue instead of armed struggle. When I was released in 1992, I had come to the conclusion that war solved nothing. Also, the entire atmosphere was different, because it was the time of the Oslo Agreements. There was no Intifada and people had become tired of that. They were desperate for a solution. The shock of surprise was that the same torturers, the same killers and the same criminals that I had witnessed in Hebron and Jenin, that had attacked the Palestinian young, were now welcomed with flowers! When I saw that, I couldn't believe it. How could people go up to those soldiers, those criminals, and give them flowers? At the same time they were going to leave the Occupied Territories. It was a big message! Go home in peace! And it was a very moving experience, because deep inside, the Palestinian people do want peace and they do want to live with the Israelis in peace.

Shortly after that I got married to my wife Salwa and I wanted to have a normal life. We started a family, which made me very happy. We got six children and for four to five years I was working at the Palestinian Ministry of Information. I became active in the Fatah movement and attended some of their meetings. But in this period of time, before the Second Intifada, I became convinced that we would never succeed with armed struggle, because it would only continue the same cycle of violence. When I was still in jail I believed in the armed struggle, but after I was released I only wanted to speak about peaceful solutions.

Naturally, it is very difficult to sit down and speak with your enemy. But you have to make that choice if you don't want to go around wanting to kill all Israelis and all Zionist people. But who are they? Who is the enemy? Until then I had only met soldiers, settlers and prison guards. I had never met normal Israelis! And I oppose the killing of civilians. It is against my religion and my moral code. So some of us within the Fatah movement began to think differently, in a more liberal direction. We had many meetings and discussions. But I felt that I don't want to wait for our President or our ministers. I am not zero, but of account, and I must do something myself. I cannot do something against a tank by throwing a stone. I need a different courage.

'The most difficult meeting of my life'
You know, I have heard about Israeli *refuseniks*, those who refuse to do army service, especially because of the situation in the Occupied Territories. Common soldiers, tank commanders and pilots who refuse to go and serve their country in the Occupied Territories for moral reasons. The first time I heard about that, I immediately wanted to meet them. I wanted to know whether they refused because they are not ready or afraid to die, or maybe because they have Palestinian wives. But it took me

three years before a friend asked me: 'Would you like to join us and meet with some Israeli ex-fighters who refused to serve in the Occupied Territories?' I hated soldiers, but I felt curious and said: 'Yes, I want to meet with them!' This was in 2000 and the first meeting was in the Everest Hotel in Beit Jalla near Bethlehem. There were three Palestinians and seven Israelis. It was the most difficult meeting of my life. We didn't know about their background and we could only imagine what they had done in the past. And how many Palestinians they might have killed... I said to myself: 'Those are the criminals that I fear.' I looked at them with much hatred, because through them I saw the entire history of the occupation. But we sat down together.

One of them started to talk. His name was Noam Hayut and he used to be the commander of the Kalandiya checkpoint for two years. It was one of the worst checkpoints, because many people pass through it between Ramallah and Jerusalem and from Jerusalem to all over the West Bank. I was amazed. This was the officer, the criminal, responsible for this checkpoint! And also he was the commander of the unit that damaged Al-Mukataa, the building where Yasser Arafat was stationed. I wanted to attack him. His unit was responsible for cutting trees, harassing little children, arresting and torturing people.

'You're staring at me all the time,' he said. 'Who are you? Say something.'

'I just want to believe that you are a Jew and that you are Israeli. You were a soldier?'

'Yes, I was.'

'But you look too sensitive to me.'

'I don't think I am the worst man in the world.'

'And you are a criminal?'

'Yes, I am,' he said. He agreed with everything I said and I couldn't pick a fight with him. So I said: 'Do you mean to say that everything you did was just terrorism?'

'Absolutely,' he said. 'That's why I am here. I was a criminal.'

Wow, I thought to myself. Maybe he is crazy.

'Say something about yourself,' he then said. All the things that he had said to me, I then told him as well. I said that I had shot many soldiers, just to make him nervous and give him the impression that I had done the same kind of things. But after we really became friends, I told him that these things were not true

The odd couple

'A Palestinian and an Israeli are traveling together in a car...'
As told by Avichay Sharon, Israeli activist in Combatants for Peace

This may sound like the beginning of a joke, but it isn't. This evening, 20 January 2008 at 10.05pm, two friends are traveling together in a car after a meeting with a group of 17 American supporters in Jerusalem. I happen to know both men: Bassam Aramin and myself, Avichay Sharon.

We are on our way to Anata in east Jerusalem to get Bassam home to his family. Suddenly a police motorcycle pulls up next to us, with two of Jerusalem's finest Special Police Unit. One of them signals me to open my window as we stand side by side at the Shivtei Israel corner stoplight.

'Who are you?' the police officer asks. 'We're just two friends who live in Jerusalem,' I answer, naively forgetting that friendship between an Arab and a Jew is unimaginable. From this point on an unpleasant interrogation regarding our ties begins – to put it mildly.

'You, friends?!' the police officer asks. And then he yells: 'Pull over!' From this moment on each of us is thoroughly interrogated separately, the car is searched, as well as our bodies, almost to the point of stripping. 'Where do you know him from?' Again I answer, adding: 'I can't understand what is so strange about two people living in the same city who are also friends.' The police officer gets even madder and orders me to stop mixing my answers with politics.

A quick look at Bassam's papers reveals to the police that his permit to enter Israel has expired five short minutes ago. 'We will arrest you,' and that I had said this just to see their reaction.

Another Israeli soldier told me: 'My grandfather was in Germany at the time of the Holocaust.' And I responded: 'Sorry, what does that mean here? You did not tell me that they were in Hebron or Jenin on the West Bank. I am not from Germany, I am from Ramallah! Don't make the Palestinians responsible for

---

the officer warns, 'for being an illegal alien and you for transporting an illegal alien.' Next to that, he also announces they will confiscate my car for 30 days and impose a fine of thousands of shekels. 'It has only been five minutes,' I answer, 'and we really were on our way to Anata to get the illegal alien back to his legal place of residence.'

The police officer still wishes to fathom the depth of our relationship. 'Are you a couple?' In response to this question I snicker involuntarily, so he begins to search my car for hashish. He does a thorough job, turning the whole vehicle inside out, flipping over even the mat in the trunk and every last cigarette butt.

In the mean time, Bassam is taken aside, undergoing the same interrogation about why he is in my company and whether we're a couple. After a quick ID computer check they discover his security past and begin to question him about his legal record. Bassam, in his amazing level-headed way, simply answers: 'I resisted the Occupation'. As usual he does not wait for the police officers' questions and begins to voice his beliefs about justice and life together. The police officer who was busy with me then asks: 'Did you know this man has a "security record"?' I snicker again, which makes him all the more furious. He asks why I laugh and orders me to stand against the wall. 'I really don't need you to tell me about Bassam,' I tell him. 'I know him well enough…'

If you thought our story ends here, well, it doesn't. The police now begin to question us about our criminal past – still separately, of course. Naturally, dangerous Arabs must be kept apart from Jews, even damned lefties. 'List all your past arrests,' one says. 'This information is easily accessible on your computer,' I answer. But naturally this does not satisfy

what the German people did to the Jews.' And this is a recurring pattern. When Jewish people talk about the Holocaust, they get angry at the Palestinians. This link always returns. They are traumatized by the past, by things that happened in Europe during the Second World War. I understand that. But they project it onto the Palestinians, which I cannot accept. All this happened during that first meeting and you don't know what direction it will go and what to decide. You don't know whether they are good or bad, whether they are serious or whether they are secret agents that organized the meeting to set a trap!

But we agreed to meet again and in the second meeting we began to talk more personally. We asked whether there was something we could do, through newspapers or in any other way, against the war, the violence and the occupation. When we met for a third time, we realized that we would be in this together for a long time. Before all this, if you had offered me a million dollars to sit with Israelis and talk with them, I wouldn't have

---

him. 'I have been arrested in the past for participating in demonstrations against the Occupation.' 'Aha! See, I was right! You really are a leftie!'

The whole ordeal took about half an hour, during which Bassam continued lecturing the other police officer. But then they are suddenly alerted to another incident, and decide to show consideration and let us go rather than arrest us, since Bassam's permit expired only five minutes before they stopped us. Naturally they write down all our particulars, including my car license number. But no, this is not the end yet. Now I am told I'm not allowed to give Bassam a ride to the checkpoint. He must walk. If he gets in my car, we'll both be arrested on the spot, and if he enters a cab or any other vehicle, then... I ask the officer to exercise his judgement. After all, he'd be letting an illegal alien loose much longer on foot in Jerusalem... I even suggest he follows us to watch me bring Bassam to the checkpoint and leave him there. 'I couldn't care less,' he answers. At this point I tell him: 'I refuse to go before my friend is released

---

done it. But now I am most willing, especially with the Israeli soldiers, to meet directly, because we have the same interest. So killers, criminals and soldiers meet and talk – the same soldiers that before searched and tortured you and destroyed our houses. Now they say: 'We are sorry and we can never be part of your suffering. We don't know what to say to you.' These discussions led us to working out the principles of Combatants for Peace. We agreed first of all that we are totally non-political, but we do have a political message. We accept the two-state solution, because the majority of the Palestinian and Israeli people support it. We want 100 per cent peace, the same for everyone. And we want to struggle together, a joint non-violent struggle against the occupation and the violence. The occupation is the source of the violence. And we don't accept terrorism and reject it as a way to achieve this.

Then I said to my fellow Combatants for Peace: 'We must include another great principle. And that is that we will continue

---

and I'd like to know how in the world he's supposed to get home!' 'That's none of your business and it shouldn't interest you in the least,' he says. 'Even if he were your own brother, you shouldn't be concerned'. I park the car and we begin walking, Bassam and I.

So an Israeli and a Palestinian traveled together in Jerusalem, just like that. What were they thinking, these hoodlums? An Arab and a Jew together in the same car! As we're walking, Bassam sees I'm upset and angry and says in his usual calm way: 'You shouldn't get so excited. This is our reality.' With his charming half-smile he adds: 'I'm even a bit glad it happened, because it allowed me another opportunity to air my ideas to two more Israelis, even in uniform!' Two hours earlier, Bassam had been explaining in English to the group we had met why he does not seek revenge upon the murderers of his 10-year-old daughter Abir. He seeks justice. The Special Police Unit men made sure to remind Bassam and me where we were, and why it is we seek justice.

---

to talk *under any condition*. If tomorrow we have a suicide bombing in Tel Aviv, the Israelis may say 'goodbye, that's it!' and likewise the Palestinians may say this after another killing on the West Bank. We must set a strong example that we believe that violence and armed struggle will never achieve anything. We must strongly express our message to politicians in this way and remain committed to nonviolence under any condition. And in case any one of us happens to be the first to pay this price, he or she must give the example.' So we based Combatants for Peace on these principles. But I had no idea that it would be *me* who would be put to the test so soon.

My child, their child

On 16 January, disaster struck. My 10-year-old daughter Abir was seriously wounded. She was walking arm-in-arm with her sister and two friends, down the streets of Anata, a Palestinian village not far from Jerusalem. Border police of the Israeli Defense Forces were patrolling the school and an adjacent boys' school. Most Palestinian witnesses testified that the border police had opened fire at the students and that there had been no provocation. One of them said he had seen a rock being thrown by one of the students. Clashes between rock-throwing students and border police using tear gas and rubber bullets are routine for Anata. But this time it took the life of my daughter. Abir was rushed to Mukassad Hospital. And I insisted that from there she would be taken to the Hadassah University Medical Center at Ein Karem.

As soon as we had arrived, Jewish members of Combatants for Peace visited us in the hospital room. They wanted to know what I would say. I was devastated, but I told them: 'This incident will only strengthen us. We must become stronger for the sake of our children. Abir died, but I still have five living children. We will fight this case through legal channels.' My Jewish friends remained with me until Abir died. They spent three days and nights with me and we began to connect like a family. I felt that my child was their child also.

I had no doubt that the border police shot and killed Abir and I am determined that the alleged killer be apprehended and punished by law. And despite the state prosecution decision to close the file, I am certain it will happen. Michael Sfard, a prominent Israeli attorney, told the *Jerusalem Post*: 'Abir was fatally wounded on a Tuesday morning. The police did not open an investigation that day. Nor the next. It was only after I was given the case and complained that the police began to investigate – on Thursday evening.' That delay turned out to be crucial. During those two days, the rain had washed away the border police jeep's tire marks and Abir's blood stains. Disagreement followed between the members of the patrol and Palestinian eyewitnesses as to where the jeep was standing when Abir was fatally wounded. The police version places the jeep at an angle making it impossible for its occupants to hit Abir. The Palestinian eyewitness testimony as to the location of the jeep does make it possible.

Sfard said to me that police investigators are trained to solve such problems and determine where the jeep stood. In this case, they could not. Furthermore, he said that even if the investigators could not establish that the border police had actually killed Abir, there were other, lesser charges that could have been laid, such as improper use of firearms. Sfard made these arguments in his appeal. But the key problem in deciphering the cause of her death is that the two pathologists who examined Abir's body reached different conclusions. The pathologist hired by my wife and myself found that Abir died of a rubber bullet wound to the back of her head. The police pathologist said it was impossible to determine what had caused her death. But I was not satisfied with that, because I wanted justice. The Attorney-General Menahem Mazuz gave us 30 days to appeal and no further comments. But through my lawyer I petitioned again. Next, they closed the case for 'lack of evidence'.

The case for Abir is still ongoing. But think of this: over the last seven years, from 2000 until now, more than 970 Palestinian children have been killed and no-one is held accountable. 970 children in seven years! I told the police: 'This is my life. And I want to bring this hero, this killer, this soldier to justice.' I owe it to Abir, but also to Arin, her sister, who held her hand when she was hit. One time I found Arin crying at home saying 'I don't believe in God.' She was crying for more than an hour and I kept wondering why. 'Who hurt you?' I asked her. 'Was there someone who told you something bad?' 'I want Abir back!' she said angrily. 'Abir went to paradise on her own. I hate her for doing that, because she will be gone for a very long time. When she comes back, I will go away for a long time!' I never forget these tears of Abir's sister. And my son, who will be 14 next month, said: 'I want revenge!' But I must also prove to him that nonviolence will succeed. Nonviolence is true justice. You can choose justice and you can choose revenge. But revenge will not get you anywhere. It will take a long time. But it is a matter of principle.

Speaking from the heart

So far I think the Israeli Government doesn't care about our work in Combatants for Peace. But in the future they will and there are already many articles about the work of Combatants for Peace in American, Israeli and European media. Together they send a signal to the Israeli Government and the army. They *will* care. And there is also a lot of support on the Palestinian side. We have also met with President Mahmud Abbas and he said: 'We are ready to do everything for peace. It depends on the young generation to make this peace.'

One of the first people that supported us was Palestinian general Jibril al-Rjoub, who was also the President's adviser on national security. He spent 17 years in Israeli jails, but he is a very strong leader and has offered his assistance. The most important thing, however is, that our power comes from the people on both sides of the conflict. Will we succeed in turning people that support us into ex-fighters?

I am an ex-fighter myself. The majority of people say: 'We believe in this peaceful road, but we are not yet ready to join you.' Some Israelis say that it is possible to have a dialogue despite the Separation Wall. Others feel that the Wall gives them peace and they can hide behind it. But the Wall doesn't work. Many Israelis are now finding out about the background of Palestinians and about how they think. I often give lectures and meet with them. But when I speak with them, it is very sensitive to speak about the Holocaust, especially if you're an Arab, even if you sympathize. 'No!' I tell them. 'I *must* speak to you, *especially* about the Holocaust.' They in turn tell me that they don't agree with my comparison. One of them said: 'I speak to you as a friend. But please don't speak about the Holocaust. They will close their ears and they will not hear you.' 'Let me speak to them from my heart,' I said. 'I never care about who is my audience. Intellectuals, workers, women, men, generals, students... I make the peace for myself and I can bring it to the others.'

I believe Israeli society carries the trauma of the Holocaust and it has set their mind pattern. They live it as if someone tells them every day from the early morning onward, all the time: 'Holocaust, Holocaust, Holocaust.' All the time. It has produced a victim mentality. And in their fear of being the victim, they found the Palestinians, a victim of the victim. It is very strange.

When the Israelis celebrate Rosh Hashanah, their New Year, they also celebrate their liberation from Egypt and the values of freedom. Once I had the chance to speak about this on the Israeli radio. 'Your message is "Happy New Year". Just know that when we, the Palestinians, hear that, we hear "Happy New Closure". Because you close the Palestinian territories and the

West Bank and the Gaza Strip. We cannot go anywhere and have to stay in our villages.' Those people, who know the value of freedom, must enjoy it. But we are their slaves in our jails and in our rooms. It was a very strong message. How can they celebrate this holiday of freedom, while taking it away from others? Some Israelis explained it this way: 'We are occupying you because of our fear.'

The Holocaust and the Nakba

I think the Nakba, the disaster that happened to the Palestinians in 1947 and 1948 *totally* relates to the Holocaust. Have you ever heard of Deir Yassin? It's a Palestinian village – now called Har Nof in Hebrew – where there was a big massacre in 1948. Altogether 330 men, women and children were taken, many of whom were killed. To motivate the soldiers to commit these acts, they were shown a picture of Auschwitz before they went. I could bring a picture of my own daughter, who was in the hospital and the picture has a lot of blood on it. I could put it in my bedroom. And if I look at it every day thinking of her killer, then I can only want revenge. So I would say that Israeli society doesn't only have a victim mentality, but also a revenge mentality. But they're taking revenge on the wrong group of people, who are not guilty! The Palestinians are a substitute for the Germans of the last century. When I speak with Israelis about this, I find they have never thought about this. And some of them simply don't want to know or don't want to see.

I don't compare Israeli extremists with Palestinian extremists. We are under occupation and have a right to fight, even if it is the Israelis that have suffered so much that are occupying us. And of course, not all Palestinians are like Gandhi. I have become moderate and peace-loving myself, but the point is that the Palestinians are under occupation and therefore have a right to rise up against their oppressors. The Israelis call them 'extremists', but what does that term mean? Those so-called 'terrorists' and 'extremists' only want to lead a free and normal life.

Hamas, after the election, became very clear. They said: 'We accept the Palestinian state and the borders of 1967.' That's it. But if you don't allow them that solution, they will still be extremists, simply because they have no other choice. I saw it with those people in Jenin. They had the choice of bringing flowers or to continue fighting. They brought flowers. Their message is that when they feel sure the peace is real, they will bring flowers and life will be good. They want peace, even when someone has killed their own child. Revenge is not the solution.

I told the police officers that are working on my daughter's case: 'I don't trust you. And I don't believe in you and your network.' So even while I am trying to make peace, at the same time I am still fighting the legal system that allows the occupation and the injustice of being dishonest about the death of my daughter. Not because I want revenge, because it would be very easy to carry a small gun and kill ten of their soldiers. But I would not feel any triumph about killing someone and also I might go to jail forever. It won't bring Abir back and it wouldn't be good for my family. When you feel revenge, you don't think about the fact that you might die and you don't care about the other. But in Combatants for Peace we care about civilians and we want to raise our children in a good atmosphere. I have a great love for this group, because we are unique people. And some Israelis are right in wondering: 'This is very strange. You don't want revenge?' I told them: 'Relax. I don't want revenge. We will double our efforts to work for peace.'

Of course, before this I had reason to be angry and think of revenge. But this simply arose in me. I am not an academic or an intellectual; I am from the grassroots, from the streets. And my decision in favor of nonviolence has simply come from my own experience and my own beliefs. Also, you don't have any choice. Hatred of the Separation Wall won't bring you very far. So if you want to be an example, you must demonstrate nonviolence to the politicians and the fighters. If everyone continues the cycle of war, occupation and revenge, nothing will change, unless you break it. That's what I am trying to do. And I feel that this message is beginning to make an impact. I see it happening, because I give lectures, I meet people. Some people have never met a Palestinian close-up.

Supporters and refuseniks

When we started Combatants for Peace, there were only three Palestinians and only seven Israelis. We now have more than 300 people, most of them ex-fighters. But there are many more supporters and we must have met with more than 7,000 people. Many Israeli and Palestinian people now see us as unique people with a unique message. And even former extremist people now give us a lot of encouragement. Some Israelis still do not accept us. But occasionally, after a lecture, they invite us to their homes. They say: 'You can talk about anything, good or bad, even the Holocaust. But don't go to meet with those *refuseniks*, the conscientious objectors that refuse to serve in the Israeli military, because they should go to jail!' As a Palestinian, however, I don't mind meeting and speaking with them. But I do warn those parents: 'Those young men and women, your sons and daughters, they are going to Nablus, Hebron and Jenin to defend your country against terrorists. And now that they refuse, they must go to jail?'

I have spoken with many Israeli generals and politicians, the president of the Shabakh, the Israeli Security Service and an assistant of the Israeli Ministry of Defense. It is very strange talking to them. They speak a totally different language. They say: 'I am very, very sorry about your daughter. We will not keep silent about it.' 'But you do give your soldiers the order to kill!' I tell them. 'How can you say you don't know what is going on?' It is very strange. And at home, while raising my son not to look for revenge and raising my children to develop themselves, to get an education and a good life, they keep saying: 'We still haven't heard of that soldier going to jail!' 'He will go,' I tell them. 'I promise. Just keep going to school and do your best. And we will see after a few years.' If you want revenge, there is no time. If you choose nonviolence, there is time. Soon there will be another appeal in court and if that doesn't work either, we will take the case to the High Court. It will be very difficult for them to refuse another investigation. But if the Israeli High Court also refuses, I will take the case to the International Court of Justice. I promised my children: 'One day, this man will face justice. Don't worry.' You know, I think the justice for Abir's blood and the loss of her childhood is more important than the Separation Wall. Abir will never come back, but our children are the closest thing to our heart.

My mission goes beyond anger and beyond fear and my hope for the future comes from the Palestinian people and of course the Israeli people. Whenever I am invited to people's homes, I tell them I am coming with my brother. You know my Israeli friend Rami Elhanan? Whenever he speaks, he refers to me as his brother. And when I speak with Nurit, his wife, she says: 'I am Salwa's sister.' They give me a lot of courage. We have experienced the same. We both lost our lovely daughters. Their daughter Smadar and our daughter Abir are victims of the same conflict. Both of them were not guilty of anything and they were killed for nothing. And the killer is the same: the occupation and the oppression it causes. I think that people like Rami and Nurit and also their sons Elik and Guy, who are part of Combatants for Peace, are real partners, real people who refuse the torture and murder of innocent people. They are a good example.

If you imagine people who have lost one of their children, there is an important word in the Qur'an called *hasra*. It means pain, but I don't think there is a good translation for it in any language. Hasra is a continuous pain that you experience 24 hours a day. With the loss of children, parents experience that pain. No matter who you are, the feeling of loss is the same. No-one can imagine what it feels like, only the people that have gone through the experience. And we have a strong message for the Parents Circle, the people who lost their sons or daughters. It's different for the Israeli side and the Palestinian side, but the feeling is equal. That's why the Israelis should indeed prevent their children from going to the army and going to the Occupied Territories. For it prevents hasra on both sides. Once it happens, you cannot turn it back. But nonviolence saves you from this loss. It paves the way for a shared future for both Israelis and Palestinians.

3

Reconciliation
One Heart at a Time

Introduction

THE ANGKOR WAT, arguably the most outstanding monument of Southeast Asia, is perhaps only rivaled in its fame by the horrors of the 'killing fields', the legacy of the Pol Pot regime of the Khmer Rouge. But the country is the same: Cambodia.

Whoever visits Cambodia's foremost monument will also come face to face with its more recent history. At various places around the ancient site are small orchestras, many players of which are amputees. Cambodia is the country with the highest number of amputees in the world, a consequence of the presence of at least four million landmines buried in its soil. These mines are still causing death and injury, ripping through the lives of children, farmers and families that need to till the land for their survival. Every day, two people step on a landmine.

This too is part of the legacy of a long period of civil war, war with the Vietnamese, bombings by the United States, and the Khmer Rouge. The Khmer Rouge regime so terrorized its own population that many remember exactly when it came to power, how many days it lasted and when it ended: from 17 April 1975 to 6 January 1979. Inspired by the Russian and Chinese communist revolutions, the Khmer Rouge led by Brother Number 1, Pol Pot, aimed to return to the 'year zero' by eradicating all traditional and foreign cultural elements. They did so with unrivaled rigor: executions, torture, imprisonment, persecution, separating families and forced labor all ensued on a massive scale. Their theory, worked out in the abstract, had no regard for human factors.

Once in power, the Khmer Rouge employed spies everywhere, acting as 'eyes like a pineapple' and informing the xenophobic regime to help it suppress the population, seeing enemies behind every tree. Their pursuit of a nation 'overflowing with harmony and happiness' required one horrifying measure after the other. The Vietnamese minority was virtually wiped out; the Muslim Cham population was halved and only 1,000 of the 60,000 Buddhist monks survived. For a while, even the unfortunate King Sihanouk was a 'red prince', the first royal head of state of a communist regime. Privately, he could only weep over the fate of his country. When Pol Pot's regime started, the population was already exhausted and it is estimated that 1.5 million Cambodians perished. After the regime was deposed, the Khmer Rouge continued a guerrilla war from the jungle for another 20 years, finishing only two years before Pol Pot's death in 1998.

Many 'children of Angkar' that joined 'the struggle' at one point or another are therefore still alive today and its history hasn't disappeared from living memory. Khmer Rouge cadre and supporters have simply been absorbed into Cambodian society and since 1979 Cambodian regimes have included Khmer Rouge members and sympathizers, up to and including its present Prime Minister Hun Sen.

Victims remember too. Some people still live with the hope of seeing their loved ones return. And people in their late thirties still remember assisting their parents in re-education camps, clearing fields or doing chores for the greater glory of Angkar.

Meanwhile, amid the five-passenger motorbikes and busy market stalls of the capital, Phnom Penh, there is a 50-person-strong office on Preah Sihanouk Boulevard, working with executive director Youk Chhang to document the Khmer Rouge regime of Pol Pot. It's an incredible achievement, considering the fact that Chhang at one time was only able to stand outside the Texas University campus waving a cardboard sign that read 'Stop the Killing in Cambodia'. There, Chhang contacted genocide researchers and volunteered to help. He ended up, in 1995, being hired by Yale University's Cambodia Genocide Program to run the field office of the Documentation Center in Phnom Penh.

But this hasn't been easy, not least because many Cambodians fear – or have reason to fear – the reopening of the past. Nonetheless, Chhang has documented the three years, eight months and 20 days of cruelty and genocide that characterized the Khmer Rouge regime. There are now 600,000 pages of documents, maps of 20,000 mass graves and 4,000 transcribed interviews with former Khmer Rouge soldiers that describe the crimes and atrocities of the regime in detail.

The Documentation Center records and preserves the history of the Khmer Rouge regime for future generations and organizes information that can serve as legal evidence of its crimes. It also promotes memory and justice as a basis for the rule of law and genuine national reconciliation. Much of Cambodia's modern history has been obscured by the flames of war, but the Documentation Center is reconstructing most of it. And as the Khmer Rouge cadre wanted to demonstrate their loyalty, they were meticulously detailed in their record-keeping. Every little detail was registered. And yet, to this day, most Cambodians know more about what Pol Pot did through the film *The Killing Fields* than through what they might have learned from Cambodian sources.

Investigations are under way, judges are preparing and surviving leader Nuon Chea, Pol Pot's most trusted deputy, has been indicted and arrested near the Thai border. 'His involvement is clear as daylight,' said Chhang. The arrests are also urgent, as some of the architects of the Khmer Rouge regime were living out their lives freely or dying of old age, such as Ta Mok, also known as 'The Butcher'. Pol Pot's deputies are now men in their seventies and eighties. Until now, no-one has been punished, partly because it took such a long time for the UN and the Cambodian Government to agree on the scope of the tribunal and its funding.

Chhang no longer considers himself a victim or a survivor. But, in his opinion, there is no future without making peace with the past. The long-awaited tribunal should allow the world to hear the architects of these crimes speak but, more importantly, it should offer a chance to heal the wounds of Cambodian society. Many Cambodians still suffer from a profound sense of dislocation due to the loss, bereavement and deprivation that they experienced. While many have survived by 'bending with the breeze', as the Khmer saying goes, they have been traumatized for the rest of their lives. The Documentation Center aims to 'build something new' to counterbalance this and to reconstruct the historical narrative. Cambodian society needs a firm footing for a better future. 'Reconciliation will happen one heart at a time.'

Youk Chhang
Cambodia

'Cambodia is like broken glass. Without justice, we cannot put the pieces together.'

Youk Chhang (born in 1961) is the executive director of the Documentation Center of Cambodia, which gathers evidence of human rights violations of the Pol Pot regime. In 2006, Cambodian and international judges were publicly sworn in as members of the Tribunal during a ceremony outside the Royal Palace in Phnom Penh.

TELLING YOU ABOUT my life and experiences might be a very long story. I don't remember everything, but what I do remember I really treasure, even though it includes many bad things. I was born into a middle-class family. My mother was a peasant growing rice and my father worked for the Government, and I am the youngest son of the family.

Perhaps you should also talk to my mother. You know, what does it take to be a mother? Not a PhD or to be rich. She is very poor. When I was eight I taught her to write her own signature. It's the only thing she knows how to write and she cannot calculate. But the love of a mother is so powerful that it can shape your future. I survived because of my mother's dream.

When, after the end of the Pol Pot regime, I came back to my mother's home village, my mother could not recognize me because I was starving and had a lot of rashes on my skin. She gave me a shower. As I went to sleep, I overheard her talking to the neighbors. They had not expected to see me alive again.

'You had a dream,' they asked her. 'What was it?'

'I remember Youk sitting on the Buddha's Eye Mountain and looking toward the east. I knew then that he would survive and that someday my boy would be somebody. And my husband

77

gave him the name "Long Life", so I knew he would come back.'

That dream is part of what made me today. It is always with me. The love she had for her child was so great, it made sure I would succeed. And those things are all you need.

We lived in a small house in a village not far from the city, only 20 minutes from Phnom Penh. I was born in the house and I grew up there, so the house is like me, it was ancient to me. Not long after this, the Vietnam War started. It was 1969 and I was about nine. Even before the war began, a lot of refugees fled the country, but the war continued into the 1970s. Many relatives that were fleeing the country came to stay with my father and mother to avoid the fighting in the countryside. All these cousins and uncles changed our living environment, for we were only a small family. Every banana, every grain of rice was rationed and my parents were very worried that bad things would happen to my sisters, so they devoted a lot of time to protecting them.

In the beginning I had absolutely no idea about the war. As a boy and as the youngest in the family, I was just walking around, assuming that I would be all right. I wasn't given a lot of attention by my parents, because I had many brothers and sisters and also because of the family members that were fleeing the war. So I grew up spending a lot of time on my own and I learned simple things like making my own kite from newspapers, growing plants and orchids, playing, fighting and having fun with the boys in the neighborhood. I survived. When I look back, that is how I lived my life. In some ways, being on my own prepared me for life under the Khmer Rouge.

Before the Khmer Rouge arrived I did hear a lot of shelling of the city from across the Mekong River. So I was aware of the war, but we had no idea which country was firing the shells – the Vietnamese or the Americans – even while the bombs and grenades were falling all around us or while we were in the cinema. Many things were closed and at times I couldn't go to school. And because of the bombs I knew that it wasn't safe to go out or travel around. Then I saw that two of my cousins had joined the army when they came home in their uniforms. And my father, who was an architect, was drafted into Prime Minister Lon Nol's army as well, and one of my cousins became the spokesperson of the Khmer Republican Government. So suddenly I could feel the war was all around me, because of all these army uniforms and the presence of a lot of foreigners and reporters. I started to observe these things and I began to understand that there was a war going on around me. The school was closed often because the teachers were on strike due to the fact that the salaries were very low. I still remember that the teachers made the students walk around the school and that we were singing, aware of the fact that there was something we could not change.

Alone and abandoned

In 1975 the Khmer Rouge had already developed and had become more widely known, emerging from the countryside into the cities. But at that time I didn't even know the word 'Khmer Rouge'. When the Khmer Rouge soldiers marched into Phnom Penh and into my village, I was home alone. The reason for this was that my mother and my sister, who had a baby of a few days old, were sufficiently worried that they had relocated the family to another place in a high brick building for safety, but I had got separated from them. My mother was hoping to collect me later but it was too late. The roads were blocked, and the Khmer Rouge were approaching. I remember that our Chinese neighbor saw me on my own and asked me to come with her, but I refused. Long after that, 30 years later, she found me again through a newspaper article and we talked about this. At that time she was so sad because she saw me and said: 'You are alone and without family. Come with us!' But I said: 'No!' because I was hoping that my mother would still come to pick me up. But she never came. So the Khmer Rouge came into Phnom Penh and the surrounding villages and everyone was told to evacuate to the countryside.

When the Khmer Rouge took over Phnom Penh, one of the first things they did was to expel people from the cities. Many people say the Khmer Rouge said that Phnom Penh would be bombed by the Americans, but to be honest I never heard that. I did see people making announcements with a microphone, but it was very hard to follow what they said. Maybe I was just too young to understand at that time.

But I do remember seeing the Khmer Rouge soldiers come in on a jeep. It looked a bit like scenes from a *Captain Hook* movie;

The Khmer Rouge

'To keep you is no benefit. To destroy you is no loss.'

(Khmer Rouge motto)

The Khmer Rouge was a term coined by King Sihanouk for various communist parties in Cambodia that later referred to the Communist Party of Kampuchea and the Pol Pot regime. In the early days, the Khmer Rouge looked to Ho Chi Minh (Vietnam) and Stalin (Soviet Union) for guidance. After 1960, it developed its own unique political ideas.

Khmer students returning home from scholarships in Paris took command of the party in the 1960s. Pol Pot (1928-1998), who had also studied in Paris and acquired a taste for the French classics and the writings of Marx, rose to the leadership. Other leaders had earned doctorates from the University of Paris or Phnom Penh and were talented members of the élite from landowner or civil servant families. Yet they launched one of the bloodiest and most radical revolutions in modern Asian history.

Having established the regime of 'Democratic Kampuchea', the Khmer Rouge imposed an extreme form of social engineering and agrarian communism on Cambodian society. They closed schools,

---

the way they dressed was definitely like pirates. They didn't have proper clothes and they had no proper shoes, but wore Ho Chi Minh sandals made of old car tires. And their heavy accents made me realize that they were from the countryside, like they were from the jungle or something. That was very scary. But nevertheless I felt very peaceful on the day the Khmer Rouge arrived. I felt so peaceful, because the bombing had stopped! It was the most peaceful and quiet moment in my entire life to that point. For such a long time, as I grew up, there had always been shelling, and we always had to be very careful and hide many times and sleep in different buildings for almost five years. So I was sick and tired of that. Even at school, there were many times that we couldn't play

---

hospitals and factories, abolished banking, finance and currency, outlawed religions and confiscated all private property. Cities were evacuated and these so-called 'New People' were relocated to do forced agricultural labor and to become part of a classless society of 'Old People'. They worked 12 hours a day non-stop. Family relationships not sanctioned by the state were banned, and family members could be put to death for communicating with each other. The total lack of agricultural knowledge possessed by the former city dwellers made famine inevitable. Even the simple act of picking wild fruit or berries was seen as 'private enterprise' for which the death penalty applied. The regime was removed from power in 1979, though the Khmer Rouge survived as a resistance movement and was only fully dissolved in 1996 due to a peace agreement. Pol Pot died in 1998, having never been put on trial.

In the 1990s, the remaining leaders apologized for the 1970s genocide. By 1999, most of them had surrendered and the Khmer Rouge had effectively ceased to exist. Although the psychological scars still affect many families, Cambodia is recovering. Until recently, the Government did not require that educators teach children about Khmer Rouge atrocities, but the Education Ministry has approved plans to teach Khmer Rouge history in high schools beginning in 2009.

---

outside because we were in the middle of the city. So when the Khmer Rouge came, everything went 'stop!' and I felt incredibly peaceful on that day. Suddenly everything went silent.

But next we all heard footsteps, walking... When I went outside I had no idea where to go. Our neighborhood was completely deserted, so I started walking. Along the way I heard people say that they were going to their home villages, so I decided to go to my mother's home in Takeo province. I simply made my way, walking about 85 kilometers from the city. As I had no food with me I asked the Khmer Rouge soldiers for some and they gave me round palm sugar cakes. After some weeks of walking I arrived at my mother's home village. In the meantime, my mother had tried to cross the border into Vietnam, but the roads were blocked. So fortunately I was able to reunite with her four months later.

While I was staying in a place in the south, one of my cousins had a brother who was working as a spokesperson for the previous Government. He arrived in the village. The village chief, who was the childhood friend of this man and like a brother to him, grabbed a knife and instantly killed him! It was a terrible shock to our family because we had never seen or heard such a thing in our lives! This man simply believed that the previous Government was bad and that his former friend was lacking respect and was corrupted. He killed him for no other reason. It was the first time we ever witnessed someone being killed right in front of us. And he was only around 30 years of age. Instantly! There was a terrible scream that could be heard from a distance, throughout the village. You can imagine that, as the killer was his own childhood friend, the shock was even greater. The name of the victim was Bu Phy.

Many people were trying to escape, because they were afraid of being found and being sent to re-education camps. Because if they were caught and were sent to a re-education camp, it usually meant that they would 'disappear' – effectively you would die.

So many were trying to escape across the Thai border, including several of my family members. My brother-in-law, however, came back, because he was missing his wife – and he is still alive today. He survived because he went into hiding in a sugarcane farm until the Vietnamese came. But my uncle, who pushed forward to escape to Thailand through the bush, has never returned. And to this day my mother doesn't want to believe he died, because she went to a fortune teller who told her that he is alive somewhere. But as for myself, I think he must have died by stepping on a landmine.

According to my research, people traveled in groups and many of them lost their lives by stepping on landmines. I think my uncle died there and that his body made it safe for others to cross. The ones that had died, made it safe for the others, you see. So he must have died there in the jungle. I heard about this from a second group that had escaped via Thailand and made it to the United States. A lot died; the few that didn't die on the way succeeded in escaping the Khmer Rouge.

A stick, a basket and a net

I myself was not in a re-education camp, but in a children's mobile team digging canals. You live in fear, you're separated from your family and led by a young adult from the Base People of the Khmer Rouge, and you work from early in the morning, sometimes till midnight. You have few clothes for the whole year, and no proper food to eat. When I think back to this or when I dream, I always feel my stomach, because I was so hungry and around me there were a lot of people who died of starvation. I remember thinking of baguettes with pâté that I loved to eat and I thought about that almost every night. But I never thought I would die. I had a stick, a basket to carry dirt and a mosquito net to protect my face. And if I lost any of these things, I would have lost my life! When I rested during the night, I was lying on my back and looking through the holes in the basket at the stars.

I learned how to swim across the river because I wanted to steal mangos. The mango tree was full of ants, so most of the time I would get bitten, but I was so hungry that I didn't feel the pain. I wanted mangos! Also, I learned how to kill and eat snakes and rats and how to find edible leaves in the jungle. And one time I dived in the water when a field of sugarcane was flooded four to five feet deep, to cut sugarcanes with a scythe. But I cut myself badly with the scythe going into my leg right here, as I was very weak. I had to pull it back, but I couldn't get it out. I still have that scar today. But meanwhile I was proud of myself and I still am today, because I just wanted to live!

I think human beings, even when they know 'this is the last split second of my life' or you know that someone will kill you, you still hope you will survive. That's human instinct. And I strongly believe in human instinct; I believe in humanity. Humans are very capable of growing, and very capable of destroying. In any desperate situation, humans will still look for a way to survive.

I witnessed the killing of a couple near the Buddha's Eye pagoda. They called a meeting after it was found that this boy and girl had fallen in love without permission. The Angkar declared that it was not allowed, so they gathered a crowd, and asked them: 'What shall we do with them?' And the crowd answered and cheered: 'Kill them, kill them!' And so they killed them. As a young boy of 12, I witnessed how they hit the man with a hoe and the blood spurted out of his head, turning his whole body red. I could see he pushed his face back, because he refused to give up and die. And next they hit the girl. I don't think they were dead. Without ceremony they buried them at the same place and the memory of that still haunts me today.

I visited that site 25 years later. I went back to come face to face with the village chief that I hate. So when I sat there talking near the site where this took place, I was shocked, because the place of the killing was so close! At the time when I was young it had seemed so far away. That couple had been killed so near to where we were that I was amazed and said 'This is it?' Where I sat, it was right there! 'Yes, right there,' the man said. And as I had seen all this with my own eyes, I tried to remember what I could and I wrote about this story some years ago, when Ieng Sary, the Khmer Rouge minister of foreign affairs, defected. When he defected, he went to that same place to give honor to the Buddha. That moment reminded me of this event and the place where it happened, the pagoda named the Buddha's Eye. And you know what? Almost 20 people called me to tell me: 'I was there too!' Many of them had cheered then. But as I was a little boy at that time and they were children too, I didn't know any of them. Many of them have since become friends of mine and visit me to share their stories. And I can still see it in front of me as I speak – I was this close. I still see these events, as if my mind has taken photographs of every moment.

The price of disobedience

I was still young and had no idea about any of the political movements and so on. I didn't understand anything except the fact that I hated the village chief of the mobile team, who was bad to me. I witnessed killings, I was sad and hungry. I missed my mum and saw my uncle disappear. And I witnessed my sister being accused of stealing rice. A soldier slashed open her stomach to prove her guilt. Her stomach was empty. She died a slow and horrible death. This is one of the unspeakable truths that have gone not only unpunished but unexplained. I also dreamed about all kinds of food all the time. Even today, when I see hungry children in the streets of Phnom Penh, it upsets me. And I wonder why they cannot have enough to eat now that we no longer live under the Khmer Rouge. I see myself in their hungry faces.

Another of my sisters was pregnant. And as she was one of my favorite sisters, I went out to get her some food. They caught me for eating grass and collecting mushrooms and I was beaten up in front of a crowd and in front of my mum, ending up bleeding. When I called my mother for help, she walked away from me, after which I was put in jail. I did not understand until many years later that by doing that she saved my life. Had she tried to help me, she would have shown support for the crime. But a crime is a crime, so she didn't. And I was very angry with her for almost 10 years about this. But later I realized that if I had the chance to go back to the Youk Chhang of many years ago, I would have told him not to steal. It was a turning point in my life. I can justify it because I was hungry, there was no food, and give myself many reasons. But deep down in my heart I felt it was the wrong thing to do. Even though my sister was in need and I was hungry, stealing was the wrong thing to do. I should have asked. And you were told everything belonged to the Angkar, even your own life, and that you had to ask the Angkar first. It was not that I believed in the Angkar, I simply obeyed.

The Angkar was the authority. We lived in a community where you were told what to do and you had to obey, otherwise you were out! So when I did not obey, I knew the punishment. The consequence was that I was beaten up and bleeding and then put in jail. And in jail I was the youngest person. Fortunately I met a person in jail who knew my family and who asked the village chief to release me. This guy managed to convince the village chief that I should not be in jail, that I was too young to be locked up with the adults. At his request, the village chief released me a couple of weeks later. You know what happened to that man? He disappeared. And I have forgotten his name! But I want to find it. I think they killed him, for he was later accused of having relatives in enemy areas. I feel very bad, because I can't remember his name. He saved my life and I just want to see his surviving family members and meet them.

So within the whole research that is going on here in the Documentation Center, there is also my personal quest to find every small bit of information. The first thing I am looking for is my uncle's name, so that my mum can be happy and can be at rest. Today she still doesn't want to say that her brother died. I look for anything, part of my brain is all the time looking for his first name, his last name, anything until his name will appear in front of my eyes and he will be found. But so far, we have never found him. We have a long list of names, of neighbors, of family members and many other people, but no-one ever even mentions him.

Crossing Death Fence

My own survival was partly due to luck, partly to acts of kindness from family members and even from total strangers and Khmer Rouge soldiers. And partly to my persistence in swimming across the river for food. In any inhumane situation there is always an act of kindness, of humanity. In the darkness there is always a light somewhere. I was given that light and that life, and I treasure it. The times were so dark, but somehow I have found a light that has saved my life.

All I remember is that my mum was worried I would be trapped by the Vietnamese army, and therefore said that I should go to the border of Thailand and hope to find some way of getting to America. It was a dream, but the point was that she knew she could no longer take care of me and that I had to leave the country. By that time my mum was a widow. My father had died of natural causes and she had to take care of a lot of children and therefore felt I had to leave. So I left early one morning around four or five o'clock. Someone knew a guide. But you had to pay him to take you and I didn't have the money. All my mother gave me was 10 US dollars. That was all we had. So we promised this man that one day when we did have the money, we'd pay him back. He was kind enough to take me with him. So we went and when we were at the old stadium near the bridge there were a lot of Vietnamese trucks. At this point I hid inside a Vietnamese truck that went a long way. It's a long story, but anyway, the guide managed to bring a whole group of about 20 people to the Thai border.

We were told to keep silent, even the babies, for if we made any sound, somebody would shoot us. The guide explained how we might avoid the Khmer Rouge and the Vietnamese, allowing us to escape. Around three o'clock in the morning we went across the Thai border through barbed wire. 'Death Fence' they call it. If you pay a lot of money you go a different way, because you can bribe a Thai soldier, giving you easy access. But we had no money, so we went the hard way. With another two boys I remember, and with my sister, my brother-in-law, and two of my nieces that were just little babies, we went along, carrying them in our arms. My niece, who is now a PhD student in Wisconsin and also studied in China, still has a picture of me carrying her like a little baby. She treasures that picture, because it is how I carried her across the border.

Later that morning we had to run fast. I was told that some did not make it, because of landmines. Or the Thais shot them. They also raped many of the women. Some did make it alive. I made it to one of the camps. Our guide had told us to go to a specific house number and we met there. And he joined us there! He had obviously arrived earlier with the 'first-class access', ha-ha. I think my sister and my grandmother have since managed to give him money to thank him for guiding us safely across the Thai border. I don't know where he is now, but we may meet again.

Upon arriving at the camp, we were illegal refugees. Every day the Thai border patrol came by and if you didn't have an ID card, they would send you back to Cambodia. They sent back a couple of thousand people across the mountains, many of whom died by stepping on landmines. But many of them made a second trip. One of my neighbors even made a third trip before managing to make it across. Through the help of friends, I managed to make it across to America.

It's a long story how I got to the United States, but it took me no time at all to adjust. I was well prepared. It was a childhood dream. I wanted to speak English, become a reporter, and go to America. I just bought this book – I love biographies – about my hero, John Kennedy and his wife Jackie. While I was still in the United States I wanted to go to Kennedy School, simply because I wanted his name on my résumé. Because I loved Kennedy so much, I wanted to work for the community night and day. And I did, you ask them! I wrote for the Dallas newspapers and also served as a community relations adviser to the Dallas Police Department, while living in a high-crime area. Then I got a scholarship, one from Yale and one from a Catholic school. And I decided to go to the Catholic school, because Kennedy was a Catholic. So I said no to Yale.

But when the journalist Samantha Power interviewed me, she said: 'If you love Kennedy so much, why don't you go to Harvard's John F Kennedy School of Government? You will have his name on your résumé for a lifetime.' So I applied a number of years ago, but I had to return to Cambodia to get the preparations for the trial off the ground. But I am prepared to go back to the United States just to get his name on my résumé!

While studying at the campus, I held demonstrations calling for attention to be paid to the events in Cambodia. But very few people understood what this was about. Each time I talked about it, I got these questions:

'Where are you from?'

'I'm from Cambodia.'

'Isn't that where there was a lot of killing? Is it true about the Killing Fields? Is it true that a lot of people died in Cambodia?'

'Yes, I don't know how many, but I lost most of my relatives there. And all the people that live there have similar stories.' I felt upset, for how can you explain the death of your sister, your parents? Then I realized a story is just a story. You have to explain it scientifically. People got frustrated with hearing the story of a refugee. They felt sorry for me and said: 'Look at this skinny

Cambodian refugee.' But I felt in my gut I had to do something and I got angry with them for questioning me. 'Why should I lie to you about the fact that a lot of people died?' I would say to them. It shouldn't even have been a question.

Salvation through education

But thinking about what my mother told me and several scholars confirmed, I decided to go back to school. They said the country was so poor and the people were sick and diseased and that I should appreciate what I have. But I said: 'I don't take your word seriously until I go to school.' And when I was there, it reminded me of what my mother had told me: you need to research the Khmer Rouge scientifically, you need to document it and explain it to people. That's what my mum always told me: education is the salvation of your life. So I said to myself: this is it. When I go back to school, I'll write and research, and I will prove and explain it. But I joined a campaign with the aim of asking the United States not to support the Khmer Rouge, so I tried to catch up with this big story. I was young and naive, trust me! But it was a matter of the heart, and my heart was in the right place. After school and after work I went from door to door showing people videos about the Khmer Rouge in support of the campaign to kick them out of the UN. It certainly gave me the time to practice my English and to become fluent in it.

Then people started saying that I had to meet groups of people and make a noise. So one time there was a phone call from Texas for a meeting at a school. It was far away, a five-hour drive, and I came prepared with flyers, brochures, a speech, and dressed up in a jacket and a tie. I drove up there in my blue Toyota. It took me hours to find the place but finally I got there, still on time. But for some reason the organizer hadn't shown up. They asked me instead. I stood there for five hours in front of these students. Only four showed up. One was the girlfriend of the guy that was there, one guy was a hippy PhD student with sunglasses, and the last one was a Thai lady who had seen the advertisement including the word 'Asia' so she came by to see me, a guy holding a sign saying 'Stop the Killing in Cambodia' – so stupid! But I said to myself: even though there are only four people, I made it! Even during the 1991 Gulf War I wanted to report on Cambodian or even black soldiers, because I was seeing all this news focusing on white Americans. I was just stupid. But when I look back it makes me happy, because I learned from it. At one time I spoke to one of my colleagues, Craig Etcheson, who is an investigator of the Extraordinary Chambers in the Courts of Cambodia. I drove him to my home village, and the road to it was full of dust and sand and he asked me: 'How did you make it to Texas from here?' I answered: 'I don't know!'

Setting up this Documentation Center has taken ages, at times surrounded by criticism, lengthy negotiations and financial difficulties. However, I have already been working here for eleven years. It's not just my personal mission, it's faith. I believe in it. You have to feel it in your heart. And what I feel is this: humans make mistakes, whether it is in a war or any other time. And it is something that is all about us: it's about our families, our neighbors, my mother or my sister, anyone of us. And it is all right to talk about this, even about the fact that you stole. People steal. In our family, I was ashamed about the fact that I stole, and I was pitied by the others. As a boy and as a man, I brought shame to the family, but I told my mother: 'I will be strong. I will do things to support the nation, and make you proud of me; I will make a new life.' So I'm doing this work for her, and because I believe in it, not because of the job, politics or money. I just love this thing, and I feel that everything we do and find sets me free and helps me grow. It gives me back my strength.

People often ask me whether I have nightmares. 'What nightmare?' I say. 'I'm happy! I am a survivor, not a victim. I am Youk Chhang. I have moved on from my victim mentality.'

Likewise, they ask me about the upcoming tribunal. You know, I don't have hate. When I was young, I did hate people and I wanted to take revenge on the Khmer Rouge. But I realize I no longer have that. And that's because I feel so free. Naturally I also do it for other people, like the widow named Phum. 'How can I feel happy,' she asked me, 'when Chhoch, the one who killed my husband, freely rides his bicycle past my house every day?'

An audience for killers

I interview a lot of people; I want to hear what they have to say. Most of all I want to know what the killers have to say, and

---

The horror of Tuol Sleng

Once the site of a high school, alive with children in the playground, Tuol Sleng in Phnom Penh became the notorious Security Prison 21. It was used by the Khmer Rouge regime between 1975 and 1979. The name means 'Hill of Poisonous Trees'.

After the Khmer Rouge won the civil war, the five school buildings were enclosed in electrified barbed wire and the classrooms were converted into prison cells and torture chambers. An estimated 17,000 people were imprisoned here. Usually they were former Khmer Rouge members and soldiers, accused of betraying the party or the revolution and probably seen as potential leaders of a coup against Pol Pot. Prisoners' families were often brought en masse to be interrogated, tortured and murdered. Upon arrival, they were photographed and required to give detailed biographies. After that, they were forced to strip to their underwear, taken to their cells and shackled to the walls or the concrete floor.

Water boarding was one of the 'enhanced interrogation techniques'. Prisoners were routinely beaten and tortured with electric shocks and searing hot metal instruments. Methods for generating confessions included pulling out fingernails while pouring alcohol on the wounds. Females were sometimes raped, even though sexual abuse was against

---

many have come to us. But I no longer see them as killers. It is true, people have guilt and they also need guilt, for it is good to feel guilty if you have done something wrong to others. But the way I understand our culture, how people express guilt, their response to guilt is different. And now that I have mastered some kind of understanding, you know it's actually wonderful to talk to a killer? You can speak to his heart. He will tell you: 'I killed this guy and there was this and that.' You know, the killer is not a machine. He may have killed one of your family members, but I am not here to judge. I am not a judge. I want to understand and somehow justify what happened to me

---

Khmer Rouge policy. Typical 'confessions' would be true events interwoven with imaginary accounts of espionage activities for either the CIA or KGB. One such 'confession' ended with the words 'I am not a human being, I'm an animal'. The vast majority of prisoners were innocent.

Many of the 1,720 prison staff were teenagers taken from the prisoners' families. The chief of the prison was known as Comrade Duch, a former mathematics teacher. A documentation unit typed up tape-recorded or handwritten confessions and maintained files including prisoners' photographs. Not being allowed to eavesdrop on interrogations, to take naps or lean against a wall while on duty, the guards themselves were just as terrified. Whoever made serious mistakes ended up being a prisoner themselves. This could be the 'mistake' of beating prisoners to death without permission.

Camp rules included: 'While getting lashes or electrification you must not cry at all'. Photographs, rusting iron bed frames, shackles and instruments of torture testify to the horrors that happened here. After the Vietnamese army invaded, Tuol Sleng was reopened in 1980 as a historical museum memorializing the Khmer Rouge regime. The museum once housed a 'skull map', composed of 300 skulls and other bones found by the Vietnamese during their occupation of Cambodia. The map was dismantled in 2002, but the skulls are still on display.

---

personally and understand it. Therefore I also met with many former friends who joined the Khmer Rouge revolution and they told me their stories.

I also met a woman that I hated when I saw her 25 years ago. She was a very mean woman, but when I met her all that time later, she was crying, waiting for her son to return home. I found a photograph and a cassette tape of a prisoner and because of the war documentation there was a file. I brought it all to the village. And there, this mother had been waiting for this thing for 30 years! And I had hated her so many years ago. But now she is an old lady, crying at seeing the photograph and hearing her son's own voice. You know, there is no need to judge her. What she did was her responsibility. But my job and my research is

---

An improbable rendezvous in 2009

Vietnamese cameraman Ho Van Tay, now 76, traveled to Cambodia in 1976 and 1979. Among the first to discover Tuol Sleng prison, his video footage included bloody walls, and fat chickens pecking at human corpses. Ho made award-winning films produced at the Ho Chi Minh City Television (HTV) station.

1976 By official invitation, Ho visited neighboring Democratic Kampuchea – the new Khmer Rouge name for Cambodia. But reporters were tightly controlled. Their lodging was patrolled by Khmer Rouge cadres and they could only visit predetermined places when picked up by a car. 'Pol Pot wanted us to spread the news that since his takeover, the country and its people were stable and thriving. But what I saw instead were deserted homes in Phnom Penh, scared hotel workers in Siem Reap, and a pool of crocodiles being fed human corpses. Apparently Khmer Rouge leaders enjoyed raising crocodiles.'

1979 When Vietnamese troops overtook Cambodia, Ho returned. 'As

---

trying to understand these things, the downside and the upside, including her part of the story and those of others. Similarly, I can deal with the opposition that exists in Cambodia today. Many Khmer Rouge cadre members have been reabsorbed into society, some being village chiefs, district heads or they are active in politics today, all the way up to Prime Minister Hun Sen, himself a former Khmer Rouge cadre member. I have met them all and talked to many of them. I write to Hun Sen on a regular basis to inform him about the research. And I communicate with several ministries and the Tuol Sleng Museum, our partner. We have developed a database with more than 30,000 biographies of Khmer Rouge and ordinary citizens. We have interviewed over 10,000 former perpetrators, not to mention victims. We

---

we were driving, my crew – an assistant and a driver – were confronted with a pungent odor. In search of its source, we found an abandoned compound surrounded by barbed wire: S-21'.

They alerted the Vietnamese troops, suddenly finding they were not alone. 'Five children were inside, some crying and some asleep, children of Khmer Rouge cadres that Pol Pot had sent to prison.' Hiding under a pile of discarded clothes, they were emaciated and on the verge of death. Among them was eight-year-old Norng Chan Phal and his brother and sister, Chanly and Rumduol, aged five and three.

2009 The Documentation Center of Cambodia invited Ho to Phnom Penh to attend the hearing of Brother Duch, the notorious leader of S-21, charged with crimes against humanity in 2007. Although now retired, there is a good chance that Ho still wishes to complete his filming of Cambodia.

His return marks another important chapter in Cambodia's history, if only for the fact that Ho will meet Norng Chan Phal, one of the five child survivors of S-21, for the first time in 30 years, at the Club of Cambodian Journalists.

---

talk to everybody.

I found someone, a lady who was the head of the irrigation project in Battambang that my sisters and I worked for. Her name is Um Chhem, Grandmother Chhem. Her name is equal to the character in Western folktales, you know the lady with a hat and a broom that flies through the air... She was a witch at that time. When she pointed at you, you would die. You would never stare at her. But today she is the village chief! How people can change! And this is at the biggest irrigation project in the country, where thousands upon thousands of people died at her hands. My sister and I were there. When you go there now, people tell you its history and it's a tourist site where people witness beautiful sunsets in the evening and people pay to have a look at it. The thing is: she is in charge of the whole project. But in the past she wanted to make sure that this job got completed before the arrival of the rainy season. And if you didn't obey, you would be killed and buried right on site! That's Grandmother Chhem.

Um Chhem has two telephones. While I was there talking to her recently, they kept ringing. One time it was about the access road; another about a visit to the pagoda for a ceremony; yet another about visitors from the city. She is simply working and happily going around. Grandmother Chhem! It's amazing, almost a completely different reincarnation. 'Do you remember me,' I asked her. 'No, I don't,' she said. 'There were thousands of people.' But she doesn't hide who she was. Before, there were so many sacrifices; it was a nightmare, a hell where thousands of people died. And if you ask the young people of that time, they will remember that place very well. But today, she is the village chief.

Former Khmer Rouge cadre or supporters are present in every part of society today, they are everywhere you look. The Documentation Center only seeks to speak the truth, like in our magazine 'Searching for the Truth' that has been appearing since 2000. My job is to speak only the truth. I don't make the analysis, I merely say this or that person was born on this day, this is what happened, this is what he did. We only document the history, we don't judge it. And also, I simply don't know. For me, any perpetrator's story is not that of a criminal. I may have met his sister, his mum and his childhood friends and his friends at college. I know what he did, but what he may be charged with regarding his responsibilities is something that the court will decide.

I have met with King Sihanouk occasionally and we have stayed in touch. In the past, the King has tried to steer Cambodia towards neutrality, but I don't believe in neutrality. I believe that if you walk in the middle of the road, you'll be hit by a car. End of story. This is something I disagree about with the King. Humans cannot remain neutral. You have to take sides. You need to be on the left side or on the right side. Which one? There are two sides in life, like when you flip a coin. It won't stand on its side. Neutrality sounds great, but you're human. Even your heartbeat changes and your reasons for doing things change all the time. So I don't think it is possible to remain neutral unless you're dead. It was something I learned from taking courses in theology and studying the Bible. I wrote a paper about passion and reason and firmly believe that humans have to take sides. They cannot remain neutral.

One of King Sihanouk's concerns is with justice. There are a lot of people who committed grave crimes and murders in the past, while today people who commit small offenses or petty crimes are in jail; the big names are still free and at large. But this is a post-conflict country and a poor country as well. It is easy to politicize. There are a lot of poor people. I think what is lacking here is something they can trust, a model, someone they can look up to, a vision they can follow. Ask around on the streets: who is your hero? Many will answer it with the name of King Rajendravarman who had a hundred wives. So in Cambodia, we don't have role models in society, in history, at home. We don't have a vision. I can sit down with you and make all kinds of arguments and reasons. But am I honest? Do I really intend to help people advance? That is something you need to ask. You have to understand that after a period of genocide... what is left? We lost family, property, nationhood, we lost everything! Some people even say we lost our soul.

Leaders lacking leadership

But there is one thing that is left and that is hope. And because there still is hope, there is a tendency in people in Cambodia today to say 'yes' to everything. To money, to food, to donors. Sometimes what they do is wrong and stupid, but they do it nevertheless.

But how do we shore up their hopes, their vision? Cambodia can become hell or heaven! Right now we have money coming in, a lot of money – we can have jobs, set up private companies, make something and sell it to the Chinese. 'Let's make money, it will solve everything.' But at least what I can see now is that hope is still around. People need that, but they should also have a vision of what our country should be like and start to fight for it. But if the leaders are short of vision and cling to power, afraid that they might be defeated, that vision will be short-lived and tomorrow will not be possible. Very simple. Who is willing to leave government office when they know, if they do, they will only make $20 a month? Instead of decreasing the number of staff, by comparison the Cambodian Government is nine times bigger than the French Government. It's not so much corruption or lack of vision; it's lack of leadership.

I think, therefore, that a challenge to the leadership is necessary to ensure that they are on the right track and the country can prosper. But these days there simply is no opposition to Cambodia's Government. That's why there's no point in talking about democracy. There is also a fear of taking risks or following advice from donor nations, because that might be seen as political interference in the national affairs of Cambodia. So the Government is just going on its way, trying to step aside from any diplomacy issues relating to foreign governments. On top of that, there is very little opportunity for young people to emerge. Around 60 per cent of our population are under 25 years of age. Young people, who are idealistic, are anxious to change things and have the energy to do so. But by the time the next two elections have passed, they will have already grown up, married and had children. And by that time all they will care about is a job to make sure they have enough for their children.

There is a lot of talk about so-called 'Asian values' these days, which they stress so that the West cannot impose democracy and human rights issues. They keep stressing 'Asian values' and that is very sad. When leaders are like that, there is no vision for the country, except for their own families. Cambodia will survive, but after all these efforts and investments in globalization, what does it teach us about Cambodia? What have we learned? There is this famous slogan 'never again', but many times history repeats itself and Slobodan Milosevic did not invent it. So my hope is that with all those resources and technology for globalization we can shape up Cambodian society, as we are still very far behind in global issues, economy and investments. 'Why is it impossible to stop globalization?' asked a scholar from Yale University. 'Because there's nobody in charge.'

Ideally, for the next chapter of the book I would have liked to recommend John F Kennedy and Jacqueline Kennedy, but they are in heaven now. And I really love simple people. You see that painting behind me? It's called 'The Widows' and it is made up of faces of women who lost their husbands and children during the Pol Pot regime. It was given to me by the Dutch ambassador Laetitia van den Assum, now based in Kenya. 'You know Youk,' she said, 'this is a picture about Cambodia. And I heard about your mum.' So for me, the best person to talk to would be to the women of Cambodia who have suffered so much. That is also why I have dedicated the work of the Documentation Center to the memory of all the mothers of Cambodia.

4

Dreams and Abilities

Introduction

YOU KNOW PERFECTLY well how to reach for a cup of coffee, open the door and get from A to B all by yourself. But what if your arms and legs simply won't perform what seem to be the easiest of daily routines? People just like you who have cerebral palsy also think just like you. Their limbs, however, don't follow their thoughts.

A common misconception about people with cerebral palsy is that they are less intelligent. But this condition often only affects the part of the brain that controls movement and does not define a person's intelligence. The muscles become less versatile, limiting their movements. This makes it more difficult for people with cerebral palsy to express themselves, as it confronts them with a multitude of problems. And whether you have a motorized wheelchair or not, someone always has to check out the accessibility of transport and locations.

Once you are more 'disability-conscious', you see it everywhere: in buildings, public spaces and on the streets. There is a need for architects and designers to fully understand the needs of people with physical impairment,' says leading Johannesburg entrepreneur Eunice Forbes, who is herself physically impaired. 'Most architects are ignorant or apathetic regarding the needs of the physically impaired. They do not seem to realize that it goes far beyond just obligatory ramps, a few wide parking bays and toilets for the disabled.' As many architects, designers and planners are not prepared to risk offending clients, they often do not stand up for the rights of – and facilities for – the disabled.

While disability consciousness is growing, for people who are physically impaired it naturally starts at home.

Meet Chaeli Mycroft, who knows what it is like. 'What Chaeli can't do starts even before she gets up in the morning,' says her mother Zelda. 'When she sleeps, she cannot turn herself or kick her blankets off when she is too hot. She can't dress herself, brush her teeth and eating takes a very long time. She can't do this, can't do that, but she doesn't mind. Chaeli doesn't focus on what she can't do, but on what she can.'

Together with her mother and dance partner Jesse Randelhoff, Chaeli travels from Cape Town to London for a presentation at St Helen's School for Girls. They promote The Chaeli Campaign, a non-profit organization that 'mobilizes the minds and bodies of children with disabilities'.

'Good mor-ning Mis-ter Hoff-man,' all the girls greet the schoolteacher, Morne Hoffman. He introduces Chaeli, Zelda and Jesse to a crowd of girls in green school uniforms. Hanging from the ceiling are statements: 'To go further than I thought'; 'To run faster than I hoped'; 'To reach higher than I dreamed'; and, in one of the out-buildings 'It is more important to try my best than to be the best'. It's a good environment for The Chaeli Campaign.

Presentations are given to two large groups of girls between 9 and 16. They consist of an introduction by Zelda, CEO of The Chaeli Campaign, the screening of a DVD and then Jesse and Chaeli show what wheelchair dancing looks like. A momentary shock goes through the audience of girls with braces and ponytails when Chaeli lands on her head in one of the wilder moves. But all ends well: Chaeli takes a long time to recover, but only from her own laughter. After the presentations they have some time for lunch and talk. But Saturday is off limits, for Chaeli and Jesse insist on a tour of London 'with all the bells and whistles'. Chaeli makes a drawing with a message for the girls and staff of the school: 'Thank you for having me.'

The Chaeli Campaign was started by Chaeli, her sister and friends (between the ages of 6 and 12 at the time of founding). They raised 20,000 Rand – about $3,000 – in just seven weeks to purchase her motorized wheelchair. After that success, their efforts transformed into a campaign that promotes and provides the mobility and educational needs of children with disabilities – giving them the same hope that Chaeli now enjoys. Zelda: 'What we are doing is paying forward the blessing of Chaeli in our lives. Chaeli's family and friends are the wind beneath her wings that have enabled her to fly and it is now our privilege to breathe hope into the lives of other differently-abled South African children, to encourage them, too, to soar.'

Following their tour of England, Zelda, Jesse and Chaeli go to the Netherlands to participate in the International Wheelchair Dancing Competition. There are 19 countries competing, sometimes with several teams. With a flag ceremony, and representatives from Malta to Mexico, it is a very colorful event that changes people's perceptions about people with disabilities, themselves and each other. Chaeli and Jesse end up third and fifth.

Once back in Chaeli Cottage, the campaign's headquarters in Cape Town, things are just as busy as before. Zelda welcomes and thanks the Chaeli Riders, cyclists who have been raising funds, and explains: 'The Chaeli Campaign was started in a garage. Not a room with a view, but a room with a vision.' She introduces Jenny, Luke and Leigh, who work in the kitchen and coffee shop, showing a miniature blueprint of what an inclusive society can be like. And another Zelda (yes, there are two of them!), who manages the coffee shop.

What does she like about this job? 'Everything! It is so rewarding to work with Jenny, Luke and Leigh. Before, there were two things I never had: patience and the confidence to speak out. But since working here I got both overnight!'

A lot of administrative work is done by Lana: 'Two years ago I was working at the Learning Center. At first I cried when seeing disabled children, but now I do so many things. I'm planning a golf event for August and other things for September.'

The snowball of The Chaeli Campaign gets bigger and bigger and the campaign is supported by many famous South Africans, including The Nelson Mandela Children's Fund. 'Children are the most vulnerable citizens in any society,' says Nelson Mandela, 'and the greatest of our treasures.'

Even now that Chaeli and her friends have a little book about the campaign, she will remind you: 'Don't judge a book by its cover.' And as inclusion is central to The Chaeli Campaign, this chapter is – passionately – told by mother Zelda and everyone else.

Chaeli Mycroft
South Africa

'You have to believe in yourself, because nobody thought we could actually do it.'

Chaeli Mycroft (born in 1993) is a young girl who was diagnosed with cerebral palsy. But with a loving family, great friends and a will of her own she makes things work. Mother Zelda: *'If there is anything The Chaeli Campaign shows, it's how much one can do with a positive attitude.'*

MY TWO DAUGHTERS Erin and Chaeli are the best gifts ever given to us, their parents. The experience of Erin's birth, our eldest, was unique. With Chaeli it was different. I had been there before; there was a lot that was different. That is because she, too, is unique...

At 11 months Chaeli was diagnosed as being cerebral palsied and this is the single greatest blessing associated with her disability. I have always been thankful that Chaeli's disability was not diagnosed at birth, as I believe that many newborn parents, when told that their child is disabled, can't see their child for the disability. We were privileged enough to get to know our child first, to have her personality impact on us, have our hopes and dream our dreams for her. Her disability has never defined who she is.

Chaeli has a sharp mind and that showed early. She can plan. Even when she was only two, when doing physiotherapy, she had to pull herself up using big foam blocks. But when she found she couldn't raise herself to a fully standing position with her hands and her fingers, guess what she did... she used her teeth to climb her way up! There was no conventional way of doing it, but she came up with her own plan to ensure that what she wanted to do would happen. And that's why, even though her hands are small and weak, she can still do things like artwork and writing. She has a spirit that attracts people and I think that's her gift.

The greatest concern my husband, Russell, and I had when Chaeli was little was her social inclusion. We have been very fortunate to have family friends in the Terry family and their three daughters, Tarryn, Justine and Chelsea. Together with Chaeli's sister Erin, these five girls have been one another's sisters, playmates, confidantes and sounding boards for their entire lives. What a privilege! Social interaction and knowing that you belong in a group is an essential human need and Chaeli's right to belong was of paramount importance to us. Having Erin and the Terry girls as friends made it a lot easier. They were given the choice initially: 'Do you want to play with Chaeli? Then these are your responsibilities: don't leave her by herself; change your games to include her as much as possible and make it work. Wherever she goes, you go.'

And if they didn't meet these responsibilities? I moaned at them and asked them how they would feel if they were excluded. As her mother, I felt that it was my responsibility to educate

Chaeli, 'campaign founder' and 'public relations manager'

'We are ordinary people with everyday needs. When I was young, I had a pretty normal life. I had friends, I got moaned at and I got irritated with my sister. But to be more independent, I needed a motorized wheelchair. My friends were always very supportive and when I was nine we came up with the idea of Sunshine Pots, sunflower seeds that people could raise themselves. By selling these, we raised funds so that I could have a motorized wheelchair.

'Much later, in December 2005, we went to Johannesburg to meet President Mbeki, because he wanted to acknowledge the work that we were doing. When I grow up I want to be a graphic designer. But I still want to be involved in The Chaeli Campaign! I always say: Don't treat disabled people differently because they're not different.'

Chaeli

'Cerebral palsy is the name they give to problems that come from having scarring on the brain. It means that my body doesn't work like everyone else's, because my muscles don't always do what I want them to do. I had various therapies which tone your muscles and help them get used to moving normally. But when I was six, my muscles stopped getting stronger and got weaker instead, especially in my arms and legs. Some nerves are damaged and my muscles don't get the necessary exercise.'

Chaeli's friends about how she should be treated and what their responsibilities were. I persevered in what I instinctively felt was the right thing to do. Chaeli didn't need to sit in adult company all day. There's no quality of life in that – just a displaced little person, bored out of her mind. The alternative was placing her in the hands of her peers. They needed to push her wheelchair, create new games and to get irritated with her as they learned the patience to slow down some of their games and eventually know that they love Chaeli for who she is, just as she loves them as they are.

Of course there was a calculated risk involved. If we gave her four-year old peers and playmates responsibilities for her physical well-being, then there was a real chance of her being hurt. How is this different from able-bodied youngsters? They get hurt, scuff knees, and fall out of trees and off bicycles. Chaeli has also been on top of a fire engine riding around the streets of Sedgefield, on the back of a camel in Muizenberg and screaming down Monkey Falls at Ratanga Junction. Why should our cerebral palsied child be denied the same growing experiences, especially if these came hand-in-hand with friendship and fun? We thought that it was a risk worth taking.

We have always believed in compromise. But compromising total physical safety for quality of life. Is this viable? Chaeli is a normal child with normal needs. Her wheelchair does not make any of that different. Children are very accepting and very curious and we used this to her advantage from an early age. As a schoolteacher it was important to me that, when children asked questions about Chaeli's disability, she and the rest of us were equipped to answer them. We have had long conversations with little people, complete strangers, in shopping malls. I have taken Chaeli to schools and chatted to them about what she is physically able or unable to do, but also about her fiercely independent spirit. We have engaged anyone wanting to know more in conversation. And the most important part of this is Chaeli seeing her disability as a bridge to communicate with people she might otherwise never have met. She manages to convey to them that her wheelchair limits her physically only – that she has choices in deciding how she lives her life and these choices are as multitudinous as any other normal child's choices.

At the age of six Chaeli was also diagnosed as having a degenerative neuropathy. But blessings come in weird places. Had this not been discovered, she would still be sitting in a special needs school which she had attended since the age of three. When her occupational therapy was discontinued, my husband and I decided to do a totally unconventional thing and

Chaeli

'When I was four, two friends who were in charge of my wheelchair were going too fast and they tipped me into a rose garden. Fortunately the roses had just been pruned, but my mom says I resembled a tortoise with a wheelchair shell. My face and arms were full of scratches and I had to cry. And my friends also cried! But afterwards I realized this experience taught us all a lesson. I have also been a goalkeeper in soccer games. I did very well, because no-one dared to shoot for fear of hitting me!'

Chaeli

'My parents enrolled me at Sweet Valley Primary School where my sister goes, with able-bodied children. For four years I had a facilitator who helped me do things at school and to get around. Her name was Precious. And she really was *precious*. But she recently started a new job, so that I now no longer have a facilitator. Nokuthula, who works in our home, now comes to school to help me go to the bathroom at first break. My school friends now help me to get up the stairs and into the classroom. It gives me a feeling of freedom and independence and it's great that my classmates at school are now also like a family to me.'

hire a facilitator for her physical needs, because she is a bright kid. This happened when she was nine. Within a week we got her an assessment session at our local mainstream school. We felt that if her body was letting her down, we needed to provide her with the opportunity to fly with what was working perfectly: her bright mind. And we have never looked back!

Without her mainstream experience I believe that Chaeli would not have been as challenged – intellectually and socially – as she has been. 'Challenge' seems to be every second word I say! But through this experience I have formed the opinion that when we pander to our children's disability we do them a disservice. It's a form of 'spoiling' that they can ill afford. Chaeli has been in mainstream education for three years now and went from a class of 13 to a class of 33. When asked what she enjoyed the most about her new school, she said: 'Sometimes I have to shout to be heard!'

Passive or active?

In her first three years at the special needs school we were told each year that she was passive in group work. Hmm. Can a child with a disability find her place and feel that she belongs in a mainstream environment where she is the only wheelchair-bound learner? Here's a checklist of her activities: she has been in the school choir for four years. Her diction is not always great but she is very musical and loves it! As a Brownie, she got her Golden Hand in 2005 and went on to be a Girl Guide. She has done drama and played chess. She has done extra math lessons – her own choice, because she reckons her maths sucks! She has done individual singing lessons in place of conventional Speech Therapy. She has done Boccia, bowls for the disabled. She was an avid supporter of the netball and hockey teams and for the last two years she has been doing ballroom dancing for the disabled. Whenever I see her do the wheelchair dancing, I get a lump in my throat. I think it's one of the most beautiful things in the world.

Chaeli has a lot of fun and quite a full social program, including an hour of private physio each week. She has a standing frame which she uses each day, but now refuses to sit in the special desk we got for her. She doesn't want to be 'different' so we

Jesse Randelhoff, Chaeli's dance partner

'When we practise, we wear tracksuits with 'SA Dance Team' on our backs. But at the real dance competition Chaeli wears an evening gown and I wear tailcoats and a bow tie. We do Latin American dances like chachacha and rumba, followed by ballroom dances like waltz and quickstep – nine dances in all. I have been doing ballroom dancing since I was nine.

'When I started dancing with Chaeli, at first I treated her like a porcelain doll, because I was afraid that she might hurt herself. Chaeli is quite skinny, her arms and wrists are quite thin and her elbows 'click' because they don't get extended that often. It took me a while to understand her arms were not going to break. So now I can just whoop her around the corners and have fun, even at the International Wheelchair Dancing Competition.'

Chaeli

'At Sweet Valley I was the only one in a wheelchair. But it was a push wheelchair and I wanted to play the games that my other friends also played. One day we had to take it for repairs and they had a motorized wheelchair in the workshop. Martha, the manager, let me have a ride in it and it was so much fun! I kept thinking about how much more I would be able to do if I had a motorized wheelchair. But it was very expensive. It cost 20,000 Rand, which was too much for my parents' pocket. Then my sister, friends and I came up with an idea. We went around the neighborhood and we sold Sunshine Pots and cards and we took orders for Saturday morning muffins. On the first day we raised 280 Rand and in seven weeks we got the 20,000 Rand.'

found another compromise: the right-sized desk and a footboard that keeps her feet in the correct place and helps to position her correctly in the two-man desk. Has she fallen out? Yup, this happened a while ago. Fortunately Matthew, who sits next to her, is a star athlete who plays rugby. Thanks to his good reflexes he caught her before she slipped out of her desk completely. As they were writing exams at the time it caused quite a commotion! And of course, one of the major things that has happened as a direct result of Chaeli's inclusion in mainstream education is the creation of The Chaeli Campaign. And that has been so good in so many ways...

When Chaeli went to school at Sweet Valley Primary School in Cape Town, it was the first time that we realized that you get motorized wheelchairs that are custom-made for little people. And when Chaeli saw it, she was absolutely blown away, because she is quite an adventurous soul. She wanted one, got a ride in one, and got the knack of it immediately. She zoomed all over the showroom.

The fact that a motorized wheelchair was not part of the

family budget didn't stop Chaeli from wanting it. And Martha suggested to Chaeli that as she was a Brownie, she should encourage her friends to sell cookies and raise funds for the wheelchair. Chaeli, her sister Erin and her three lifelong friends Tarryn, Justine and Chelsea Terry came up with the campaign, because as Chaeli said: 'Being with your parents all the time is boring!' In any event, Martha's suggestion had planted a seed in Chaeli's mind and she then became the driving force behind all five girls brainstorming the idea. They created the entire concept themselves. They scanned the internet for ideas and decided on Sunshine Pots, miniature do-it-yourself pot plants and self-made cards with Erin's and Chaeli's artwork on them.

The power of dreams

How many of us still have big dreams? Three years ago, 20,000 Rand for five children under the age of 12 was a huge dream. That was their goal. And I really believe that we too have to have huge dreams. I believe that The Chaeli Campaign has a role to play in the disability sector on the world stage. That's why we asked the mayor of Cape Town, Helen Zille, to send letters of introduction to the mayors of London, Amsterdam, New York and Los Angeles. These girls started all that, because they saw themselves as quite capable. Most people do a SWOT analysis – of Strengths, Weaknesses, Opportunities and Threats. But their focus ends up being the challenges. Had we, as adults, imposed our skeptical business viewpoint on them, we would have told them not to do it. But it was their exuberance and the belief in themselves that gave them wings. Opportunity is there all the time, but often we don't see it. And that's one of the lessons that we have learned from these children. They grasped it.

Pre-sale orders for the Sunshine Pots and the cards came in fast, especially as the team had persuaded friends, classmates, teachers and even the business community to participate. And to make the Sunshine Pots? Sometimes big orders came in. Filling these orders was very difficult to do, so they asked an entire class to come and help at a work party. We provided the cool drinks and they provided the hands. They made 1,300 Sunshine Pots in only six days. And they ended up reaching the amount needed in just seven weeks.

But we were daft when we started doing this, because the profit margins were minimal. We took Erin and Chaeli's artwork and scanned, printed and laminated the cards at home. We sold them individually without envelopes for only three Rand and two cards for five. And so much labor went into the Sunshine Pots as well. We took all of those, covered them with raffia and cellophane and sold them for five Rand too. But consider: $1 is 10 Rand... so we realized that we need to charge more for the actual physical labor that goes into it. We now sell it for 10 Rand. But the money didn't stop coming in once Chaeli received her wheels on 11 June 2004 at a school assembly.

Chaeli

'The wheelchair was handed over to me in assembly, so the whole school could see and that day is one of my happiest days ever. And when I got it, it wasn't so difficult to operate it. My therapist, Nim, says that it's because I have good motor planning. I can easily determine which actions should follow. '

The campaign we run now does physiotherapy, occupational therapy and communication programs. And we also run a parents support group. We say: one person can make a difference. And once I had my wheelchair, my friends and I started thinking about how good it would be if all children with disabilities could be more independent. Sometimes families are embarrassed about having a child with special needs, but mostly it's because they can't afford to help their children. But if I can get a wheelchair, then other children should be able to get what they need too!'

There came a moment when their 'team' approached the school principal, which is the moment it stepped up to another phase. Something of a more lasting effect was happening and it was decided to formalize the campaign as a non-profit organization, provided that the original founders always remained involved in growing the work that they had started. When the money started rolling in, it affirmed what these girls were doing; it affirmed their relationship, their empathy for Chaeli and the acknowledgement of Chaeli needing to be more independent. They gave life to the fact that disabled people need their dignity – even if it's just through an assistive device – in order to be more functional in an able-bodied world. It changes their lives.

In June 2005, I stopped teaching and after running The Chaeli Campaign part-time for one year, I became the first full-time employee. Now I often joke saying: 'Our pre-teen children created full-time jobs for mum and dad!' It's a wacky perspective, but it's very real and important. I have been a teacher most of my professional life, and therefore I have the advantage of knowing how to manage people. The campaign has really taken off and the team has raised enough funds for the mobility needs of 200 children from disadvantaged communities. And a host of other things! Most people we support have cerebral palsy. And the major things that help them are custom-made motorized wheelchairs, standing frames and laptop computers.

We live in a world where people feel that admitting to basic decency and compassion is hard. It seems nerdy and it is not

---

Chelsea Terry: 'Because we love Chaeli'

People often ask: 'What is Chelsea's job?' She's the youngest. And we always say that she is there to win hearts with simple truths, because she always starts with: 'We started The Chaeli Campaign because we love Chaeli.' And that is the essence of it.

'cool'. You need to build up a wall and work from behind a facade. But The Chaeli Campaign is based on love and relationships. I believe that you have the world at your fingertips, if you have the will, the drive and the passion. When you do what your strength is, you can achieve anything. And that achievement could be simply kindness. These kids have known each other all their lives. They love one another enough to fight and still remain friends and we're not ashamed to say: 'It started because of love'.

Chaeli being the face of the campaign is important, because she is bright, she is alive and she exudes a confidence that people see immediately. It radiates from her. It is also important to note that the spirit of The Chaeli Campaign is the teamwork that exists. As I said, blessings come in weird places and we need to claim them when and where we can. Chaeli's disability has given her a quality of life and recognition as a 'young woman of worth'. At 10, she was the youngest-ever finalist in the Woman of the Year 2005 competition of Shoprite Checkers, a huge shopping chain in South Africa. Her physical challenges have created qualities of courage and independence that inspire those around her. Her friendships have already lasted a lifetime. She and Justine have started planning the house that they intend sharing 'when they grow up' and she has a vision for her life of independent living and holding down a job, even though her future job aspirations keep changing... She has claimed her rightful place in society and has added quality to the lives of the people she has touched. Through The Chaeli Campaign she has become a positive role model for thousands of disabled children who often cannot dream of a future in which they fulfill their potential.

I feel privileged to have been given the awesome task of raising two beautiful daughters. Erin's part in Chaeli's success is never acknowledged enough. She is the stabilizing force – the sibling who tells Chaeli: 'You're just being lazy!' But she loves her to

Russell, Chaeli's father and office manager

'My task is to run things successfully from an administrative point of view, as I'm more comfortable in the background. In a way, my work simply evolved from sorting out problems with computers and things started from there. My main objective is to make The Chaeli Campaign completely self-sustainable.'

distraction and helps her more than anyone else in the world. I am humbled to have a partner in Russell who puts up with a woman who is strong-willed and often difficult to live with.

I'm also blessed to have been able to love Chaeli for who she is and not to have allowed her disability to shut her out of our lives. Chaeli has been 'lucky' to have friends and family who have nurtured her in a very affirming way. But what Chaeli has added to our lives is also immense. She has opened our eyes to an otherwise unseen world, taught us lessons that only she can teach and enriched our lives with her feisty spirit. In the grand scheme of things I think we're all winners...

Chaeli's need for increased and more effective independence was the catalyst that started this campaign to mobilize the minds and bodies of children with disabilities. As an organization started by children for children, our five founding members have a huge role to play as social leaders of the future and they constitute our Junior Committee – hence our slogan 'administered by adults, powered by kids'. But the organization manages public funds, so it is essential that adults handle the administrative and financial duties and the day-to-day running of the organization. The job descriptions of Tarryn, Justine, Chelsea, Erin and Chaeli are tongue-in-cheek, but that doesn't make their contribution any less. The objectives of The Chaeli Campaign are to promote and provide the mobility and educational needs of disabled children under the age of 18 throughout South Africa and to work together with other organizations to 'change the life of one differently-abled child at a time'.

We have a vision to grow and that was understood perfectly by a small girl called Amber Gardiner. She created a picture that shows the world with Africa at its center, circled by children. It shows that our focus is Africa and more specifically South Africa and that our key mandate is children and that inclusion is central to our work. But we see ourselves as capable and essential partners and facilitators in the disability sector worldwide. People – and specifically children – with disabilities have the right to function effectively and happily from within their own communities, as equal citizens in a world where they do have a valuable and exciting contribution to make! And

---

Oscar Pistorius, patron of The Chaeli Campaign

'Differently-abled' is a phrase coined by Oscar Pistorius (born in 1986), a young man who had to learn to run without legs. Also known as the 'the fastest man with no legs' and 'Blade Runner', Oscar won the gold medals in the 100-, 200- and 400-meter sprints at the 2008 Summer Paralympics. He runs with carbon-fiber artificial limbs. Being differently-abled himself, Oscar understands the challenges of The Chaeli Campaign and his success as an athlete demonstrates the possibilities of pushing boundaries and expanding horizons.

When he was 11, it was diagnosed that Oscar had 'congenital absence of the fibula' in both legs. As a result, his legs were amputated below the knees. But while attending Pretoria Boys' High School, he played rugby, water polo, tennis and even did wrestling. In 2004 he was introduced to running. Oscar currently studies business management and sports science. 'You're not disabled by the disabilities you have. You're able by the abilities you have.'

---

our Junior Committee are pioneers in this field, providing a blueprint of how inclusion should and can work in reality. And on top of all that, we are very fortunate to have Oscar Pistorius as our patron.

One thing these girls have in common is a wonderful skill. Despite their very young age, they're not afraid of public speaking. But they do not want to do it in front of their own school. They will speak to corporate people and other schools, but at their own school it embarrasses them. They feel the peer pressure of their schoolmates and that they would be teased about it. And they don't allow me to promote anything at their school. I think they're

Chaeli's sounding boards

Erin Mycroft, Chaeli's sister and computer boffin

'We had always done Kids TV marketing on Market Day, an entrepreneurs' program presented by Kids TV. We did that every year, so we sort of had a little bit of experience. We were always making things on our holidays, so we decided that we should do it for Chaeli. We went to school and sent out forms for Sunshine Pots and cards. And on the first day when we went to see how many there were in a box at the secretary's office, the box was overflowing! And in the first envelope we opened there was a 500 Rand donation. People are still donating money even now that Chaeli has a motorized wheelchair.

'We then decided that if we can make Chaeli's dream come true, why not pass the blessing forward, so that we can help other children too? By now, we have helped so many children with wheelchairs, mobility aids, laptops, hearing aids and so on. The five of us focus on the promotion of things, so we go to talks and we make some of the products and we do the online newsletter. Chaeli is definitely changing people's perceptions about people in wheelchairs. That they can do stuff and do not just sit around in a wheelchair.'

scared that their mother will make a fool of herself or of them!

Chaeli is the face of The Chaeli Campaign; the spirit is the teamwork. Chaeli, as a differently-abled person, is a functional member of an able-bodied group of people. Without her, her sister and their three friends, this would not have happened. Chaeli's need was the catalyst, but now it is the needs of other children that drive our work. As a legal entity, the adults have to run the organization, but in order for it to maintain the integrity that started it, the children have to remain involved. Many top businesspeople actually think that the five girls run The Chaeli Campaign as they do all have functional roles that they play.

Justine Terry, 'marketing manager', Chaeli's adviser, confidante and best friend

'Chaeli and I have always been best friends. She is only four and a half months older than me. She has known me my whole life. Chaeli is my best friend, because she is one of the people I can always talk to. Chaeli and I go to schools and we give the school a challenge and see whether they can raise the funds for another disabled person's wheelchair.'

Tarryn Terry, 'financial adviser' with a big heart

'Chaeli is like a sister to me. I've known her forever and we all love her. She's awesome. In a way there never was a decision to do The Chaeli Campaign. Chaeli wanted us to help. Yes. And now I am the secretary of the campaign, so I take minutes at meetings and then I type them up.'

Chelsea Terry, 'goodwill manager', agrees with the other girls

'Working for The Chaeli Campaign means we sometimes miss out on school or on tests. And sometimes our friends get jealous, because they feel we get too much attention. We have learned many new things and we are confident in speaking in front of people – without the keywords that you see people use on TV! We're very lucky to get these experiences.'

They do run certain aspects, but they are children and their first 'job' is school!

From small beginnings, The Chaeli Campaign has grown and it now has five full-time employees, and six contract therapists who provide services to over 85 children in three centers around Cape Town. We're a social development business, a business with heart. And we have provided custom-made assistive devices to over 200 children – anything from wheelchairs to hearing aids

'Hope in Motion', the sister organization of The Chaeli Campaign in Zimbabwe, led by Sibongile and Never Chanengeta

With an initial supply of three wheelchairs and a conference on fundraising and leadership, 'Hope in Motion' is on its way. The main drive is to raise awareness of disabled children's right to be a part of the community, their right to dignity, to be recognized and acknowledged. Sibongile and Never do this in an unbelievably selfless way.

Sibongile

We are a support group of 16 families. Each family has a differently-abled child. Two years ago, I phoned Zelda and The Chaeli Campaign, because Never and I had read a magazine article. Our 12-year-old daughter Leona, who had brittle-bone disease and who was often in pain, inspired us to contact them. People with brittle-bone disease are very tiny, so she was in a class with the nine year olds. Since then, with their help, we have created a sister organization.

It took us a long time to realize that Leona was disabled. At first she was treated for polio, then tested for HIV. She had had problems since the age of two, but only at the age of 11 did they discover that she had brittle-bone disease. Over the years, her bones started becoming thinner and we were concerned that she might break them. After that, she was no longer able to walk, so we carried her on our back and laptop computers for children who don't have functional language. The challenge is enormous. In South Africa there are 45 million people, of which approximately 3 million are differently-abled. I don't like to say 'disabled' because everybody has abilities. They are simply different. But there is a cultural resistance to include disabled children. They are often seen as a curse of ancestors and neglected, sometimes in appalling conditions. But with The Chaeli Campaign we hope to show

to school. Or to hospital. Her older sister, Linette, brought her water and did everything for her, as if she was simply playing with Leona. But Leona was also short-tempered. She always insisted that something she needed was done immediately. If not, she asked: 'Why?' If she knew the reason, she was comfortable.

A doctor in Harare explained the whole truth: 'Leona's chest bones are caving, so she is experiencing pressure from her bones that are squeezing her heart, lungs and internal organs. The bones are contracting and that makes breathing difficult. There is nothing we can do, not even an operation... What you can do is: give her whatever you can afford.' But for me, I didn't want the truth, because I loved my child so much. I was hoping for a miracle from God, for my child to be well. This was in 2003.

Over a long time Leona got more and more pain. She loved watching the religious channel, because that gave her hope. And at one time she said: 'Mama, I want to phone in to Bishop Deya Ministries in Britain myself! When is he going to pray for me?' So she phoned in and Bishop Deya said: 'OK, we agree to pray for you on Monday 26 November.' The Bishop, junior ministers and sister Mucha would pray for her. The sister spoke Shona, our language, and would translate it for Leona. But Leona passed away the day before, Sunday 25. She was only 14. At 6 o'clock British time the Bishop phoned again to speak to and pray with Leona. They cried on the phone, when they heard that she had passed away. It was a very sorrowful day. *[continued overleaf]* there is oomph and something positive happening at the bottom of our continent!

Some of our contract occupational therapists work at Fish Hoek-Kommetjie-Noordhoek Welfare Association's Special Care Centers: Ocean View, and Sinethemba, which means 'We have hope'. Lezanne de la Rey, CEO of the Association, and the staff deliver daycare for children with special needs, creative stimulation programs, recreational activities, counseling, parent support groups, adult and youth support groups. And due to the partnership with The Chaeli Campaign, exercise, occupational and communication therapy as well as transference of care

---

Never

We went to South Africa and Zelda said: 'Right, we're going to provide you with a wheelchair for your daughter.' When we got home, we put Leona in the wheelchair and it brought so much joy to her life! She started getting more friends and enjoying window shopping and outdoor life, feeling the fresh air among the trees. Her life was lifted up and she was shining! And at school, the whole class and the headteacher were also very happy for her. We sent Zelda photos. That started our relationship.

'What about other children in Zimbabwe?' Zelda asked. 'Do you want us to help?' We decided to register an organization under the umbrella of The Chaeli Campaign. But it had to be registered under another name, so we chose the slogan 'Hope in Motion'. It was difficult. In Zimbabwe most NGOs and charity organizations are banned or closed down, because the authorities believe that many NGOs are just a front for subversive organizations. People in power are scared, because a lot of opposition is channeled through human rights and non-profit organizations. We were interrogated for three days. But we managed to go through all the paperwork. After that we had to advertise this in *The Herald* in Harare for three weeks and if there was one person that would have objected, it wouldn't have been registered.

---

skills are also offered. The staff is very dedicated. During one of our talks, Lezanne said: 'Many people do things beyond the call of duty and we have made an amazing journey. It's a 360-degree revolution from where we started.'

There are certain things that you don't have control over. But you do have control over the choices that you make. Our biggest mission is to move people away from a sacrifice mindset. Often when a differently-abled child comes into a classroom or any other environment, the first thought people have is: what do we have to sacrifice to include her – space, attention, time? I believe that people need to move away from that 'sacrifice'

Fundraising in Zimbabwe is very difficult, because the little money people have they need to buy food. Whatever we had in the beginning, all came from The Chaeli Campaign. They also advised us to make things from wood, like the logo of the organization. They are made in Zimbabwe and sold in South Africa, which allows us to buy things. Some of the money goes to the single mothers that make it; some of it goes to our organization. Zelda is always there for us. She inspired us and was very patient.

Leona said: 'I really want that organization to be there, also for other children. You must go, mama!' And when we came back, she would have a big smile on her face. Leona's spirit lives on and she has made us think about other children with disabilities and fight for those in need. Our organization now includes a man who studies teaching children with disabilities and a physiotherapist. And we hold meetings with parents to share ideas about how to look after children with disabilities and to show that it's no use being sorry for yourself and that you are not alone. You know, many of Leona's classmates come and visit our place after school – 15 young girls that knew her in Grade 3. Since she passed away, they have been coming every school day: 'We really loved Leona,' they say. 'We come to comfort you.'

Chaeli

'So far, we've already helped hundreds of children and it gives me such a good feeling to see how we're making a difference. I will never forget how good I felt when my friends decided to help me get a wheelchair and I would like everyone else in the whole world to feel that special.'

mindset to a mindset of abundance: what are these other 30 children going to learn from this experience? What are we going to gain from this? And the high school that Chaeli now attends has that kind of mindset that is growing the school community in a special way. They are embracing the special lessons that Chaeli has to offer and it's wonderful.

5

One of the One Million

Introduction

WHEN 'PROLETARIANS OF all lands unite', what do their sons and daughters inherit? In Karl Marx's view, they had 'nothing to lose but their chains'. Around the world, communist revolutions have indeed brought about incredible changes, but often at great human cost and suffering. Creating state institutions that serve society turned out to be a greater challenge than anticipated on the basis of manifestoes of 'historical necessity'. Yet, the proletarian revolution and class struggle were accompanied by an unfailing conviction that these ideas had universal validity for the progress of humankind.

After being adopted by Russia, Marx's and Engels' ideas were re-interpreted by Mao Zedong and the Communist Revolution in China. For decades, China was controlled by the Communist Party with an obsessive personality cult surrounding its leader. Everywhere you went, there was a huge poster of Chairman Mao: Mao the swimmer, Mao the poet, Mao the thinker, Mao the family man.

But from the beginning there was dissent and opposition resulting in millions of prisoners and victims. While replacing the bourgeois and landowning class, the Communist Party essentially followed the line of imperial dynasties, replacing a dictatorship of one by a dictatorship of 3,000: the National People's Congress. Anyone opposing their ideals was classified as a 'counter-revolutionary' or 'enemy of the state'.

From 1949 onward, labor camps were set up, in which 'hostile elements' would 'reform through labor' – the meaning of the Chinese word *laogai*. At one point there were more than 1,100 labor camps. They spanned – and still span – the land of China, from highly industrialized factories in the east to isolated farms in the west. In the early decades, prisoners planted, harvested, manufactured and processed all kinds of products for sale in domestic and international markets. But as the rules of supply and demand affect China as much as any non-communist nation, the focus has changed to consumer goods, often contracted by domestic and foreign businesses and then shipped around the world.

The products may sell. But the system that produces them 'brings its victims to their knees and leaves them to crawl'. Today, there are still around three million laogai prisoners.

In the 1980s a new wind started blowing under Deng Xiaoping. Deng's 'socialist market economy' and 'open-door policy' allowed more foreign businesses, joint ventures and trade. These policies became famous by Deng's catch phrase: 'It doesn't matter whether the cat is black or white, as long as it catches mice'. Ever since, foreign businesses have been quite happy to 'catch mice' – do business – with the Chinese. Deng, *Time* magazine's 'Man of the Year' in 1978, is commonly thought to have had 'backroom control' until his death in 1997. The Great Leap Forward that was supposed to take place from 1958 to 1961 could be said to be happening today.

Decades of Chinese Communist Party rule produced many

victims – but also some remarkable survivors. One of them was a 'counter-revolutionary rightist' named Harry Wu. He was rehabilitated in 1979 after having experienced every misery of the Chinese laogai system for 19 years. Born in Shanghai, with a seemingly bright future, Wu's fortunes changed dramatically after the 1949 Revolution. While studying at the Geology Institute in Beijing he was arrested for speaking out about the Russian invasion of Hungary and the concept of 'comrades'. He was sent to do forced labor in 1960 and was tortured, nearly starving to death in places 'where they send our misfits, our outlaws, our dissidents, our class enemies, our thinkers, our questioners, our doubters, our dreamers, our scholars, our optimists, and our pessimists – anybody who thinks or feels – millions of us.'

Wu later left China for the United States and wrote about his experiences in *Bitter Winds* and *Troublemaker*. In 1992, he established the Laogai Research Foundation, a non-profit research and public education organization, and the China Information Center, both located in the Washington DC area. The Laogai Research Foundation is recognized as a leading source of information on China's labor camps. Wu has testified before various US congressional committees, as well as the parliaments of Britain, Germany, Australia, the European Union and the United Nations. He has exposed the laogai and many other failings of Chinese society, including the death penalty, the harvesting of organs from prisoners on death row, the side-effects of the one-child policy and the lack of judicial reform. Research has shown that at least 200 different 'products to avoid' are produced in today's laogai. The products range from tea to rubber boots, clothing to cotton products, binder-clips to diesel engines.

Although Mao died in 1976, his legacy and that of earlier Communist policies is in some senses still intact. A never-ending reservoir of laborers is helping China realize its double-digit economic growth percentages. And this part of 'market socialism' is underpinned by entire books published by the Chinese Government itself training officials on the efficient use of forced labor and on allowing the laogai to operate as a profit-making enterprise. Just imagine working with toxic substances without protective gear – tanning hides while standing naked in vats filled with chemicals. Or working in improperly run mines where accidents and explosions are common. For 15 hours a day. On rationed food. With torture, sleep deprivation, shackling, solitary confinement and starvation.

Wu feels the Chinese Government should respect the rest of the world *and* their own people if they wish to continue selling their goods around the world. 'Somebody must remind them. This is my job. I appointed myself. I live in another country now, but I cannot forget.'

Harry Wu
China

'I want to expose the system. I am the needle in the heart, the bone in the throat. Truth is on my side.'

Harry Wu (born in 1937), activist for human rights in China and founder of the Laogai Research Foundation. He spent 19 years in the laogai, the Chinese labor camps.

'My major at university was in geology. After that, for 20 years, my major was in tilling the earth!'

I AM 70 NOW. Before I was born, the Japanese had launched large-scale attacks on China in the 1930s. They took over Manchuria, bombed Shanghai and Guangzhou, and committed the Nanking Massacre. When I was a child, at first I did not feel we were living a very wealthy life, for we still had a lot of economic problems. But my father was working for a bank in Shanghai, and after he got promoted, from 1945 to 1949, our life was becoming much better.

One day my father even ordered a new car, a Buick, although he never received it. My father also enjoyed hunting and he owned a couple of guns. So at that time, our family was reasonably well off. For a short while I even studied the piano, but we had to sell it again after six months. The rest of my childhood was a time of peace and pleasure. After elementary school, my father sent my brother and me to the Catholic St Francis College. There, my most memorable teacher was Father Capolito, who taught me to stand up for my beliefs, to ask questions, to be smart, stubborn and logical.

The connection between my father and me was very weak. There were eight children and my father particularly cared for his first daughter and his first son, my elder brother. But

129

I do remember an important moment. After my own mother had passed away, a special service was held in our home. My father gathered the whole family together to commemorate her. The service was held in a Chinese way with incense and many candles and cups of wine. It was very funny, because it really still was a kind of Buddhism mixed with Christian things, but my father didn't want to talk about it with me. But after I graduated and went to university in 1955, I insisted: 'Why did we hold that service for our mother in that way?'

'Because your mother was a great woman and we wanted to remember her in a special way. But I am neither a Buddhist nor a Catholic, so I asked myself how to do it in the best possible way. We used elements of both religions to remember your mother. That's all.' Later he married my stepmother.

Another time, my father took me out to the shopping center to buy reading glasses. It was the only chance I ever had to sit down by his side. 'Are you doing all right at school?' he asked. 'Yes,' I answered. 'But what about those people over there, the people that are selling the silver dollars?' He said: 'That's OK. These people really understand the current situation and the economy of Shanghai. They will be all right. In any country and in any society, every man has to depend on himself. I don't have any money for you, so you have to study hard and provide for yourself.' That was his most important advice to me.

Only two years later, the Communists took over all private property, including that of my father, even though he was not very high up in the bank. In 1952, there was a strike due to the so-called Strike Tiger Movement. My father was accused of the crime of capitalism. One evening, he didn't return from his work. My brothers and sisters were waiting for him and we asked Mummy: 'Where is Daddy?'

'Eat your dinner,' she said. 'Don't ask about it.'

Meanwhile, my father and all the bank managers were detained in the bank building. One month later he was finally released.

He came back home and simply said: 'It's all right.' He didn't tell us what had happened, but after that, the bank was gone. 'I'm not the boss of the bank,' he had told his captors. 'Are you sure?' they had said. He had explained that at Yang's Brothers Bank all the chief managers were from the Yang family. 'I have only one stock, but I don't own the bank.' Still, they considered my father to be a capitalist. They did not give him a jail sentence, but Mr Yang had to go to jail for five years.

During the period from 1949 until 1957 my sister was in the United States and my elder brother had gone to graduate school. From then on, at home I was at the head of the family. But as education was the most important thing, children were not supposed to be involved in finance, politics and so on. Father said: 'Whatever you want to do, you study. And if you need money, ask Mummy and she will give it to you.' Even though our life at that time was quite tough, we did not feel anything was wrong. But the piano got sold, the carpet got sold, the refrigerator got sold and two telephones became one telephone. And then finally we had no telephone.

Upstairs there was a storage room with my father's and mother's possessions. My mother always quietly went up, packaged something, moved things around and went outside. But we didn't know they were actually selling everything! – silk, garments, valuables. One day, I went up myself. 'O, my god,' I said. 'What is this?' Among many other boxes, there was a big suitcase from the time of my mother's marriage. She had come from a very rich landlord family. But all the boxes were open and empty! Since 1952 my father had gone from the top to the bottom. Now he was only able to work at a table in front of the bank, handing out deposit or withdrawal papers to people. For the rest, he depended on selling things. From that time he became very tense and pensive and he suffered a lot.

In 1957, at the age of 19, I was accused of being a 'counter-revolutionary rightist'. In April something happened that surprised me. My first love, Meihua, graduated from school early, two months before the normal graduation time in China, which is in June. She sent me a letter saying: 'I have graduated from the school and I have made arrangements. Maybe they will consider me and my fiancé for a job in Beijing.' But later she wrote me another letter: 'I am sorry that I cannot come to Beijing. I will go away.' She disappeared.

Red flower, white flower

At that time the Government was running the so-called One Hundred Flowers Campaign. Mao said: 'Letting a hundred flowers blossom and a hundred schools of thought contend is the policy for promoting the progress of the arts and the sciences and a flourishing culture in our land.' This sounded promising. But it was a disguised way of finding out who was *for* and who was *against* the Communist Revolution and to unmask 'thought reactionaries'. The Communist Party asked everyone at the university to speak out. My class had 30 students. Of these, 7 were Party members and 16 were Communist Youth League. So they were *red* students and the remaining seven of us were white. Whatever it meant, we were a minority. I did not feel it was a problem that the Communists were leading. But then a girl, who was secretary of the Communist Party branch of my class, asked me: 'You want to go to Shanghai to see your fiancée, your girlfriend? Then you have to ask the head of department for approval.' I got approval and boarded a train to Shanghai to see Meihua. So far I didn't have any problems.

But when I came back, the secretary of the Communist Party said to me: 'We want to ask you in a friendly and straightforward way: what are your views about politics?'

'I have no views,' I said. 'I'm a major in geology. I am captain of the baseball team and I'm getting ready for a training session this afternoon.'

'No, no, no!' she said. 'You have to come! Stop the baseball practice. Whatever you have to say, we want to listen to you.' I entered the classroom.

'Well,' I said, 'the Soviet involvement in the Hungarian revolution last year was right, because we are a socialist country and Hungary was involved in counter-revolution. But I think that one country's military intervention in another country's political affairs is a violation of international law.'

The second issue I raised was this: 'Chairman Mao has said many times, even today, that everybody wants to join the construction of socialism and that we are all comrades. So why is it that you, as a Communist member, always say: 'OK, comrade students, today we call a meeting and so on...?' It means that you are telling the 23 members of the Youth League and Party members that they are comrades. But we, the rest of us, are not comrades; we're students. You're dividing people in first and second class. If I take a bus or a train, I say to the driver: "Comrade, I want a ticket". And when I go to the department store I say: "Comrade, I want to buy a cup". We're all comrades!' You have to know that in China at that time everybody called everybody else *comrade*.

A couple of weeks passed. The student body gathered again in June. 'Today we will criticize Harry Wu!' they said, to my astonishment. They arranged for some students to come forward and talk about the two points I had raised.

'So you disagree with the Soviet invasion? It means you disagree with the policies of the Communist Party. You are a counter-revolutionary rightist.'

'What is this?' I said. 'I'm innocent.'

'No, you're not!'

On 20 October the school put up a big poster, using the big characters in the style of newspapers: 'Harry Wu is a counter-revolutionary rightist.' From that point on, I was forced to make confessions, to tell on my classmates and accept the lead of my Communist League classmates. The Communist Party appointed two people to watch over me. I had to report to them, tell them where I went, what I was doing and what I was thinking. I lost freedom.

Enemy level 3

My classmates had always been my friends. But now, not only did they denounce me, but nobody would talk to me anymore. I had become their enemy, an 'enemy of the Party', an 'enemy of the people' and an 'enemy of the Chinese Government'. I felt utter shock at this sudden change. It meant *total* exclusion. Across the whole school there were hundreds of students, teachers and workers, who were all wearing a hat – in a manner of speaking – with the label of 'counter-revolutionary rightist'. And each had loyal members of the Communist Party assigned to watch over them. This remained so until February the following year, when Chairman Mao made it Government policy to divide students into different levels of punishment. Level 1: you go to a labor camp right away. Level 2: you're expelled and do not continue in a school or university, but go to the countryside or to a factory to labor. Level 3: remain in the school as an enemy of the people, but with surveillance by other students. Level 4: no punishment, but retaining the label of a counter-revolutionary rightist. I was in the third level. But many students were expelled from school.

So some of us remained in society – in schools, in hospitals, in offices – but we were different. At school, all the counter-revolutionary rightists remained under surveillance. This was all part of the Communist Revolution. It divided people by class. This is why much later, after I had made *laogai* a popular word, I coined another word in 2003: *classicide*, not genocide. The word genocide became well known due to the fate of the Jewish people in Hitler's concentration camps. European Jews suffered a terrible ordeal. And later, people in countries like Rwanda and Yugoslavia experienced a similar fate. But the concept of genocide cannot explain the killing in China, because there the Chinese killed their own people, indistinguishable from each other. They had divided people by *class*. That's what classicide is, killing people on the basis of their class. The nationalist Kuomintang killed Communists, landlords killed peasants, revolutionaries killed landlords, and Communists killed Catholics, Tibetans – anybody who disagreed. Chinese killed Chinese.

On 1 May 1958 there was another significant campaign. The whole country came to a stop. Why? To kill sparrows. Mao Zedong said there were four major pests: rats, flies, mosquitoes and sparrows. So all the people went out to kill them, the whole country, everybody. At night, they went into the streets and they were looking in every corner and making a lot of noise. The birds kept dropping from the skies. Sparrows were seen as especially harmful, because they ate too many seeds of grain and disrupted agriculture. Everyone was running around banging pots and pans to make sparrows fly away in fear, tear down their nests and kill any surviving birds. But with no sparrows to eat them, locust populations rapidly grew. They swarmed the countryside and together with bad weather they caused even greater problems.

From 1959 through 1961 an estimated 38 million people died of starvation. People had killed millions of animals, but for what? To test you. The truth behind the campaign was that Mao wanted to see how you responded and whether you believed in Communism or not. Looking back at it, it was as if the entire nation was in a psychotic state. People wanted to save their lives, so they remained loyal to Mao. In the same period, from 1958 until 1961, the Great Leap Forward started. It was an economic and social plan to change China from an agrarian to a modern industrialized society. But meanwhile, people were starving to death.

In the countryside, whether you were poor peasants, middle-class peasants, rich peasants or landlords, everyone had to register their class background. In the cities likewise. You filled in questionnaires saying whether you were a worker, a government official, a capitalist and so on. And I belonged to the so-called capitalists because my mother was from a landlord family and my father was a banker. And these two classes, the landlords and the capitalists, were destroyed and their property was confiscated. It was in this period that my 19 years of imprisonment began – 19 years of hunger, deprivation and torture; 19 years of so-called reform, menial work without pay; 19 years without explanation, without hope.

And if you want an idea of the entire system, all you have to do is multiply my experience by 50 million. It still goes on, subsidized by corporations, by the World Bank, and by all the governments that encourage trade with China. But I didn't fully understand what was going on, because there had been no court and no trial. At school I had been under surveillance for almost two years. Then they said: 'Your behavior is not good enough. You go to the labor camp.' So in 1960 I was 'upgraded' and I became a prisoner. The police simply came to the school. 'Now would you follow us, we'll go.' They said this very kindly and they didn't handcuff me. We went to my dormitory and I gathered my belongings. I was put onto a jeep straight away and into a prison cell. The doors shut.

Punishing poisonous ideas

I was shocked! And during the first night, at midnight, I was called up to the interrogation room. I went in and there was a police officer behind a small table and there was only one light in the room. He yelled at me: 'Sit down!' I couldn't sit down, because there was no chair. So I squatted on the floor and he shone the light right into my face.

'State your name, age, occupation and the nature of your crime,' he said.

'I am a counter-revolutionary rightist,' I said. 'In the One Hundred Flowers Campaign I attacked the Communist Party. And I still have a lot of poisonous ideas.'

'Do you know your sentence?'

'I don't know.'

'How come you don't know?' he shouted.

'Nobody told me.'

'Nobody told you? Oh, that's all right. I will tell you.' He opened a file. 'You have been sentenced to life.' I was utterly shocked. Life imprisonment! 'Yes, you need a lot of time to reform yourself.' He then said: 'Tell me your crimes. List them carefully.' He took note of all the crimes that I 'confessed' to him.

'All right. I have to give you an education,' he said. He stood up and walked to the wall and kicked the door open to another room. I was still squatting on the floor and he said: 'Look!'

God, I thought! One man was hanging on the wall with his arms tied behind his back, naked. Another was on the floor, naked. He had lost consciousness. They just poured water over him. What on earth is this, I thought! The interrogator said: 'I'm warning you. I'm giving you a one-day chance. Tomorrow, come back here to finish your first interrogation.' And pointing to the other room: 'Otherwise you'll go this way!'

I said: 'I will say anything!'

'Don't yell at me!' he said. 'Tomorrow, very clearly tell me your crimes. Don't miss anything.' It was the worst time of my life.

I know the interrogator wanted to ask me about the 300 yuan that I 'stole'. While still at school, in my youthful overconfidence I had thought of a plan to escape punishment and flee across the Hong Kong border. Together with three other students I had set aside 300 yuan and we had even devised secret gestures so as to communicate without detection. But our plan never worked, because the time had come for me to face an interrogator with my 'final thought summary'.

The next day the interrogator asked me again: 'What do you want to tell me?'

'Yes, there was the 300 yuan that I took.'

'You *took* it? Or you *stole* it?'

'Maybe I stole it,' I said, 'but I returned it.'

'That's OK,' he said. 'You have to know, you're also here because you're a thief.'

But what could I say, squatting on the floor? You know, most people are simply used as a labor force. But as I was a graduate student and there were only a few of them in prison, they first sent me to the laboratory of the chemical factory.

Every day was labor, torture and the teachings of Mao. Was I expecting something? Yes, I was! I was expecting freedom! Despite my life sentence I was hoping that something would happen. That maybe they would excuse me and free me. I was only 23 and I was still thinking of my family. Why did my mother not write to me and where was Meihua, my girlfriend? I had all kinds of thoughts, because the connection to the outside was still very strong in my mind. I cried. And then I prayed to the gods: 'Will you please help us? If I really am a bad guy, what about the rest of the people? There are so many innocent people here!' I felt terrible. But praying didn't help. And every day I focused on the food. I was trying to keep my full weight, but at one point I weighed only 36 kilograms!

I only spent five months in the chemical factory, because I violated the rules of discipline. As nobody cared about me and I was really starving, I stole a cucumber from the vegetable garden and ate it. But unfortunately one of the guards noticed. He reported me and I lost my job. At the end of December I was therefore put back in the study class and later I was sent to Yanqing, a big steel factory. After a while I went to different iron mines – it's very complicated, because altogether I did forced labor in 12 different camps. I mined coal, built roads, cleared land and harvested crops. Much later, the chemical factory and the iron mines were closed and many of the camps were shut down. But at that time there were about 1,000 prisoners in the chemical factory and 2,200 in the iron mines. After that I went back to till the land at a place called Tuanhe Farm. I don't know exactly how many people there were, probably 50,000 to 60,000 doing all kinds of prison labor.

Living like a beast

Every two months they reorganized the prison camps and the labor. They put you in different companies and different small groups. Every day I did labor. Whatever – digging the roads, cutting the grass. And every day I had to fulfill the labor quota. One particular prisoner, Xing Jingping, nicknamed Big Mouth Xing because of his voracious appetite, taught me how to be tough. 'Nobody here will take care of you,' he said. 'You have to take care of yourself. And if you don't hit another first, you won't make it. If you're not tough, you won't survive.' Big Mouth Xing was three years younger than me. He was a peasant and a thief from a poor village. But in prison he was the most influential teacher of my life. Gradually you become just like an animal, a beast. I almost completely forgot about my family and my schoolmates and I didn't care about anyone any more. And actually nobody cared about me. I only cared about myself and I was only able to survive by reducing myself to my most primal state. My first concern was always: food. Sometimes I fought over food and if there was any chance of stealing anybody else's food, I would. I didn't care.

Often, I would just close my eyes and sleep. Why sleep? To save energy. When you think, you use up a lot of energy. Shall I think about freedom, about my family? No. Even later, when I heard that my stepmother had passed away, I thought: 'Even if she's still alive, it means nothing to me!' So that was my life: even while I was walking, I was sleeping. If you woke me up, I would say: 'What? What do you want me to do?'

My brain stopped working and that is how I survived. What expectations could I still have? A visit from a friend? A visit from my fiancée, my love? A package of food? No, there were no expectations any more. And if at any point I had said: 'I was right in criticizing the Party...' I would have been dead! You're punished, you can never survive!

I had to write a confession and self-criticism, uphold Communism and support Mao Zedong. My confession is still there, in the prison camp. In Mao's opinion this was good. Even though his mother had been a practicing Buddhist and his Confucian training included the importance of a 'moral compass', he was ruthless. And so were the captain and the police of our camps.

'What are you? You're nothing! You're just like a stone to piss on. Bad smell and dead heart. And if you want to commit suicide, go ahead, do it! That will only pollute a small piece of land.'

In one of his essays, Mao said: 'Marxism maintains that the State is a machine of violence for one class to rule another. The machine of violence is operated through the army, police, courts, prisons and other necessary facilities... The Laogai, as a part of this state machine, is a facility of violence. It is a tool representing the interests of the proletariat and the masses to exercise dictatorship over a minority of hostile elements.'

His police officers acted upon it. 'Good labor, good food. Less labor, less food. No labor, no food,' they said to me. So if you felt sick or tired and said: 'I can't work, I am staying here,' you would have a very low level of food: no meat, no cooking oil, no eggs, nothing. Just a little vegetable soup and perhaps two pieces of *wotou*, corn bun.

So out in the fields I was looking for edible weeds. And I was also looking for rats, frogs and snakes in irrigation ditches. Someone educated me about rats, common knowledge among prisoners. I learned not to *kill* the rat, but to *follow* it. Because if you followed it, it would lead you to its burrow and the places where it stored its kernels of grain and other food. It became part of my gut knowledge of how to find food.

You have to survive, don't you? For many years I didn't have chopsticks, a fork or a spoon. No, I ate with my bare hands or with my hands tied behind my back and just with my mouth, when I was given extra punishment. Every morning we got up and we received a bucket to clean ourselves and we went to labor at the farm right away. And around noon two prisoners pushed two big wooden carts with buckets. One contained soup, the other corn. But it wasn't enough. Many people starved to death, particularly in the first few years.

'Labor makes a new life'

Even today, now that almost 30 years have passed, it is still fresh in my memory that I was in prison camps for almost 20 years. So when I came to the United States many years later, my first interest was in visiting an American prison. I wanted to see the difference, so I did. And my conclusion was: if there is any chance, I'll stay in an American prison! There you can borrow a book, you can write, you get food, a doctor will care for you, there is air-conditioning and you will not be cold. So it's a comfortable place.

What does freedom mean? Freedom means I can think what I want to think, I can say what I want to say. And I think American prisons provide those basic conditions; that would have been much better for me. But in Chinese prison camps, there is no freedom, despite the camp slogan 'Labor makes a new life', similar to the words above the entry gates of German concentration camps: *Labor liberates* [in German: *Arbeit macht frei*]. They forced you every day to study Chinese newspapers and documents that uphold Communism. You *had* to. The food wasn't free, the living conditions were horrible and all the space you had was two-and-a-half feet.

During my time in prison, the Cultural Revolution of 1966 took place. Mao issued instructions to eliminate the 'four olds': old thoughts, old habits, old customs and old culture. You see, the Communist Revolution of 1949 had been a great success. Almost everyone joined the Communists; people listened to them and did what they wanted. 'Follow us, you peasants working on the land.' Everybody worked and everybody shared. And the poor people just joined together, killed the landlords, the capitalists and the bourgeois class and divided the land. There were no courts, so they were simply punished and killed by the peasants. All the banks, factories and department stores became government properties in only four to five years. Religions were abolished. Catholics out, Christians out, Buddhists out. Everybody only upheld one thing: the thoughts of Mao Zedong. All that happened before 1957. And even today, when they talk about the rights and wrongs of Communism, they only talk about what happened after 1957. But from 1957 onwards they saw *inside people* as the enemy – not capitalists or landlords, but workers, peasants or intellectuals. Out of the five or six million intellectuals, the Communists picked up one million to be punished. And if, as a 'counter-revolutionary', you disagreed, you would only hear: 'Shut up! Shut up!' Or they would shut you up.

The last few years I was working in a coalmine, doing shifts of 12 hours a day. It was really incredible. Every day was a list of human rights violations and I witnessed so many people pass away... One time, after seeing the burial of fellow inmates, I thought: 'Human life has no value here. It has no more importance than a cigarette ash flicked in the wind. But if a person's life has no value, then the society that shapes that life has no value either. If the people mean no more than dust, then the society is worthless and does not deserve to continue. If the society should not continue, then I should oppose it.' You would think there must have been many people who felt that something was not quite right. But nobody dared to speak up. Only one voice was allowed: those who were loyal to the Communists and to Mao. And if you did raise your voice, you would be classified as *imperialist*.

When Mao Zedong died, on 9 September 1976, all prisoners were very scared. We might be released, but we might also all be killed! So we just quietly waited, carefully listening and reading the newspapers about the struggle for power between Deng Xiaoping and the Gang of Four. Six months later we still didn't know, but some people got rehabilitated. Some of my fellow prisoners came up to me and said: 'We can tell people what went wrong and that Harry Wu's case does not relate to the stealing of those 300 yuan. We want to clear things up.' One of those men was separated from me at Xinjiang, but he sent a letter about my rehabilitation. I received the letter and talked to the officer in charge. He said: 'I am going to the capital to have a meeting, where we will discuss your case.' When he returned, he said: 'All right, your case is over. The central policy is that many people will receive rehabilitation. And you're on that list.' So I got rehabilitated, 'corrected'. This is Chinese policy, Chinese reality. You never know what a policy is.

What does it mean: this is a policy?! What does rehabilitation mean? The boss says: 'You're rehabilitated,' so you're rehabilitated. If he says: 'You're prosecuted,' you're prosecuted. There is no constitution, no law, no justice, nothing.

Being *nice* for survival

Much later, after my release in 1979, I went back to Shanghai and saw my father again. He was 80 years old then.

'I don't know why,' he said, 'but I felt very sure that I would see you again soon.'

'How come?'

'You know, when you were arrested, your mother committed suicide. So I decided that I had to wait until you came back.'

'But I was sentenced to life imprisonment! I would never come back!'

'Yes, I know. But there was some indication that told me you would come back. And I am happy that finally I see you again. And more importantly, you stand on your own two feet.'

'Yes, I stand on my own two feet.'

After a pause, he finally said: 'I am retired and have nothing to do. But you still have a big problem.'

'What's the problem?'

'You cannot survive in this country.'

'Why not?'

'Because you don't know how to serve the people.'

'Serve the people? I will do that!'

'No. You don't know how to be nice to the people in power.'

That was true of course, because I didn't want to say nice things to the people that are in control to get benefits from them. And I still don't.

'So, you have to leave the country,' he said.

'How?' I said, because I had never thought I would leave the country.

'Your sister lives in America,' he said. 'I will ask her to help you go to the United States.' But then there was another problem: I didn't have any children. Because, while still in prison, I was married to a woman who could not give birth. And by that time I was 47 years old. And so my father had my brother's daughter transferred to me. I adopted her. Those are the two things my father did.

The next year, in 1980, I was in Wuhan, working at my university as a teacher. And suddenly my father sent me a telegram: 'Come home. I need your help.' So I went back home and he said: 'There is an English gentleman who has come here to see you.' He told me about Mr John Cassuack. He was number one in the British business community in Hong Kong, who had come back to China, but he had retired and his nephew had taken over his business.

'I cannot see him,' my father said, 'for how can I show myself to other people like this? All my furniture is old and broken, it's ugly. But Mr Cassuack is like a friend. More than 30 years ago we went hunting together. So can you please go and represent me?'

'My father cannot come to see you,' I said to Mr Cassuack. 'He is ashamed of his condition.'

John Cassuack is a good man who said: 'I am sorry I cannot see your family. Because of the Communist occupation we missed 30 years. But I always remember your father and have always thought of him as a good friend.' He then said: 'I am in a position to offer you financial support with whatever you need. I can help you.' Shortly after this encounter, my father passed away.

Getting started in the United States wasn't easy. I received an invitation from the University of Berkeley. They had to free money to give me a stipend for my living arrangements. But when they finally managed to do so, I said I had enough money to live on, even though I didn't and I had already sold all my property and my books. So even though I got appointed as a visiting professor of geology, I was sleeping in bus stations and on park benches. Some people gave me money, but I only had 40 dollars in my pocket. I asked my sister, who lived in San Francisco, but she didn't want to help. To reach her, I had to cross the Golden Gate Bridge every day. But every round trip by metro cost me $5.25. So after just a few trips, I said to myself: 'I can't continue going over. I have to save that precious money that I spend on the metro.'

It was hard. Every night I was sitting in the office and by 9pm I had to leave the building. I couldn't sleep in the office, so I walked the streets and returned at 5.30 in the morning. I really didn't know where to go, just that I would survive. That was my whole life at that time. But eventually I got a job in a donut shop, making 72 donuts during the night shift. It was wonderful, for finally I had a roof over my head and I wasn't homeless any more. The coffee was free and so were the donuts and the ice cream. But I can tell you that today I can't stand donuts any more!

Still, I felt quite sure that, whatever happened, I would have a good life in this country. If I was honest and if I worked hard, I would be fine. And if I compared my life here to my life in the labor camps, nothing could be better! So I said to myself: 'No labor camps, no China. Stay away! I want to earn money. I want to have a good life.' And I could have milk, eggs, chicken legs, bread, almost free! What else could I want?

So during that time I didn't talk about China and I didn't tell anyone about my personal experiences. But then, in 1988, something special happened. There was a student who was writing his thesis for graduation. His name was Jeffrey Ling. 'I heard about your story,' he said. 'Can I write about *you?*'

'My personal story?'

'Yes, your story and the labor camps.'

After he finished writing, his professor was amazed and wanted to see the guy that the story was about. So I talked to him and we met at the University of California in Santa Cruz. This made a significant change in my life. I received an invitation to give a lecture about my experiences. When I arrived, there were about a hundred students and I sat in the middle.

'You're free,' they said. 'Whatever you want to say, say it.'

So I said: 'All right. I am a storyteller. I am not Harry Wu. I will tell you a story about Harry Wu in the third person.'

I had only just begun, when suddenly I stopped. I couldn't prevent the tears from running down my cheeks. The audience was shocked and quietly waiting. I was crying for probably 15 to 20 minutes. They let me cry. The first two years in the laogai I had cried, but after that, never. No tears for 20 years. But in 1988 it all came out.

Going back undercover

'You're crazy!' people warned me, when in the 1990s I went back to China undercover four times. 'What on earth are you doing?'

Every time I went back to China, I never did anything relating to political, military or economic issues. Except one thing: I went to the prison camps, managing to get close or inside by assuming the role of someone in the police or in business. China is a huge country, so it's just like when you live in Virginia, you don't know what's going on in California or in Texas. How many camps there are in the rest of China! I visited many victims in different places, each time I went over there.

Each of the four times I went back to China I was well prepared. I knew what to look for in this city, in that province and where the prison camps were located. First of all I would walk around the whole area, along the walls and the watchtowers, take pictures and go in front of the gate. Sometimes I pretended I was in business, sometimes in the police, allowing me to get into the camps and film the police, the prisoners, whatever. I wanted to give people an idea of the prison camps so that they could imagine what it was like. It's right in front of you!

In one of my trips, in 1993, I went to Tibet – an entire country turned into a prison camp. Since 1959 it had been depicted as a backward nation, primitive and cruel and with monks who possessed great wealth. But when I wanted to go into Tibet, at the Nepali border town of Tato Pani, someone had found out about my presence. I was nearly caught and had no way out. Five men jumped out of a Chinese Public Security jeep in front of my hotel, some of whom were taking pictures. But I was saved by the Nepali innkeeper at the reception desk. He played stupid when asked: 'Have you seen any strangers in the hotel?'

In 1987 the Chinese Government released the first laogai white paper called *Re-education Through Labor Work Handbook*. It's a typical lie. This document was released to every country in the world, essentially saying that the Chinese prison camps are wonderful, that prisoners can graduate from university and can go for regular check-ups to a medical doctor who will say that they are fine. Whatever!

'My God,' I said to myself, 'I suppose I should have stayed there! Why should I feel like a victim and suffer?' See, here is something different: the Handbook of the Laogai Research

Foundation. It's the only book in the world that gives detailed information about how many labor camps there are and where they are located. And it includes recent official Chinese Communist Party documents with instructions 'to appropriately dispose of counter-revolutionary elements' and even the 'tax collection policy for prison enterprises'. But in China no one is able to talk about the laogai. And when foreigners visit, they only get to see model camps. The real prison camps are 'state secrets', because they are a tool, a mechanism to suppress political dissent, to consolidate control and to support the dictatorship of the Chinese Government. The German concentration camps, the Russian gulag and the Chinese laogai have this in common. Everyone was subject to one policy: forced labor.

Going back undercover allowed me to obtain evidence for the rest of the world to see what is going on. For me there was only one alternative, because the United States has two different policies.

One is: *deal with China*, deal with imports and exports and buy their products. Among the people that are opposed to this are Speaker of the House Nancy Pelosi and Congressman Frank Wolf, the chair of the committee that checks the spending of the State Department. They are anti-Communists and they oppose the Most-Favored Nation (MFN) trading status of China.

The other policy is: *do not deal with China*. There are many people that have heard about the laogai system, who know it is true and who have seen the Handbook. And that raises the question: 'Why is it that today, in the United States, Germany and other countries, you set up museums for concentration camps and the Holocaust, but you don't want to hear about the gulag or the laogai?' It's a similar system, right? The concentration camps and the gulag system are gone, but the laogai is still in operation! Even if today Communism stops and there were no laogai anymore, we would still have to think about the tens of millions of people that perished there, right?! How can people kill that easily and make others suffer without any consequences! It's a basic human rights issue.

In 1990 and 1991 I took a lead in saying that there is a laogai system, and I insisted that the word 'laogai' be accepted in daily language usage and in dictionaries. In December 1992, the Chinese Communist Party passed a resolution to stop using the laogai system. Within the Chinese judiciary system there is a Laogai Affairs Bureau and many prison camps – Beijing's number 5 prison and a provincial city number 17 prison among them – have a laogai detachment. They are everywhere. And many make export products that are publicly advertised – it's all there.

So in the 1990s all this was exposed and the Chinese were really shocked. Their first response was to stop using the word 'laogai' and rename it 'prison'. But they also made it very clear that the basic policy of 're-education through labor', meaning *forced* labor, was not going to change. They changed the name; everything else stayed the same. When the Communist Party took over they must have asked themselves: 'How can we keep everybody quiet, so that anybody who says even one word against the Revolution will be silenced?' Laogai.

The last time I went back was in 1995, when the Chinese charged me: 'You are stealing state secrets.' I was arrested and held by the Chinese Government for 66 days before they sentenced me in a show trial to 15 years in prison. But thanks to an international campaign I was immediately deported from China.

'If I die today...'

You know, I am really surprised that I have come to the United States. I am so lucky to have survived! There isn't one day that I don't think about that. The number one reason for that is: I didn't know that I would ever become a free man again. Or that I would write books about things that are amiss in society. This was completely outside of my imagination, because for a young man in jail these things didn't make any sense. Today I am closer to death by age, but at that time, I was so desperate that I wanted to commit suicide by taking acid or by any other means, whatever.

So here's the problem: *before* you cross the line between life and death, what do you want to do? You want to have sex, make money, write a book, become famous? To sail in a boat on the ocean? Go ahead. Enjoy yourself. I asked myself this question about the rest of my life. But the rest of my life was too short, because when I arrived in the United States I was almost 50. I could only expect to have another 20 years, normally. So I divided the rest of my time into periods of five years. The first five years: find a woman, marry, get money, and buy a house. After that: maybe have a baby. And after that: you're not going back to school, right? So what do you want to do? Own a business? You're 55 or 60 years old... 'What else is there?' I asked myself. Now that I am 70, if I die today, I will become nothing. That's reality, whether you go up to heaven or down to hell.

So it was my choice to bring to light and show to the world what is going on in China, so that knowing the truth about today, the Chinese people may have a different future tomorrow. That is the motive behind my writing, disclosing the laogai system and giving presentations in the United States, the European Union and elsewhere.

But even though I have some ideas about it, I'm only focused on what I saw, what I read and what I experienced. All I want to do is to tell people about my experience. And all the 20 books of the *Black Series* you see here on this table are from different people who spent 15, 20, 30 years in the prison camps and who have written their own stories. After the word 'laogai' entered the dictionaries, I told the *Washington Post*: 'I am happy that

I can go to my grave with my eyes closed, because the word "laogai" was recognized and accepted around the world.'

The last words of my book *Troublemaker* were: 'People tell me never to think about going back to China again. Nobody tells Harry Wu what to do. I will go back. Front door next time.' But if I ever go back, it will be for human rights issues and for the prison camps. China is terrible. Terrible! Occasional visitors from other countries have no idea what is going on. They may have a general idea about the Cultural Revolution, about death and starvation. But is there any change? And do their countries speak out about the laogai, about human rights violations or the lack of freedom and democracy?

My major at university was in geology. After that, for 20 years, my major was in tilling the earth! No profession. Today, what my profession is, I really don't know. But before I die I want to help myself and other people who join me to leave a legacy for the next generation. But what will happen to it?

And what has happened to the advocates of democracy and the human rights activists and people who want free press in China? Let me take you back to the 1989 Tiananmen Square movement. It was a *huge* movement! Throughout the country, in all major cities there were protests led by students. After the suppression, people asked: 'Where has it gone? And where are the student leaders of 1989?' They're gone, history.

You can go to the campuses today. Is there anyone talking about politics or democracy? Almost no-one. They became disconnected. How? The student leaders are only in their late thirties or early forties. Most of them became businesspeople! It's present-day reality. The truth is right in front of you: you can't stand up for freedom if you don't have food to eat. You have to eat first and live a better life first, right?

So meanwhile you forget about freedom and work for yourself. Many of them simply gave up. Not because of fear, but because of money. That is the main power of the Central

The 'Unknown Rebel' and the 'Goddess of Democracy'

In June 1989, a man who was carrying his grocery bags home stopped four advancing tanks on Tiananmen Square. Within 24 hours the image went around the world, symbolizing the Tiananmen Square protests. The Chinese however refer to the Tiananmen Square protests and suppression as 'the June Fourth Incident', censoring its significance.

The protests seemed to lack a unified cause or leadership, but inspired people across China. In Hong Kong, people gathered in sympathy, dedicating democratic songs to the uprising. In Shanghai, similar demonstrations occurred, although these remained peaceful and without casualties. The participants, especially in Beijing, indicated they were against the authoritarianism and economic policies of the Communist Party and called for democratic reform. In Beijing, the Government repressed the protests violently, leaving hundreds of people dead in the streets.

Students from the Central Academy of Fine Arts had erected a 'Goddess of Democracy' statue in Tiananmen Square during the protest. Around the world, these voices were heard, seen and remembered. In the Polish city of Wroclaw, as an example, a memorial depicts a destroyed bicycle and a pavement ripped up by a tank track. Family members of protesters are still under surveillance today. The violent suppression of the protests caused widespread international condemnation of the Chinese Government.

Government: 'If you follow me, you can share in the money. Otherwise, you can't.'

Money over morals

People follow the money. Foreigners too, and especially businesspeople. I had a conversation with the CEO of Boeing aircraft industries, many years ago.

'Harry, I really support you,' he said. 'I know your moral standing and I know what you are fighting for. It's wonderful. But I'm sorry, I cannot agree with you. I cannot cancel the purchase orders for our aircraft with the Chinese. Why can't you see that? Otherwise I have to close down two factories and lay off maybe 4,000 workers including myself. The Chinese will simply say: if you don't want it, we'll give it to Airbus.'

That's the reality. Boeing is a big company. And money is more powerful than morals. People need to eat first before they can contemplate freedom. In the long term, morals may defeat money. But in the short term, if I were a student leader and the people said: 'Here is a proposal and here is your budget...' I would be quiet, accept that proposal and that budget. But the same power that is making the Chinese Communist Party so powerful today will ultimately destroy their own systems. Now that capitalism is becoming so popular everywhere, is anyone still talking about the Communist Revolution? About liberating people and spreading socialism across the world? I don't think it will happen.

In 1997 Jiang Zemin, President of China from 1993 to 2003, visited the United States and delivered a lecture at Harvard University after visiting the White House. I also received an invitation. But Jiang Zemin was to speak from 11 to 12 in a small church called Memorial Hall. And I spoke from 1 to 2 in a church just opposite. So the people went from one gathering to the next, simply by crossing the street. Everywhere there were protesters that opposed each other, chanting 'Free Tibet!' or 'One China!'

'Let me remind you of one thing,' I said. 'Today we're in November 1997. Does anybody remember what happened in November 40 years ago? Communist Party leaders from all over the world gathered in Moscow to celebrate the 40th anniversary of the Russian Revolution. A big celebration! At that time many people were convinced that the world would get a new socialist society. They already had Russia, China, East Germany, Czechoslovakia... it was growing all the time. Even the French Communist Party almost conquered France.'

Mao thought that capitalism was just like the setting sun, while socialism was like the rising sun. Everybody remembered it. But 40 years later, in 1997 or today for that matter, where is Moscow? Jiang Zemin even went to Wall Street! 'What?' I thought. 'You are the Chinese Communist leader. And as a Communist, your number one priority is to destroy Wall Street, right!?'

Do you think that Chinese Communism will last another 40 years? Until 2037? Impossible! It's history. Whatever the current leaders call their policies, like 'market socialism', Communism is history. What's happening in China today has *nothing* to do with Communism, all right! They allow people to own property, more privacy and more religious freedom. By 2037 I will be gone, but so will Communism. It's only a small step in history. This is what has happened to the work of Lenin, Stalin and Mao Zedong. It's over.

Today, the people complain about Mao, but the Central

'The east wind prevails over the west wind'

'There is a Chinese saying: "Either the east wind prevails over the west wind or the west wind prevails over the east wind." I believe it is characteristic of the situation today that the east wind is prevailing over the west wind. That is to say, the forces of socialism have become overwhelmingly superior to the forces of imperialism.'

Excerpt from Mao Zedong's speech in Moscow at the meeting of Communist and Workers' Parties on 18 November 1957.

Government says: 'Come on, look forward. Don't look back.' Why? You *have* to look back, don't you? If you don't have a history, how can you have a future? Why not change the Communist Party's name to the Market Economy Capitalist Party? It's too sensitive. Yes, you can call the economic system 'market economy socialism', but the problem right now is that capitalism, foreign and international businesses have become the major influences of China's domestic economy and keep the country growing. Many scholars around the world have publicly said: 'Capitalism destroyed socialism'. You cannot disagree with it. You can see many rich Chinese people these days. They seem to have survived... The Central Government has become more stable, but the laogai camps are still there. That is the big problem.

The books I have written, the undercover trips I have made and all the work we do here at the Laogai Research Foundation and the China Information Center is not being done because we want to oppose the Communists. Even if the Communist Party in China would end tomorrow, it's just like the breakdown of the Soviet Union: many people are still thinking about the gulag. And they will still speak about the laogai. This is why I have a vision to create a Laogai Museum in Washington. I'm lobbying to create a permanent reminder for something in our history: how some people have been killing innocent people with impunity. In the past I have mounted photo exhibitions in Congress, the European Parliament and in Australia. They were all enlarged pictures of photos that I had brought back from China. Here's the laogai.

You know, the Chinese recently commemorated the massacre at Nanking by the Japanese, commonly known as the Rape of Nanking. 'Oh, the Japanese invaded China and killed millions of people,' said a member of the US Congress I met today. 'And during the Rape of Nanking, they killed 300,000 people.'

'What,' I said in return, '300,000? In my time the Chinese

killed one million in just one year, 1957! Their own people! These people were the same human beings as you and me. Unfortunately, most of them cannot tell their story. But I am one of that one million!'

Today the Chinese Government estimates that only around 10,000 of them survived. The rest are gone. I don't care whether today China speaks about freedom, democracy or prosperity. I want to tell the story of the lives of that one million. How the wives lost their husbands, how the children lost their parents...

Mao: unknown, yet known

The book *Mao: The Unknown Story*, written by Jung Chang and Jon Halliday, thoroughly demystifies the greatness of Mao Zedong. The writers traveled all over the world, interviewed hundreds of people who had met Mao, including George Bush Sr, Henry Kissinger and the Dalai Lama.

It took 12 years to complete the book. The book is regarded as hugely controversial, described by some as 'an atom bomb of a book', by others as 'bad history and worse biography'. Whatever the truth may be, there is little doubt that Mao was ruthless in implementing his policies, responsible for untold cruelties, torture, famine and the death of millions of Chinese.

Mao Zedong on Mao Zedong: 'I have only been able to change a few places in the vicinity of Beijing.'

Edgar Snow, an American journalist who sympathized with the Communist Party, in *Red Star over China* (1937): 'He had the simplicity and naturalness of the Chinese peasant, with a lively sense of humor and a love of rustic laughter... he combined curious qualities of naivety with incisive wit and worldly sophistication.'

Joseph Stalin, General Secretary of the Soviet Union 1922-52, believed what is their story?

You can't just say that today we are doing big business with China. Reality is reality and I can't give it up. Fortunately I have many friends and associates, both in China and around the world.

One of my friends is the writer Jung Chang. We have known each other for a long time, since her first book *Wild Swans* was published. One time, we were both invited for an event hosted by a publishing company, so we happened to be traveling together.

---

that Mao deviated from Marxism. He called him *peschany marksist*, a 'margarine Marxist'.

Nikita Khrushchev, General Secretary of the Soviet Union 1953-64, in his *Memoirs*: 'Mao thought of himself as a man sent by God to do God's bidding. In fact, Mao probably thought God did Mao's *own* bidding.' And in *Khrushchev Remembers*: 'Mao Zedong has played politics with Asiatic cunning, following his own rules of cajolery, treachery, savage vengeance and deceit... Mao Zedong has always been a master at concealing his true thoughts and intentions.'

His Holiness the Dalai Lama: 'That was the danger with Mao. Everything he said – half true! *Half* true!' (quoted in *Mao: The Unknown Story*).

Henry Kissinger, US Secretary of State 1973-77, in *The White House Years*: 'At one point China had only a single ambassador abroad. Mao destroyed or sought to destroy every Number Two man – Liu Shaoqi, Lin Biao, Deng Xiaoping, and possibly even Zhou Enlai.' And in *Diplomacy*: 'Mao was the visionary, ruthless, pitiless, occasionally murderous revolutionary.'

Jung Chang and **Jon Halliday**: 'To deny people's desire – and right – to live was central to Maoism' (in *Mao: The Unknown Story*).

She talked about her book; I talked about *Bitter Winds*. I asked her: 'Are you free to go back to China?'

She smiled and said: 'So far, until this moment, yes.' But a couple of years later it all changed.

'Do you feel regret?'

'Yes, I do,' she said, 'even though I knew it could happen. But these days I have such a big audience and so many people want to see me. And I always remember you, because you asked me that special question. But at that moment I wasn't able to answer, because I really wanted to go back.'

The change was due to the fact that the basic facts of her first book *Wild Swans* were wonderful and good in the eyes of the Chinese Government. In the last part of her book there were some comments about the fact that China under Deng Xiaoping was showing progress and it seemed that China would have a brighter future. So Deng Xiaoping liked it. And Jung Chang could go back to China with a high profile, and many people in China wanted to interview her. But when she wrote the very critical biography *Mao: The Unknown Story* together with her husband, everything changed. It's like Chris Patten, the last governor of Hong Kong, said: 'This book almost destroyed the regime.'

China, made of china

The Chinese Government is very sensitive to these kinds of things, and, likewise, to the situation of Tibet. They are upset about the fact that, in their view, the Dalai Lama only cares about Tibetans and not about China. But I very strongly support the Dalai Lama and Tibet. Why? You see, the Soviet Union had 16 republics, but during the period of *glasnost* (openness) and *perestroika* (reform) under Mikhail Gorbachev, it collapsed.

China's regime is just like a plate. But the Chinese plate is not made of plastic, aluminum or paper. It's made of *china*, porcelain. Tibet is a big territory, but it has a very small economy and a very small population. But it wanted to go its own way and be independent. That only caused one problem: it shattered the plate. The *entire* plate. Because china isn't flexible. Communism isn't flexible. So that's why I say: 'The Tibetans have to say thanks to the Chinese. And the Chinese have to really appreciate the Tibetan struggle. They are fighting for their freedom and for their future. And their fight has broken the system. The Central Government must think that Tibet is terrible, because every year they have to spend a lot of money on Tibet alone. So far, the Chinese haven't got any benefit from Tibet, and internationally most people are on the side of the Tibetans. Why? Why not let them go? They can't let them go.

I have become quite close to the Dalai Lama. I respect him and he is a great religious and political leader. But the Dalai Lama says: 'No, I'm not going to be involved in politics. I am a religious leader.' But let me make this clear: he has a great mind. You never really know what he is thinking. And it is remarkable that the Tibetans, from such a small religious group and a very backward country, emerged onto the world stage in 1959. The Tibetan cause became known worldwide and people respect the Dalai Lama. I don't think anybody can say there is anything wrong with that.

The Dalai Lama has made it very clear that he is not a Chinese leader. But the Chinese are very keen to emphasize that he *is* Chinese, based on the simple fact that he is Tibetan, and today's Tibet is seen by the Chinese Government as part of the People's Republic of China. That is why I argue that in 1989 a Chinese person received the Nobel Peace Prize. People ask me:

'Who?'

'The Dalai Lama!'

'But he is Tibetan!'

'Wait a minute. Isn't Tibet considered to be part of China? So if the Dalai Lama received an award, it also means that the Chinese received an award. Right?'

Whatever they say, they cannot deny that the Dalai Lama, by being Tibetan, has Chinese citizenship. But I don't think he will ever become a leader in Chinese society, no. At this moment there is no-one. But most definitely one day there will be someone.

The Laogai Museum – in Wu's words 'the first museum in the US to address human rights in China' – was opened in 2008 in Washington DC.

6

Responsibilities for Leaders

Introduction

A LARGE-SCALE REVOLVER with a barrel tied into a knot stands near the United Nations buildings in New York. It is the *Disarmament Sculpture*, the Government of Luxembourg's special gift to the United Nations in 1988. When considering guns and the harm they cause, the sculpture could equally well have been another gun: the AK-47, also known as the Kalashnikov. The Russian-designed AK-47, in production since 1947, has developed a reputation like no other.

Thousands of people are killed by Kalashnikovs every year, because there is little international control of their production, sale and use. According to the report *AK-47: The World's Favorite Killing Machine* produced by the Control Arms Campaign, there are around 70 million examples of this rifle and variations on its design in the world today. They are found in the state arsenals of at least 82 countries and are produced in at least 14. But this is only a small part of the global arms industry.

The Stockholm International Peace Research Institute keeps

track of all of them: in 2006 the total world spending on guns, ammunition, missiles, military aircraft, vehicles, ships and electronic systems amounted to $1,158 billion – more than $1 trillion. Amazingly, global military expenditures amount to two per cent of the world's GDP. The United States accounts for around 36 per cent of worldwide weapons sales, followed by Russia, Britain, Germany and China. 'We are living in the midst of a permanent wartime economy,' writes John Ralston Saul. 'The most important capital goods produced in the West today are weaponry. The most important sector in international trade is not oil or automobiles or airplanes. It is armaments.'

Since the late 19th century there have been concerns that the arms trade was getting out of control. In 1940, US President Franklin D Roosevelt still aimed to develop the United States into the 'arsenal of democracy'. In 1961, US President Eisenhower warned against the 'military-industrial complex' in which the armed forces, commerce and politics become closely linked. In his *Farewell Address to the Nation* he said: 'In the councils of government, we must guard against the acquisition of unwarranted

---

One death per minute

- Small arms in circulation: 600 million
- Manufactured by: 1,135 companies
- Based in: more than 98 different countries
- Individuals who die in small arms conflicts every year: 500,000
- Minutes in one year: 525,600
- Individuals who die per day: 1,440
- Individuals who die per minute: 1

Estimates from the Control Arms Campaign, founded by Amnesty International, Oxfam and the International Action Network on Small Arms.

---

influence, whether sought or unsought, by the military-industrial complex... Only an alert and knowledgeable citizenry can compel the proper meshing of the huge industrial and military machinery of defense with our peaceful methods and goals so that security and liberty may prosper together.' Although it is now closer than ever before, as of 2009 there is still no international treaty governing the arms trade between states.

Liberia and Sierra Leone are probably not countries that spring to mind when it comes to advocacy for peace and justice. But they are two of many that have demanded an Arms Trade Treaty (ATT). Over 150 states have voted in the UN General Assembly to take steps toward making such a treaty a reality. It could save many lives.

Language, however, can at times be misleading. 'Disarmament' can be interpreted in many ways and governments usually prefer to focus on smaller goals: *partial* measures on *particular* categories in a *specific* geographical area (as in the case of nuclear-weapon-free zones). A 'freeze' deceptively sounds like things are cooling down, but it may just mean a 'mutually agreed level of increase', which of course is not disarmament at all.

For more than a century, efforts have been made to limit armaments, initially by international conferences in The Hague in 1899 and 1907, followed by talks under the auspices of the League of Nations after the First World War. Negotiations involving most countries and most categories of weapons reached a climax in 1932 at the World Disarmament Conference in Geneva. But it failed due to rising tensions among the great powers – notably Germany and France – when Hitler came to power and the Second World War became imminent.

After the war, the Cold War dominated alliances and treaties. Both Russia and the United States maintained massive capacities to inflict destruction. During Cold War conflicts such as the Korean and US-Vietnam wars, hundreds of thousands died; in the 'New Wars' in Africa, millions have died; and the current war in Iraq has led to the deaths of tens of thousands of civilians. None of these wars involved nuclear weapons, but the use of conventional weapons is quite deadly enough.

Armed conflict has also characterized the 1970s, 1980s and 1990s in Central and South America. But today there appears to be peace among nations that were once at war internally or with their neighboring states. A momentous change occurred in 1987, when five countries signed the Esquipulas II Peace Accords in Guatemala. The architect of the Peace Accords was Oscar Arias Sánchez, whose achievement was recognized by the award of the Nobel Peace Prize.

Arias has twice been elected to serve his own country, Costa Rica, as President – once from 1986 until 1990 and now since 2006.

'Costa Rica is a country that is quite uniquely committed to the rule of justice and international law,' he says. 'We unilaterally abolished our army in 1948, placing our stability and prosperity in the hands of the multilateral system, with the expectation that, as enshrined in the preamble of the United Nations Charter, obligations arising from treaties and other sources of international law will be maintained.'

Next to paving the road for the future of Costa Rica, Arias champions human development and democracy, a comprehensive Arms Trade Treaty and the 'Costa Rica Consensus' – new criteria for debt relief based on social investment and demilitarization. With the financial part of the Nobel Prize he established the Arias Foundation for Peace and Human Progress, where he is cordially referred to as 'Don Oscar'.

Oscar Arias Sánchez
Costa Rica

'My greatest hope for the world is that the priorities of those who lead it will, some day soon, move in line with the urgent needs of the people they lead.'

Nobel Peace Prize winner Oscar Arias Sánchez (born in 1940) was elected twice as President of Costa Rica, which will celebrate 200 years of independence in 2021.

'Humanity cannot wait. The poor and forsaken cannot wait.'

I WAS BORN in San José, the capital, but grew up in the small and prosperous city of Heredia, just to the north. It's a beautiful place, known in Costa Rica as 'the city of flowers'. I am the eldest of three children. My father, Juan Rafael Arias, was president of the Costa Rican Central Bank. My mother, Lillyam, a sweet, generous woman, was from one of Costa Rica's coffee-growing families. Her father had started out as a poor ox-cart driver, and made his fortune in coffee. He was a compassionate and generous man with a strong work ethic.

I had a normal childhood. I went to public elementary school at the Escuela República de Argentina, and liked to play football in the plaza and go to the movies – although my great love was always reading. My father instilled a love of learning in me at an early age, and used to read to us: stories, novels, poetry. I devoured all kinds of books as I grew up. There were some that I read over and over, such as the memoirs of Winston Churchill, and of course Miguel de Cervantes' *Don Quixote*.

In 1948, when I was eight years old, Costa Rica experienced a brief but violent civil war. It was a turning point in my country's history and would have a great influence on my ideas and on my political career. The leader to emerge from that war,

José Figueres, decided to abolish the Costa Rican army. This momentous act strengthened our national values of democratic participation and social progress. However, my interest in a career in public service didn't take shape until much later. I grew

'Ask not...'

Following in the footsteps of 'war president' Eisenhower, the American people felt that with the inauguration of John F Kennedy, accompanied by his glamorous wife Jackie, a new era began. 'Ask not what your country can do for you...' – many people can complete this line, perhaps the most memorable words of any presidential speech.

The Cold War was still raging, culminating in the Cuban Missile Crisis during Kennedy's term of office. But Kennedy took action in the area of civil rights legislation. He wanted the US to resume its old mission as the first nation dedicated to the revolution of human rights, and to that end instituted the Alliance for Progress and the Peace Corps. These were set up to bring US idealism to the aid of developing nations. During his first speech to the American public he said:

'Let every nation know, whether it wishes us well or ill, that we shall pay any price, bear any burden, meet any hardship, support any friend, oppose any foe, in order to assure the survival and the success of liberty.

'Now the trumpet summons us again – not as a call to bear arms, though arms we need; not as a call to battle, though embattled we are – but a call to bear the burden of a long twilight struggle, year in and year out, "rejoicing in hope, patient in tribulation" – a struggle against the common enemies of man: tyranny, poverty, disease, and war itself.'

'And so, my fellow Americans: ask not what your country can do for you – ask what you can do for your country. My fellow citizens of the world: ask not what America will do for you, but what together we can do for the freedom of man.'

Excerpt from John F Kennedy's Inaugural Address on 20 January 1961.

up thinking that I was going to be a doctor. I went to the United States as a pre-med student at Boston University, and I was there for the 1960 presidential elections. It was then that I began to learn about John F Kennedy. I was enormously impressed by his intellect, his youth and his charisma. It was during this time that I realized that my real passion was for politics.

I then studied law and economics at the University of Costa Rica and went on to get my doctorate in political science at the University of Essex in England. The academic space I was afforded there allowed me to study Costa Rican institutions in depth, which prepared me well for public service. Of course, I also benefited enormously from exposure to the British political traditions of debate and negotiation. Upon my return to Costa Rica, I dived into the world of politics. The 1960s and 1970s were a time of great social and political ferment. The Costa Rican model of social development was coming into fruition. I was actively involved in the social democratic National Liberation Party, and President Figueres, in his third and final term, named me Minister of Planning, a post I held for seven years. In 1978 I was a representative for Heredia in the National Assembly, and in 1979 became Secretary General of my party.

The abolition of the army in 1948, which I mentioned earlier, set Costa Rica apart from the rest of Latin America, and paid off in strong education and healthcare systems, a highly educated workforce, political stability and modern infrastructure. During my youth and the beginning of my political career, I felt the pride that all Costa Ricans share, pride in that heritage of peace. When I became President in 1986, however, that heritage had taken on new meanings – and was being questioned in new and dangerous ways. Civil war was tearing apart El Salvador and Guatemala, where Marxist guerrillas were fighting the governments, and Nicaragua, where the Sandinista Government was under attack by the Contra rebels.

While Costa Rica maintained its neutrality, the effects on our country were profound. Our economy hung in the balance, since our location in a war-torn region threatened tourism and foreign investment. Our Government was under pressure, mostly from US officials, to side with the Contras in the Nicaraguan conflict. Armed groups had staged attacks that breached our northern border. Many in Costa Rica called for the Government to re-establish our military. I resisted those calls, believing instead that the best way to ensure our country's future was not only to stay our own course of peace, but also to lead the way to peace for our region.

Region at war

El Salvador

El Salvador was blighted by repressive military regimes for more than half of the 20th century, from 1931 onwards. In the 1970s, civil society resistance increased – but so too did the repression, killings by death squads and routine human rights abuses. In 1980, Archbishop Oscar Romero, a noted human rights defender, was assassinated; in 1981, leftist guerrilla groups merged to form the Farabundo Martí National Liberation Front and civil war ensued. The Reagan Administration in the US became directly involved in the conflict, backing the rightwing regime's 'counter-insurgency' war. The conflict and the widespread human rights abuses continued throughout the 1980s, took the lives of more than 75,000 people and left more than a million in exile.

Guatemala

The longest civil war in Latin American history took place in Guatemala between 1960 and 1996. Guatemala was traditionally ruled by military leaders who guarded the interests of the US transnationals dominating the economy, notably the banana giant United Fruit, and systematically discriminated against the indigenous majority. A democratic election

I drafted a peace plan calling for democracy as a precondition for peace in the region, and began introducing it to the other presidents. That was a difficult process, to say the least; the plan faced opposition in varied and often contradictory ways. In El Salvador, for example, it quickly became clear that military leaders, not the President, would have the final say on the peace plan. In Nicaragua, the Government was against my 'pro-Yankee' peace plan, even though the US Government was opposed to it as well, since the United States sought to derail peace efforts until their support for the Contras resulted in a military

---

after the Second World War produced a government promoting democracy and socio-economic change, including land reform. The reformist government of Jacobo Arbenz, however, was ousted in a coup organized by the US in 1954, and further decades of repressive military regimes ensued. From the late 1960s US military advisers trained government troops in 'counter-insurgency' techniques. Disparate guerrilla groups formed a broad coalition, the Guatemalan National Revolutionary Unity, in 1982.

Nicaragua
The 1979 overthrow of the corrupt dictator Anastasio Somoza by the guerrillas of the Sandinista Front prompted optimism throughout Central America and in the world beyond that the standard regional mold of rightwing repression could be broken. The Sandinistas nationalized Somoza's land and industrial assets, which constituted 40 per cent of the country's economic resources, and began a major literacy campaign. In 1981 US President Ronald Reagan announced his aim of destroying the Sandinistas and in 1982 2,500 former National Guards invaded from Honduras with US support. The counter-revolutionary force, known as Contras, continued their military operations through the 1980s. Covert US funding for their operations emerged during the Iran-Contra scandal of 1983.

---

victory against the Sandinistas. US officials tried to pressure my colleagues into rejecting it and even put an alternative plan, written in English, into the hands of Honduran leaders for them to present at one of our presidential meetings. Such meddling provided ample justification for the peace plan's stipulation that outside intervention in our region needed to end for peace to be achieved.

Fortunately, I have never been one to give up easily. Thanks to perseverance; willingness to compromise and accept changes to the plan so it could gain the necessary support, and the hard work of many people, the presidents of the region signed the peace accords on 7 August 1987. The peace process did not end there.

The Esquipulas II Peace Accords

On 7 August 1987, five Central American nations – Costa Rica, El Salvador, Guatemala, Honduras and Nicaragua – signed a regional peace proposal in Guatemala, composed by Costa Rican President Oscar Arias Sánchez. These Esquipulas II Peace Accords set specific guidelines to stabilize Central America and bring peace to the region. The five Central American presidents had held many consultations with each other and worked out their differences. Representatives of the five nations finally agreed on a peace plan that called for dialogue between governments and opposition groups, amnesty for political prisoners, ceasefires in ongoing insurgent conflicts and free elections in all five regional states. It also stipulated the cessation of outside intervention – a hugely destabilizing factor in Central America.

The Procedures for the Establishment of a Firm and Lasting Peace in Central America – also called the Central American Peace Agreement or the Guatemala Plan – further called for renewed negotiations on arms reductions and to set up conditions conducive to the development of a 'pluralistic and participatory democratic process' in all the signatory states.

It took nine years for the last of the subsequent national peace accords to be signed. But by standing together in Guatemala that August day, we confirmed our region's commitment to peace. I don't think I had ever doubted that the Costa Rican path, the path of dialogue and peace, was the right way – but achieving those accords certainly provided eloquent proof.

Land of teachers

When it comes to my country today, I have great ambitions. Costa Rica has prospered in many ways over the past half-century, but when I was re-elected President in 2006, I set the goal of becoming a developed country by year 2021, when we celebrate 200 years of independence. When we reach that milestone, reflect on our history, and look around the country we have built, what do we want to see? We want a nation at peace with itself and the world. We want a nation that is equitable, healthy and educated. We want a nation capable of affording opportunities to all and protecting the fragile equilibrium of our environment. We want a nation that is proud of its past and in a position to contribute in a significant way to the future of all humanity.

My Administration is pursuing myriad initiatives with that goal in mind. We are improving our infrastructure, providing housing for struggling families, continuing to open our doors to the global economy, and nourishing our thriving tourism industry. Of all our efforts, however, the most important is certainly strengthening our education system. I have always said my land is a land of teachers, a country that chose to invest in schools rather than barracks, books rather than ammunition. Our challenge today is to live up to that legacy by ensuring all our young people have access not only to the education that would have been sufficient five or ten years ago, but to the education today's world demands.

Some of the challenges facing the other countries of our

region – reducing poverty, improving education and public health – are not unlike those facing Costa Rica, except that I'm proud to say that our country got a head start on some of them, years ago, by making good investments in social spending. One regional problem I have watched with particular concern is the increasing Latin American arms race. In 2006, the region's military spending was over $32 billion, while 194 million people languished in poverty. And why? Our region has never been more democratic. We are fortunate enough to say that in the last

A new Latin American arms race?

Observers describe a considerable increase in defense spending by Venezuela, Brazil, and Ecuador and significant arms purchases by Chile and Colombia. For decades the region has not seen a major war. But what does this build-up of arms arsenals signify?

Venezuela, flush with oil money, has spent freely on attack and transport helicopters, Russian fighter planes, and 100,000 Kalashnikov rifles. Neighboring Brazil recently asked Congress to allocate 10.13 billion reals ($5.6 billion) – a 53-per-cent increase – for its 2008 military budget. Chile had invested significant sums earlier in the decade; Colombia received hundreds of millions of dollars in US drug-war aid and now Ecuador is also spending more on weapons.

The motivation for these purchases appears to be different for each country. But problems could arise in the event of one state distrusting another's intentions, and some worry that Venezuela may be preparing for a possible attack by the United States. The expenditures on defense may be 'for any contingency'. But a 'military edge' always worries neighbors.

Reported in Time, International Herald Tribune *and other media. The paragraphs above are based on Andrew Downie's article in* The Christian Science Monitor *of 16 January 2008.*

decade we have rarely seen military conflicts between nations. Poverty and disease cry out for our governments' attention. Why, then, does our region continue to misdirect its resources?

Many leaders who spend on arms throughout the world use as their excuse the need to protect their people – but a government that allows its citizens to go hungry, to remain illiterate, or to die needlessly from diseases we know how to cure, is hardly protecting its people. What's more, a government that does not invest in education is not even protecting its own democratic system. Democracy without education is all too susceptible to the temptations of authoritarianism or demagoguery.

World without weapons

In 1988, after I was awarded the Nobel Peace Prize, I used the monetary portion of the award to endow the Arias Foundation for Peace and Human Progress. Under the auspices of the Foundation, three programs were established: the Center for Human Progress, to promote equal opportunities for women in all sectors of Central American society; the Center for Organized Participation, to foster change-oriented philanthropy in Latin America; and the Center for Peace and Reconciliation, to work for demilitarization and conflict resolution in the developing world.

As a non-profit, non-governmental organization, the Foundation has made great efforts to promote more just, peaceful, and equitable societies in Central America and has sent a message of peace to the rest of the world. The programs, projects and initiatives that we undertake are steps in the right direction. From its inception, the Foundation has been one of the key non-governmental organizations leading the post-war reconstruction of the Central American region and fighting for a world without weapons and full of opportunities. The Foundation makes every effort to understand and prevent social violence to avoid the destruction of Central America's future and that of succeeding generations.

The Arias Foundation creates dialogue with political leaders and state representatives in order to promote public policies and social changes that contribute to good governance, democracy, human security and equality between men and women. We also work on a daily basis to construct the foundation of societies by promoting the rights of women – their political participation and their business capacity – as well as by empowering citizens for democratic participation and local development.

Over the years, the Foundation has benefited from an

Women's rights secure peace

Felicia Ramírez Agüero, the Arias Foundation's Co-ordinator of Good Governance and Human Progress:

'Since its beginnings, the Arias Foundation has worked towards the construction of more just and equitable societies. This grand endeavor includes efforts to consolidate a culture of peace in Central America, as well as efforts in favor of equal opportunity and gender.

'The establishment of the Law to Promote Social Equality of Women in Costa Rica is based on a commitment to gender equality. This law allows our Foundation to develop systematic projects in favor of all women in Central America. These are aimed at the promotion of women's rights to land and property, the incorporation of gender issues in the agricultural and environmental sector, and women's participation in popular elections.

'In Guatemala, after suffering the brutal and traumatic experiences of war, and living for years as refugees in Mexico, numerous rural families and indigenous women returned to their country and resettled in lands far from their home towns. Paradoxically, the circumstances of war, repression and land seizure became a "culture medium" for defending their rights to land and property and becoming organized. It helps them to reposition themselves as people with rights, to themselves and to society.

extraordinary staff. In the 1990s, the Foundation's most outstanding work involved demilitarization in the Central American and Caribbean basin region. We published a number of in-depth studies on the transition from war to peace in various countries. We were also very actively involved in the abolition of the national armies in Haiti and Panama. I could go on and on about the work the Foundation has done – I am very proud of what we have accomplished.

If there is one message that I have sought to communicate

'The Arias Foundation focuses on strengthening their internal capacities, empowerment, leadership, negotiation and ability for political advocacy and so forth. This results in better dialogue with employees of public institutions, the recognition of women's work, and representation in key development institutions such as the Ministry of Agriculture and Livestock, Fund for Land and Fund for Guatemalan Indigenous Development.

'Following the Peace Accords, the Arias Foundation supported Central American governments and civil society organizations in a process of democratization of the region. An important aspect of these efforts relates to the lives of women, especially in the area of land and property rights.

'In Nicaragua, Haydee Rodriguez and Elida Maria Galeano share the experience of having been opponents in armed conflict, both leading armed groups. In the past they were bitter enemies: Haydee as part of the Sandinista Front, Elida as a commander of the Nicaraguan Contras. Today, they exemplify the miracle of peace and reconciliation.

'The war had left them scarred forever. At the same time, new lessons learned allowed them to plan their future differently. They exchanged armed struggle for the battle for women's rights, gender equality, and the well-being of families and communities. Now they provide training for women to defend their rights, housing solutions, and development projects – irrespective of political affiliation.'

---

to the world over the course of my career, it is that our global military expenditure is simply immoral. It's more than one trillion dollars per year – that's approximately $3.3 billion per day. How can governments continue to spend this money when people continue to go hungry, to die of preventable diseases, to languish without even a primary education? Some would say this is a sad but inevitable choice in an increasingly dangerous world. I argue that our world is dangerous *because* of these choices, and that we all have the power to change this terrible state of affairs.

And so we work to convert into a reality a global treaty that would control the international arms trade and avoid the atrocities that are produced by this most perverse business.

In 1997, I met with seven other Nobel Peace Laureates

The Arms Trade Treaty (ATT)

'Peace is not just a dream. It is hard work, and requires real-world, practical efforts to come to fruition... Humanity cannot wait. The poor and forsaken cannot wait. Now, more than ever, the ratification of a set of universal rules on arms transfers is essential, if we still dare to hope that the 21st century will be more peaceful and just than the previous one.' Oscar Arias

From the letter by the Nobel Peace Laureates*:

'The international Arms Trade is out of control! There is as yet no co-ordinated mechanism or global criteria to be used in a harmonized fashion and applied equally to all arms exporters and importers. Irresponsible arms transfers foment violent conflicts, perpetuate poverty and underdevelopment, and contribute to countless violations of human rights and humanitarian law. Every day, thousands of people around the world are tortured, injured, or sent fleeing from their homes by forces armed with deadly weapons. Every minute of every

---

in New York to draft the International Code of Conduct on Arms Transfers. A draft of a comprehensive, legally binding Arms Trade Treaty (ATT) grew out of the principles set forth in the Code of Conduct. In brief, the ATT would prohibit the transfer of all arms that are likely to be used for violation of international law or human rights, or that significantly impair the goals of sustainable development. The ATT differs from the UN Program of Action to Prevent, Combat and Eradicate the Illicit Traffic of Small Arms and Light Weapons in All Its Aspects (PoA). The PoA's current recommendations are not legally binding, do not regulate licit transfers, and only relate to small arms. The problem of the global arms trade demands a broader solution.

I am happy to say that dozens and dozens of nations around

---

day, someone is killed by armed violence. Further, a person living in the developing world is twice as likely to die from arms violence as a person in the industrialized world.

'As part of a comprehensive approach to enhancing human security, states must work to establish strict national, regional and international arms transfer criteria that are consistent with their existing responsibilities under international law, based on common global principles. The development of such national criteria was mandated in the UN Program of Action to Prevent, Combat and Eradicate the Illicit Trade in Small Arms and Light Weapons in All its Aspects. Various other international, multilateral, and regional processes further the promotion of these global principles.'

Signatories of the letter declaring this position include Amnesty International, the Dalai Lama (Tibetan Autonomous Region), Shirin Ebadi (Iran), Rigoberta Menchu (Guatemala), Desmond Tutu (South Africa), Lech Walesa (Poland), Jody Williams (United States; International Campaign to Ban Landmines), and others.

---

the world have thrown their support behind this effort. In 2006, the UN General Assembly approved a resolution ordering the Secretary-General to create a Group of Governmental Experts to examine the feasibility, scope and draft parameters of an eventual ATT. Members of this group are continuing to meet periodically and I am confident that they will reach a consensus regarding the urgency of an ATT.

We face significant differences of opinion on our path to making the treaty a reality. Some delegations disagree about whether the treaty should cover all conventional weapons, which is essential; helicopter gunships and armed humvees can be just as deadly as pistols and rifles. Others argue that the proposed guidelines infringe on a nation's right to defend its security interests. This argument holds no water. I believe we can all agree that no legitimate security interest is ever served by providing weapons to those who seek to violate human rights.

'Where there is a Costa Rican... there is liberty'

To some degree, my commitment to disarmament is a result of the very specific experiences I had as President during a violent and dark time in Central American history. On the other hand, however, that commitment is inherent to me as a Costa Rican. Julio Maria Sanguinetti, the former President of Uruguay, once said: 'Where there is a Costa Rican, no matter where he may be, there is liberty.' You could also say that a Costa Rican, no matter where he or she may be, carries close to the heart a firm belief in the power of peace, and shares that belief with others. In my view, that's our country's great gift to the world.

Another of our gifts is our history of conservation, and our struggle against another kind of war in the world today: the reckless war we are waging against our own planet. Last year, my Administration launched an initiative we call Peace with Nature. It includes domestic commitments such as becoming a carbon-neutral country by our bicentennial, and international commitments such as lobbying for financial incentives for developing countries that curb deforestation. As the name of the initiative implies, I see this effort as a direct continuation of my lifelong work against war and violence; for what we are doing to our planet is violent indeed. We are blasting CO_2 into the atmosphere at an unprecedented rate, dynamiting our oceans, attacking our forests.

Sometimes I worry that our blindness to these very obvious dangers will continue. In general, though, I am an optimist. I have seen people forge peace with each other in unlikely circumstances, so I believe that the human race will find a way to forge peace with nature.

I've been blessed with many remarkable experiences throughout my life, and most of all with the chance to know many remarkable people. It's been particularly wonderful to receive a second chance to help my country in this very direct way, all these years later.

As I look to the future, I suppose my basic vision of the world is this: that my great-grandchildren will enjoy a world in which each government is democratically elected, is able to fulfill its people's basic needs, remains at peace with both its neighbors and its internal opposition, and uses the tools of economics and science to the benefit of all its people.

To put it another way, my greatest hope for the world is that the priorities of those who lead it will, some day soon, move in line with the urgent needs of the people they lead; that feeding the hungry, and lifting up the poor, and educating our children, and protecting our environment, will finally be seen as the overriding responsibilities that they are.

7

Daughters with a Future

Introduction

ALTHOUGH 19TH-CENTURY CHINESE immigrants brought prostitution to Thailand, there is a long-standing Thai tradition of men having concubines. Even today, the concept of *mia luang mia noi* – major wife, minor wife – is socially accepted, especially for wealthy entrepreneurs, politicians and organized crime leaders. In the south, the sex trade is still controlled by ethnic Chinese, but prostitutes come from almost any ethnic background in the Mekong Delta: Thailand, Cambodia, Laos, Vietnam, Burma, Malaysia and the Yunnan province of China.

The Thai king Rama VII banned polygamy in 1934 and prostitution was declared illegal in the 1950s. But despite these measures, prostitution flourished during the Second World War and increased again during the US-Vietnam War. The Ministry of Public Health estimates that sex services involve around 90,000 Thai citizens, but the United Nations and the Chulalongkorn University's Population Institute put the number at more than 200,000.

Unlike many Western countries, where prostitutes are managed by pimps, in Thailand there is an extensive network of intermediaries that control the trade, all taking their share of the sex-service fees. In some places the girls are ranked according to their beauty or skills by wearing colored tags. In back alleys men may be 'serviced' for 40 baht ($1), but entrepreneurs and government officials visiting member clubs may pay up to 5,000 baht ($125). Thailand has become a virtual playground for sex addicts and pedophiles with little to fear from the country's government.

Some accept the sex trade as it is, glorify it or make allowances for it by referring to indigenous customs or to the Buddhist notion of *fah likit* (Thai for 'destiny') or *tien ming* (Chinese for 'Heaven determines'). Western men take advantage of this permissiveness, while the Thai Government seems unconcerned. But the sex trade has many dark sides and few excuses. It leaves young girls (and boys) uneducated, uprooted and extremely vulnerable. On top of that, their 'working life' of about 12 years leaves them, even at the young age of 24, unemployable, dependent, estranged from their families and communities, and often suffering from diseases and psychological trauma.

Some, however, are rescued from this fate. In 1989 Sompop Jantraka identified the root causes of the sex trade and convinced 19 at-risk girls and their families that they could have a different life. He established the Development and Education Program for Daughters and Communities (DEPDC).

'Sompop is willing to go to any length,' said filmmaker Christopher Osborn. 'He will sacrifice his money, position, even his friends – to help children.' Nominated twice for the Nobel Peace Prize, Sompop feels embarrassed about praise. He told a CNN reporter: 'When someone calls me "hero", I turn my head and see my staff and my daughters who help me and who wake up before me, cook and take care of me and I feel bad.'

In 2008, Sompop received Michigan University's Raoul Wallenberg medal for 'outstanding humanitarians'. Meet Sompop, and it quickly becomes clear that he doesn't waste time: 'Save them today, because tomorrow it is too late.'

Sompop Jantraka
Thailand

'Sometimes I almost cried, thinking: Wake up! Speak up! Stand up!'

When Sompop Jantraka (born in 1957) saved 19 girls from the Golden Triangle's sex trade in 1989, he had no idea he would found an NGO that has rescued thousands of girls. It is now led by some of those first 19 girls, while Sompop expands the formula throughout the Greater Mekong sub-region.

I SAW THE same things that the police, the governors and everybody else saw. But they didn't do anything and at first I didn't realize that they were never going to do anything. That's why my work focuses on prevention and protection first, and return and repatriation later.

I was born in Surathanee, in the south of Thailand, into a poor family with seven brothers and sisters. My father didn't have an occupation, but took all kinds of jobs, anything he could get: cleaning houses, cutting wood, gardening, clearing forests, carrying materials, a million different things. My mother and my sisters worked in a mineral mine and when I was 10 or 11 I was working together with them. It was very difficult.

Not every child in the family had the opportunity to go to school or to finish their education. My brothers' and sisters' education was limited and they only learned how to read and write. But I was lucky, because I was the first son of the family. I was sent to school and stayed with my grandparents, because most of the time my family moved from one place to the next. They moved all over the south of Thailand, across the district and across the province, depending on where the mining company set up business. When they had finished digging up the land in one place, they moved to another, searching for more minerals.

After three years they moved and then again after five years. So my family had to move and build a new place to live several times. Each time, my brothers and sisters had to leave school and in some places there were no schools, so they dropped one or more years. But I was doing well in school, so my mother decided to leave me with my cousin who had a house in Surathanee. And this house didn't move! So I was studying in that place for seven years, without my father and mother.

In addition to school, I had to work to support myself and help the family of my cousin. This meant that I spent most of my time on the street, picking up tin cans and plastic bottles and collecting them in a basket so I could sell them. It was a wonderful time for me, because I was free and I had something to eat. And occasionally, when I had enough money, I could buy ice cream. It was much better than living in the family with nothing. When I finished wandering through the streets, past the shops and restaurants, I secretly went into people's gardens to pick fruits. They didn't see me. It was stealing I think but, you know, I needed something to eat. And at other times I went fishing in the nearby river. I don't think I was a 'professional' street kid, because I didn't do it all day. It was just something that happened by chance and it simply provided me with some income. Sometimes I went with other boys and put ice cream in a cooling box. All day long we sold ice cream and we returned home in the evening.

While in secondary school, I moved from one cousin to another. But they didn't live far apart, so it didn't affect my schooling. When I was 12, I got a different job: digging the graveyard. New orders had come for the graveyard, so everything had to be dug up. A competition was held, because they thought there would be no-one who would want to dig up bodies. So that became my job and I did this with four friends of mine. It was good money; ten times more than we got from collecting garbage or selling ice cream. Ten times! You can imagine – it was an old graveyard and we just dug up bones, clothes and sometimes coins.

Another job I did was digging wells, one meter in diameter and up to 15 meters deep. So deep! It was very dangerous. Some of the other children died while doing it. They suffocated. But older people taught us how to stay safe. 'In the morning, when you arrive,' they said, 'you have to use a piece of paper and set it alight. Then you drop it into the well. If the fire reaches the bottom and it is still burning, it is safe. If it dies out quickly, pfft, then there is not enough air and you can't go down.' So, whenever we did that, everything was just fine.

That job was good money too. My parents didn't come over very often and my family was broken when I was 14. My father divorced my mother and left the family, so my mother had to work to take care of her children alone. I almost dropped out of school. I still worked hard, but I didn't have enough to eat, no lunch at school and no money for a school uniform. The teacher couldn't do much to help me. In 1970 there was no such thing as a scholarship.

The delight of imagination

During my first two years in secondary school I met a foreigner. Her name was Rebecca Perham, but we called her Becky. She was a Peace Corps volunteer from Boston and taught English. This was very interesting for me, because it was the first time in my life that I saw someone very different. She was an adult who talked very politely to the children and brought along interesting things like cartoons, pictures and stories. It stopped me from running away from class and missing lessons, because it was so much fun. This is why from that time my English got better and I learned a lot about culture, history, English books and the media. It changed my way of thinking and allowed me to imagine my life and the world differently thanks to stories like *Peter Pan*, *Mary Poppins*, *The Little Prince*, *Pinocchio*, *Cinderella*, and *The Sound of Music*. When I heard the music and saw those

185

people trying to do something good and improve their lives, I compared it to myself. Could I be something similar? What could I be?

I always dreamed that one day I would be able to speak English well and get the opportunity to travel. Becky was a great teacher and the children wanted to participate in almost everything. She also set up English summer camps three times for good students. And I was selected for every camp. She talked a lot to me and I had the chance to meet 25 to 30 other foreigners. I was delighted! I was able to talk to Steve, John, Peter, Mack, Philip, Debby and Judy. It was like a new life to me and it pushed me to learn English even more. Today I am still in touch with Becky and I have gone to see her many times. We have had family reunions and my children call her 'auntie'. She and her son Greg have supported DEPDC since 1996, when we met again for the first time in 25 years.

Actually, after secondary school I was planning to go and help my mother and my grandparents. But my records showed that I was the top English student in the province. 'Sompop, how could he do so well?' the teachers said. After Becky left, I continued and read a lot. Often I went to the railway station of Surathanee, the only place where I could meet foreigners. Trains from Bangkok to Kuala Lumpur (Malaysia) would stop there, so every day I spent one-and-a-half hours walking from one side of the train to the other until it left again. I would say to them: 'Hi, how are you? Where are you from? How long does it take to get from here to Kuala Lumpur?' I just wanted to practice my English and make sure it was correct. 'Are you traveling first or second class?' I would always try to ask them something different. But sometimes I would learn things that had nothing to do with language, but with how people are.

I would say: 'Hello, good morning!'

'No, I have no money!' they answered. 'Go away!'

They thought I was begging. But I would also meet friendly

people. 'Ah, you speak English? Who taught you?' And then I started practicing different accents: Malaysian and Chinese people speaking English and other people who didn't have Thai as their native tongue.

Going to high school cost a lot of money, and everyone in my class had a good family. They went to Bangkok, central Thailand or the north. For me, I only had one contact: a friend of another teacher at my school. He said: 'Sompop, if you don't have a place to go, then go to this man in Songkhla in the south.' One time I accompanied a senior friend, who was taking an American Field Scholarship. Becky took him, me and other students on a trip to Songkhla to show me that maybe in the future I might be able to go to Mahawachirawut School if I did well in English. It's a very famous school, where Prem Tinsulanonda, the former Prime Minister, also studied. Today, at almost 90 years of age, he still serves as the chief adviser to King Bhumibol. So when I studied there, from 1974 through 1976, I remembered my first trip. I was still dreaming: if I study here, maybe after a few years I can go to the United States!

A dormitory among coffins

But when I arrived with my backpack, I didn't have a place to stay, so the first few nights I slept on the street. It was another 15 days before school would start and then I would have to do an entrance examination to qualify. I had to prepare. The next day I went into the temple to pray and I asked one of the monks: 'Do you have a place for me as a temple boy?'

'Do you have an identity card or anyone that recommends you?' he said.

'No, I don't know any people in this area and I was born far away from here.'

'Then I cannot accept you.'

'Why not?'

'Because you may cause trouble and if you steal anything,

nobody will take care of you.'

I then sat there for almost half a day when I saw another boy going in and out.

'What are you doing here?' he said.

'I am looking for a place to stay.'

'Come stay with me!'

He did not belong to that temple, but he had a free space at the back of a ruined temple next to the other one, where they kept coffins, bodies and clothes. He was going to take the same examination at the same school. I went in and it was so smelly! For some bodies they didn't have coffins and clothes and pillows were stacked up to the ceiling and all over the place. It was worse than digging in the graveyard! But for the time being it was a good place for me and I didn't care. I stayed there for two weeks without permission, like an illegal immigrant. But I got 78 per cent of the questions right and passed the examination thanks to my good English.

I went back home and worked at the mining company for one-and-a-half months before returning to study. I was still poor. 'Do you have any work for me?' I asked the teachers. They did: garbage collecting, making a dog kennel, digging holes and growing things in the garden. So I had a lot of different jobs during school and the holidays that ensured I had enough to eat. It was at school that I met my girlfriend, who is now my wife. She was in the same class as me, understood my situation and supported me. One time she gave me some money and another time she shared lunch with me. She knew many other students and temple boys, but said: 'Your English is so good!'

In class, many times the teacher even asked me: 'Is that correct, Sompop?' I said: 'Sure!' or 'No,' when I had to correct them. I was much better at grammar then, now I make lots of mistakes.

By the time I took a university entrance examination, my family was moving again. One of my sisters and one of my brothers got married. Only two of them went on from primary to secondary school. And after my father separated from my mother, we lost a piece of land. My mother didn't get anything, so she relied on the support of other family members. But I was admitted to the University of Chiang Mai. So I had to go all the way from the south to the north. I collected some money, hitch-hiked to Bangkok in a truck and managed to buy the cheapest third-class train ticket from Bangkok to Chiang Mai, even though I didn't exactly know where the place was. In Chiang Mai, I was matched to a three-digit number relating to someone that was there last year – number '272'. After that, I was treated like a brother and taken care of by a very kind 'sister'. Like a buddy system. She found out that I was poor and gave me everything. 'You don't have a basket? You don't have a blanket?' And I had to do the same with my younger 'brother' next year. The seven people in my '272 family' were like parents, grandparents, brothers and sisters. It really helped me.

I started my studies with humanities, but didn't do very well. I don't know why. So I changed and took political science, but eventually my major was in humanities again. And as I had taken French at secondary school and now took German, I got terribly confused. In the end I changed three times, from History to German to Psychology, but finally I decided on Social Sciences and got As and Bs. During my time at university I played music and started a folk band called Songs for Life. I played local instruments: string, keyboard, and bamboo and pan flute, and I composed songs. We sang for justice, for the environment, for peace, for children, women and farmers. We also played for a left-wing political student movement at public demonstrations and strikes, standing up for democracy. For seven to eight years I was in this movement, fighting against certain government policies. We didn't accept military control of our country and wanted to change the system at university so that there were free elections.

I also worked outside whenever I had the time, or even when I didn't have the time. Then I simply left my classes and worked as a tour guide for Alternative Tours of Thailand (ATT). During those trekking tours I could make good use of my English and I guided groups of tourists into the hills and villages of the jungle. I learned how to communicate in local dialects and understand the cultures of the Akha, Lahu, Lisu and Karen peoples. Most of them were in the Chiang Mai area, some in the Chiang Rai area. The work was good, but I saw a lot of poor people with problems. I could offer them no help and I didn't see yet that the

'I am lucky I didn't cry today'

24-year old Tasanee, trafficked to Burma and subsequently a bar lady in Phuket:

'Do you want to know the truth about the sex trade?' Now engaged to her Swedish boyfriend Kristian, Tasanee escaped a life of misery and abuse. She shows pictures of bar life, Boom Boom Bar and karaoke. 'This kathoey [lady boy] died from a car accident. And this bar lady died of AIDS.'

'The bar ladies work as they do because they have problems with their family. If they marry a Thai man, they have no security, because Thai men can have another lady. But they cannot take care of them, because as a plumber or taxi driver they don't make enough money. In my country, men suppress women and you cannot trust them. But the women have to survive, especially after they have babies, so they start to look for farang people [foreigners]. Sex work is not good, but the money is: 1,000 baht ($25) to go with a man for one night is better than staying at home and getting only 100 baht ($2.50). A lot of girls want a new life. It's my story too.

'When I was 19, I was on my way to school, when a van stopped next to me. A man got out, pulled me into the van and drugged me. When I woke up, I found myself locked up in a room, not understanding what had happened. At that time I was waiting to be sold to a man sex trade was such a problem. My attention was more focused on how to support them with some money, because many of the people were sick and uninformed. So the next time I came, I gave them food and clothes or medicines for old or sick people. It was just common sense. Being from a poor family myself, I simply cared about them. If there was anything I could help these people with, I did.

I practiced my English and made connections with individuals and organizations, which could give me some money to continue

---

from Burma. I guess that didn't happen, because the man that took me knew I was still a virgin and liked that. So now I was locked up in a room for over a year and I couldn't do anything. And I couldn't see anything, no sun, no stars. The man who had taken me came in often to have sex with me. In the beginning I always tried to fight him, but I soon learned that that only made it worse, because he enjoyed hitting me.

'During that time I never felt clean. It didn't matter how many times I washed myself after the man had abused me, I just never felt clean. I could sit for an hour cleaning myself, crying and thinking "who am I?" There were many other rooms with girls that had been sold like this. I often called for help, but if I was screaming too loud the man came in to hit me. So I stopped. One day I escaped. I don't know how, but another lady opened the door for me. I guess she was also locked up. I ran and ran and found my way to Bangkok where my sister lives. Meanwhile I was carrying a baby for six months. But I went crazy and tried to kill myself many times. I even jumped off a four-storey building, but miraculously survived. The baby was born in a hospital when I was recovering from the "accident".

'From Nakhon Ratshisima (Korat) where my baby was born I went back to my home village, which is a two-hour bus ride. But I could not stand looking at him because he brought back bad memories. So I left the baby with my parents, because I got fucked up in my head my studies. After eight years I graduated.

While I was studying political science and researching poverty and co-operative village projects, I saw a lot of failings in the governmental projects. I was very fortunate to be invited to join a project with a Japanese friend, journalist Michiko Inagaki, when I was working in Bangkok for ATT. They focused on training, workshops and dialogue, and Michiko needed a research assistant to collect information about child abuse, sex exploitation and prostitution. Together, we interviewed 'bar ladies' and visited many massage parlors. We also made many treks and met with the families and communities from which the girls originated.

We started in Bangkok, but I couldn't see very much there, because people were simply talking about their difficulties in life, how little money they got and how they fell into the situation of working as sex workers. Many of these girls only got a 30

---

and even tried to kill the baby many times. I cannot blame the baby, but he looks like the man that abused me. The baby was born after seven months, so it is very small and needs expensive milk and food, even today. If I stayed with my father and mother, none of us would be happy. My mother had to stop working and stay at home to keep an eye on me, so that I wouldn't do anything stupid to myself or to the baby.

'To escape it, I chose to work as a bar lady and went to Phuket. I did this for one-and-a-half years. At first, I cried all day and wondered: God, what am I doing? I still have friends that work in Phuket. My cousin too. She had a problem with her boyfriend and went together with me. On her own she found it too scary. I started drinking a lot and just wanted money, to have fun and visit my father and mother. Most bar ladies have similar sad stories – same same, but different. That is why we can stay together so well – we're like a family.

'Because of the man that abused me and then working as a bar

---

to 40 per cent share of the income from the owner. And they were not allowed to say no to guests or choose with whom they would go out. Many of them had tried to run away from their contracts. They had debts and sometimes they escaped. But they were followed and taken back and often severely punished. So, many of the stories of these girls were very bad. In northern Chiang Rai the conditions were different. There were many sex trade centers, but here the girls could buy themselves out. If they paid the charge to their owner, they even ran away with their boyfriends sometimes. The rules in the south were much stricter, because of the presence of Malaysians and Chinese.

Causes and consequences

After we had collected a lot of information, the root causes of trafficking and the sex trade appeared to be the same everywhere. It pushed us to see the girls' families. The majority of them came

---

lady, I couldn't go to school for a long time. Today, when I read a book, my head hurts. And as nobody helps you, you have to help yourself. In Phuket we lived in very small rooms. How we lived, we didn't care. We cared about what we looked like. Looking sexy. The sexier you are, the more money you can make. And many bar ladies try to save money and hope one day to go back home and perhaps open a shop. For me, it was all easy money. Easy to get and easy to lose. I spent it all on shoes, clothes, makeup, drinks. Most of the girls are alcoholics, because every day customers offer you drinks and you have to accept.

'I don't expect any changes from the Thai Government, because so many people benefit from it. So it is amazing that I will now have a future in Sweden. I never thought that would happen, because in Burma and Phuket I had no future. And I hate men, I really hate men! I had to be with them, but I wanted to kill them. I was so fucked up in my head...'

---

from poor, broken or troubled families. Another cause was drug abuse, opium and heroin; they needed a lot of money to support their addiction. And yet another was parents whose health was bad and who desperately needed money for long-term HIV or cancer treatments. They had to borrow money all the time. And the girls living in the northern provinces had no residence status, no ID and therefore no rights. They couldn't get any jobs and become part of society. And finally another cause was broken relationships between boys and girls. They marry at a very young age, 14, 15, but break up after one or two years. But by that time, they already have a child and the girl has no knowledge, no job and nowhere to go. So they find a job as a sex worker.

In almost every village there are people with connections to girl trafficking and the sex business. Like scouts, they look for vulnerable girls who are easy to convince and coerce. There are lots of those people in the hill villages and especially along the border, and of course in Mae Sai. That's the place where I stopped, because I found out there was a link between the sex trade and the intermediaries in Mae Sai with all the other places in Thailand, but also in Malaysia, Japan, Singapore and so on. Everything revolved around Mae Sai, and that's why my organization DEPDC was established here.

I started research with the YMCA, village leaders, teachers, governors, immigration officers and so on. And when I went to the Golden Triangle, where the borders of Burma, Laos and Thailand meet, I visited many guesthouses and met with many street kids. I recognized the problem and the pattern. The Golden Triangle is especially dangerous for abandoned children. Many gangs operate there, because they find children from Laos, Burma, south China and several hill peoples all in one place.

'The sex trade here is small in comparison to Mae Sai,' people in the Golden Triangle said to me. In Mae Sai, the last part of my research, I saw a guesthouse with a lot of children. But I couldn't say whether they were sex workers or not. A week later I started to track many places with a guy from Australia and we went to the same places together. For the last 15 years, he had been spending most of his time in Mae Sai, just to sleep with young girls. 'You know these places?' he asked me. Altogether there were up to 58 brothels in this small city. This was in 1989.

Who owns the gold in the Golden Triangle?

Next to the Golden Crescent (Afghanistan, Iran and Pakistan) and Colombia in South America, the Golden Triangle (Laos, Burma, Thailand and Vietnam) is one of the major illicit opium-producing areas of the world. Although the term refers to the opium trade, it is also used to designate the tourist region where the Ruak and Mekong Rivers meet. The area is spread out across the mountains of the four countries, while some say it should also include the Chinese province of Yunnan. The reputation has existed since the 1950s.

Opium and morphine produced in northeastern Burma are transported by horse and donkey caravans to refineries along the Thai border for conversion to heroin. Most of the trade uses Bangkok for distribution to international markets by couriers using commercial airlines. Law enforcement is intense, as is the continuously developing industry itself. In the 1970s a whole wave of Asian traffickers was incarcerated in US prisons, but the drugs continue to find their way to major cities around the world.

Most of the people who grow opium are from indigenous groups and live below the poverty line, having no alternative ways to generate an income. The region is equally known for its money laundering and human trafficking, especially of girls for prostitution. The only ones that profit from any of these 'trades' are local and international crime rings, vast networks of intermediaries and women that extend to the girls' own family members. And last but not least: officials that prefer bribes to law enforcement.

He just went in and said: 'Hello!' and he was friendly with the girls in almost every brothel. Many of them called him 'dad' or 'papa'! And he would act funny, make noises and speak half Thai, half English, like in a play. And all the girls would respond to 'papa'. But he used many of them, even 10-year-olds. He had no sense of guilt.

'The way things are'

'This is just the way things are around here,' he said. 'Sompop, you do what you do and I do what I do. But if you want to know what I do, better than me telling you about it, you just follow me and see what it is like.'

'OK,' I said. 'I told you that I am doing a study about children working in the sex industry.'

'Why?'

'Well, they should go to school.'

'No. They couldn't go to school, because they didn't have money and nobody wanted them.'

'How do you know that?'

'They told me!'

'They may have. But maybe that could be changed!'

'Well, do what you want to do. There are thousands of children.'

I spent three months in Mae Sai studying the sex trade. It was strange, because only a small percentage of people in Mae Sai actually come from there. Most of them are from elsewhere, Burma, Laos, south China or various hill peoples 60 kilometers away. They all move there. After one to three months, their placement has been prepared with documentation and connections. The children are referred by agents to different places throughout Thailand, Malaysia and so on. Mae Sai is like a transit station, a temporary brothel where the girls get prepared for the sex trade. Many of them are still virgins when they arrive, having no idea what they are getting into. But in Mae Sai they are trained: sex training, basic language skills, self-protection and so on. Self-protection includes never telling anyone they are under 18, telling people they have parents in Thailand or that they are Thai, and never that they just came in from Burma. Sometimes parents ask an intermediary to negotiate a price for their daughters and sign papers. Lots of things are done in this border town, even ID cards, border passes and travel documents are falsified here. It involves many, many people.

This is how I obtained a lot of information. And then I realized that many of the girls from Mae Sai were delivered by the same gangs – or different gangs – to other places, because I had met and talked with many children from Mae Sai in Chiang Mai, Chiang Rai, Bangkok and in the south. The south is the biggest place for Chiang Rai children; there are about 3,000 of them there. It is part of the sex trade that the children are dislocated from the homes where they originally grew up. From Chiang Rai to the south, from Laos to Thailand and from the province of Songkhla to Narathiwat and vice versa. In those places there are about a hundred brothels, each with about 50 girls.

I started to investigate this further and went into the villages, searching for the parents of the children I had just spoken with. I met with families, local people, teachers and leaders of hill villages. They were encouraging children to go to 'work' outside their villages.

'Wait a minute,' I said. 'What are you doing?'

'Children go to work,' they said.

'Don't you have any children here that want to go to school?'

'No, no, no. Nobody here wants to study!' They were laughing at me. 'You must be joking,' they said. 'Do you have a lot of money? Give it to me and we have some good business for you. Don't ever spend it on these children to go to school.' They used a Thai proverb: 'You're breaking chilies to spice up the river! They're going to eat you.' They meant: they're going to waste your time and your money.

'Look!' they said, pointing to some Akha girls. They had already changed from their original costumes to jeans, ready to leave the village.

'Are you sure they don't want to go to school?' I asked. So I went over to the girls themselves and talked with them. 'Do you want to go to school?'

'Yes,' one of them said, 'but my mother already accepted some money, so I can't.'

'Where are you going?'

'We are going to work in a restaurant in...'

That was almost 20 years ago, when I couldn't do anything, even though these children were right in front of me. Hundreds of kids that I met during my three months of surveying the area left the villages, even while I was talking to their families and the village leaders.

In many villages you don't see girls above the age of 13. What happens to them? I turned to a few girls that were left behind and I asked their parents: 'What about these young girls?'

'They will go next year,' they said. 'She has been booked already.'

My God, I thought, she is still in fifth grade. But when she is in sixth grade, she can go. So that girl was only 13 then! She was *at risk*. And this was the first time I realized that there was this specific group that was *at risk*. I highlighted it and shared this information with UNICEF, with government officials, with journalists of CNN, ABC and BBC News and so on. I talked about these girls that were *at risk* and more and more those words were recognized as the priority of any work of prevention. That's when the work of prevention really began, in 1989.

Broken families, broken futures

In my first document for DEPDC I wrote a definition of *children at risk*: children whose families are involved in the sex trade, whose parents are drug addicts, who come from broken families, who migrate and who have no ID, no home, no rights and no hope. All these children are easy prey for scouts. And then there are children whose parents are sick and need money to go to the doctor or for medication and those who have been sexually abused. The last category is especially at risk, because everyone around these girls knows they lost their virginity. They become embarrassed, and everywhere they go people point at them. Their parents no longer want the responsibility and send them to work in the sex trade.

Sometimes we go to Burma, but working there is really difficult. We go to cities like Keng Tung and Taunggyi, but along the border it is too close: you see them and they see you. I live only one kilometer away from the border, but there is very little I can do. Yes, the border is open, but the society is closed – and not just that, people's minds and hearts are closed! We can't do anything and our projects there don't grow. They have to be cared for and nurtured, but everything is controlled and limited all the time. Health and education issues are limited. You simply cannot mention human rights. 'Rights' is a forbidden subject in Burma. It's very difficult to explain to people: 'It is your *right*!' if you can't even use the key word! What alternative is there? When you're confronted with fear, power or pressure or dictatorship, you cannot breathe and your brain stops thinking.

I met about 35 girls that were at risk. Some of them had already been booked for the sex trade; they were almost gone. So I tried to encourage parents and talked directly with the girls, the teachers, monks and village leaders to convince them that I had enough money for these girls to go to school. My Japanese friend had gone back already, but I still remained in the area, because I wanted to follow up the case and complete my research. At that point I had no plans to start an NGO – I just wanted to stop something that was wrong and that was right in front of me. I thought maybe I could use my salary of 30,000 baht ($1,500 at the time). Two months later, Michiko paid me. But when I went back into the village again, of the 35 girls that I had met, only 19 were left. The rest were gone, missing or had run away. But these 19 wanted to go to school, because during my interviews I had promised that I could prevent them from having to go into the sex trade.

'Do you want to go to school?'

'Yes, if I could...'

'Yes, you could!'

'But how?'

'I can take you and put you in a school, all right? And I will provide you with documents and some clothes.'

'Yes!' they said. It brought a smile to my face. So I encouraged those 19 girls to go to school in Mae Sai. I bought them school

---

Burma's 'forbidden subject'

The largest nation in Southeast Asia, Burma's recent history has been characterized by oppression. Despite the fact that the country is heavily influenced by Theravada Buddhism, a military junta has violently suppressed the people since 1962. What was initially called the Burmese Way to Socialism led to all business, media and production facilities being nationalized. Even the Boy Scouts are under Government control.

During free elections in 1990, for the first time in 30 years, the National League for Democracy (NLD), the party of Aung San Suu Kyi, won 392 out of a total of 489 seats. But the election results were annulled by the regime.

In 2006, the International Labor Organization announced it would seek 'to prosecute members of the ruling Burma junta for crimes against humanity' at the International Court of Justice - the crime in question being the continuous forced labor of about 800,000 of its citizens.

In 2007, anti-government demonstrations were swiftly repressed. The International Red Cross was not allowed to visit those detained or tortured. In the same year, Buddhist monks withdrew spiritual

---

uniforms and called the Japanese NGO Asian Children's Fund: 'Did you know that the girls we met in the village are already at school?'

I had only a little money left and I asked them whether they could send me some more...

'All right,' they said, 'we will support you and will get you some more money from Japan.' I don't know how they managed to do it.

I put these girls in the school, but five or six of these 'daughters' could not go back home because of the sexual abuse of their stepfather, drug addicts or gangs. And 12 girls were from far-away villages. That presented me with a problem, because I had

---

services from all military personnel, referred to by some as the Saffron Revolution. The monks were joined by nuns, leading 30,000 people in a protest march from the golden Shwedagon Pagoda in Yangon (Rangoon), past the offices of the NLD opposition.

A year later, in 2008, Cyclone Nargis devastated parts of the country. More than 130,000 people died and more than $10 billion worth of damage was done – the worst natural disaster in Burma's history. One million people were left homeless, injured or threatened by hunger and disease. Yet Burma's junta complicated recovery efforts by delaying the entry of UN planes with medicine, food and other supplies. On national television however, General Than Shwe was shown ceremonially handing out disaster relief.

Human rights organizations have reported on abuses by the Government: no independent judiciary, political repression, forced labor (especially for the Unocal oil company), human trafficking, child labor and sexual violence by the military.

The Government restricts aid, requiring in its 2006 guidelines that humanitarian programs 'enhance and safeguard the national interest' with staff from government-prepared lists of individuals. UN officials consider these restrictions unacceptable.

---

to go back home to my family and my company was waiting for me to do another trip. But these girls could not go back. They were still at risk. So I asked their parents: 'I need your permission for at least three years, enough time to allow your daughter to complete secondary school.' I made a deal with them: 'If you withdraw the contract, you have to pay back the full amount of the scholarship that I gave to your daughter.'

They said: 'Oh, that is not a bad deal!'

And I guaranteed them: 'After three years, they will complete their school education.' I signed the contracts, but had no confidence that it would succeed. But that was the start of the Daughters Education Program (DEP).

For the DEP I rented a small house that now belongs to Alinda Suya, the current director. Alinda was the first staff member. When I started the idea of the secondary school for at-risk children, I spoke with the teacher. 'You have a very good idea,' he said. 'I had the same idea, but I couldn't do it. I support you. But I have one girl that is very good, but who almost dropped out because she has no money. Would you want someone to assist you?'

'All right,' I said and I met with Alinda. She took me to her mother. She had no father and her family was very poor, but they were so kind! And they said to me: 'OK, Sompop, you can share with us and use half of our house.' So I shared their house for only 400 baht per month. And I paid Alinda 1,400 baht per month for her to take pictures, make documents and do various jobs such as washing clothes and cooking. That allowed me a lot of free time to run and solve 'my problem'. The at-risk girls had become my problem. So what could I do? That was all the staff there was in 1989! A few girls and one volunteer in the house of Alinda's mother.

Only three months later, DEPDC officially started. From the beginning I learned how difficult it is to negotiate with the parents. Sometimes I persuade them, plead, beg or berate them into allowing their child to attend school, even for free. Often I started with: 'How are you doing? And how about your daughter?' They never saw their daughters' potential and thought they were lazy and good for nothing. 'So do you give up?' I asked them. It was like a game between one who wants to save them and another that wants to take her away for the sex trade. So I had to work very hard to prove to them: 'It really works! It's much better than you think. She'll be much better off!'

It is difficult when you try to change people from a bad background and bad habits to become better. They don't know what it is. It's difficult because it is true: they were very lazy and selfish and had no interest in anything. So during the first half year, I was struggling like mad.

Under suspicion

One of the first people to visit me in Mae Sai when I was in difficulties was Dr Saisuree Chutikul, the first woman who fought with the law, the policies, the Government and with international standards. She was the former adviser of the Prime Minister and worked as the Social Change Leader. Almost 40 years ago, she started talking about human rights, children's rights, child education and so on. I was taking care of children without parents, without shelter, without residence permits and without any understanding from the Government. I needed help, so I invited her to be the president and consultant of our work. She has helped so much to protect DEPDC that I think without her it would never have grown into what it is now. Today, Ms Saisuree is the UN representative for the Convention for the Elimination of Discrimination Against Women (CEDAW). She still fights human trafficking and, thanks to her, DEPDC is secure.

There were a lot of people who misunderstood what we were doing and even abroad there were gangs that were against our work. Others accused us of brainwashing the girls to become servants of 'Heaven's Gate' or Mormons or something. But I had no idea what they were talking about.

The police came to investigate and the military warned me: 'You are destroying the image of our country in the rest of the world by openly saying that children are being abused in the sex trade; you criticize the police; you talk about the lack of education and say children don't get opportunities because they don't get government support. You talk about child labor and trafficking. You always send the wrong message...'

I had to fight them: 'The reality is making Thailand become worse and worse. Maybe we are not dealing with all the problems of our country here, but you cannot sweep the problems under the carpet.' I only said that we have problems, not that we have the solution. But given time, I think people will understand what we're doing.

'We are going to close down your center!' some threatened. Again I called Ms Saisuree: 'We have a problem. Could you help us clear it up?'

One day I got a phone call from a man who introduced himself as working for an American NGO. He said: 'You are doing a good job. But friends of friends of friends of mine told me that the Yakuza, the Japanese mafia, know you very well.'

At a party, where some of them had a few drinks, they said: 'Don't worry about Sompop of DEPDC. Let him do what he wants. It doesn't bother us, for there are thousands and thousands of girls. Whenever we want to buy some, we can simply go ahead. Maybe he can rescue a few hundred, but it doesn't affect our business. Let him be.'

They still have a business of trafficking that runs in the hundreds of thousands. For many years I have been followed and have received many threatening phone calls. 'Get out of town or we'll beat up your staff,' they say. 'We'll burn down your school. Get out before we kill you.' A friend let me know: 'These stalkers are mafia gangs. But they believe that you don't have enough money to save all these girls.'

Sometimes I almost cried for these girls, thinking: wake up! Do some exercise, work, cook, learn, speak! Speak up, speak out, stand up! I tried to change their attitude from one of fear and limited consciousness to one of opportunity and empowerment. Even though they are poor, their parents try to make them look wealthy and beautiful, ready for the competition with other girls. They try to look good and are afraid of dark skin. So I said: 'No, you're not just a girl. You're a strong young woman, all right!'

Sometimes I would take them along for a holiday trek into the jungle, crossing rivers, camping, cooking and so on. But after a while they would cry, saying that it was all too difficult. 'Go on! Do it!' I said. 'It's life!' I pushed them to work and pushed them to change.

'Read newspapers! Stand up and speak up for yourself!' So they started to read and become more aware of their environment. This is how I conducted many study tours. And while doing that, many memories came back to me, like a running stream: treasure hunts, children's games, reading newspapers, media, drama, music and word games...

'Come on, Sompop, what did you do when you were young?' I asked myself. That was the time that I recognized what I owed Becky. I challenged myself: How much do I know and how much experience do I have about children? What did I get? How did I get it? What did she say? What did she do?

I contacted her: 'Becky, tell me what is the meaning of "universality"? Why did you think I was a child that could improve? Why did you say: "Pop, you have to pop up to the top! Like popcorn!"?' She used the word 'Pop' as a nickname for me. Pop, pop, pop, pop, pop... 'Why did you say that to me?'

I said to myself: thank you Rebecca, thank you school, thank you, because I had turned from a street kid without any encouragement and without any opportunity – from almost nothing – into something. So it occurred to me that I had to use that potential and there were not so many skills that I had learned at school and at university that I could use. My God, what did they teach me those eight years at university? For a while I hated myself for what I couldn't remember and couldn't do. But soon I realized that I should not blame myself, because when I was young I couldn't imagine anything else. Instead, I should think for myself. In short: I had to put my life into the life of those children and really understand them. This is how I discovered 'inside out' education.

Many times education is approached by bringing in new knowledge from the 'outside in'. But I believe that the best kind of education is to learn 'inside out', from what we already have.

'What makes you happy in your life?' I asked the girls. And they started to talk about what made them happy. 'And what causes unhappiness in your life? How is it different?' It is a very simple thing to ask, but it allowed them to recognize things close to them. 'Talk about your parents, talk about yourself. Why did your father beat you? How do you feel about that?' It was hard to learn from this in the beginning. But by challenging them in that way, they started to think for themselves about their life and their world. And they began to understand that not only were they part of the world, but also that they were part of the problem. In itself it was not the solution, but it was the beginning of *life skills* training. That became my first subject in training the daughters at DEPDC. After that, I could reach them better – in their hates, their fears and their jealousies – and little by little their mentalities started to change. And peer groups were developed, to share, love and take care of each other like brothers and sisters, like a family. Those relationships offered them rehabilitation, like a family reunion at home. A new kind of family, and a new home.

After that I used schools, study tours, human rights

organizations, daycare centers and even prisons and environmental organizations. I brought 'my daughters' to have a look, see and learn and come back to report on what they had experienced. Like learning by dialogue, *direct education*. So the second step was direct education that helps them to develop their life skills and social skills. Being with DEPDC for five or six years, the girls become young social workers.

Since the beginning, DEPDC has linked up with women's and children's organizations, UNICEF, ECPAT International, and Ashoka – and over the past 10 years we just grew, grew, grew. Different organizations support DEPDC nowadays, allowing it to work on several new projects and expand the Center. Today there are many young people from the area that come to our Center and a whole new generation of students is coming. My assistants Num and Puangtong were from one of my classes in 1990. Ten of my former students were working here, but they have now moved to other areas. From the first group of 'daughters', two still work at the Center: Phensri Nobang, the co-ordinator of Mekong Youth Net, a training project for youth leaders from six countries who start up provincial projects in their own countries; and Ramjaj Jaijoy, the co-ordinator of the administration department. Today, there are five young women in the directing team assisting Alinda.

The bloodsucker cycle

Prevention is not just focused on the children. It's the whole environment that surrounds them that makes them at risk. Next to brothel owners and intermediaries, there is a whole 'bloodsucker cycle' of people who have vested interests in sexual slavery: parents, mama-sans, village leaders, taxi drivers, tour guides, moneylenders, police, members of the border authority, and outwardly respectable businesspeople or government officials. In such a bad environment these girls cannot survive.

Protection also has many key issues associated with it, such as rehabilitation, repatriation, reintegration, reunion, budget support, safety, follow-up, jobs with a sustainable income and so on. One special aspect is the performance of a good-luck or welcome ceremony of forgiveness when young girls rejoin their family or the community that they came from. This is very important, for rebuilding trust is difficult. These children have been away from their family and their culture for 10 years or more. So their attitude and personality have changed and perhaps they can't even communicate in their own dialect any more. They may have left at 9 and returned at 19. That's a big gap. They have to be brought up to date, otherwise after a month they don't want to stay any more.

I have put all these key issues together as guidelines, for I'm afraid I might miss some important issues. I don't know how to write a book, but this way I at least have most of my chapter headings. After 20 years of research and experience I still don't have a book! Many people say: 'Sompop, write a book, so that everybody can learn from it!' I have all these details, but I would have to sit down to do it, maybe for one year. And we have so many records, photos and other materials...

Until now, the Thai Government does not financially support us. The reason is that they believe that DEPDC is a very strong organization and has a lot of foreign support, so they don't give us any money.

The Mekong Youth Net is a training program that is now brought into the rural areas of Laos, Burma, Cambodia, Thailand, Vietnam and the Yunnan province of China. We cannot yet work through governments, but only through local NGOs. The curriculum starts with a one-year training centering on 'human being', ethical and moral issues and personality. It links to study tours, in which they can see prevention projects. Part of the philosophy behind it we borrowed from Howard Gardner's book *Five Minds for the Future*: the disciplined mind, the synthesizing mind, the creating mind, the respectful mind and the ethical mind. It involves human rights, management skills, planning and follow-up, networking, learning by doing and so on.

We recently started a project called Mekong Youth Union. The curriculum is a one-year training, during which the students work directly with an expert in law, politics or any current issues – that's how you get to understand things. People are very impressed with this project and the Mekong Youth Union is going to become another new NGO in its own right. By next year, we will already have 96 graduating youth leaders from six countries. The Mekong Youth Union will become the umbrella organization, making it possible that people can be trained in their own countries, all with the same curriculum. The major obstacle now is that the host organizations don't have enough money to support them. But in time, they will link with the European Union, Novib, Open Society Institute and so on.

From the very beginning, DEPDC's work has focused on prevention, and not so much on victims. I met with gangs and mafia members and explained to them: 'I don't mind who you are. My work is prevention. If you took a girl, it means it is too late for me to do my job.' That was already on my mind 18 years ago. Since then, we have developed a multi-disciplinary approach that includes working with governments and NGOs, a Halfway House for cross-border issues, Child Voice Radio and a Child Helpline – 24 hours a day.

Many people have been an example to me, but Rebecca Perham was the one that inspired me to use opportunities, to build up better things and to encourage people to become something from nothing. She demonstrated kindness, nonviolence and patience to see the results and wait for the fruits to ripen. You have to be both a *teacher* and a *parent* and mix these two personalities. So Rebecca was like a mother to me. She raised and taught me at the same time. She never treated me like a student and didn't think about how much time, money or energy she might have to spend on it. She simply had very high instincts of giving and change-making. I think she is still working very hard. Even though she has done a lot already, she is still working at a law center in Boston helping people who have migrated.

To see girls enslaved in brothels, it hurts. If you can protect one child, you protect future generations. If the Buddha were here today, I think he would say that selling children or accepting money from prostitution is a sin.

8

The Coming of Spring

Introduction

RECONSTRUCTION IN AFGHANISTAN? Has there been any progress? For most Afghans, the picture is dark and painful. Billions of dollars in aid have poured into the country, but reconstruction projects are limited and a lot of money has been looted by warlords, government officials and corrupt NGOs. In the UN Human Development Index, Afghanistan still stands 175th out of 177 countries and unemployment is still more than 40 per cent. Average life expectancy is now an appalling 44 years.

And what about security, human rights and democracy, all of which were to be restored under the leadership of the United States? It is evident that the US mission of Operation Enduring Freedom and the International Security Assistance Force (ISAF) have not been able to deliver what they promised: freedom and security. About this 'ghost war', writer Tariq Ali says: 'There's no freedom. There's no safety. There's no rule of law. It's all fabrication – another made-for-TV invasion that's

99 per cent fiction.' The foreign troops are having a hard time making a positive impact, while the Afghans 'endure' the imposed 'freedom'. Many have even demonstrated for their withdrawal, a demand that has only been strengthened after witnessing the poor performance of the US-backed Afghan Parliament.

The Afghans have always shown great resilience and resisted occupation and control by any foreign nation. Long before the Cold War, the country had already defended itself successfully in three Afghan-British wars. The army of the Soviet Union was defeated in the 1980s by the *mujahedin*, the Afghan resistance fighters. After the departure of the Russians, the Northern Alliance started a civil war, at least in part because the United States had poured billions of dollars into their pockets in service of its own anti-Soviet strategies and policies. Few people today ask why exactly it was this formerly US-backed Northern Alliance that came to power again when the Taliban were deposed by invading forces following 9/11. In any event, the Afghan people long for a time when they are no longer pawns in the hands of fundamentalists or foreign countries.

In 2003, a parliament was set up with US support, a landmark in the recent history of Afghanistan. One of the most prominent winners in the parliamentary elections that followed was Malalai Joya. After being elected, she took up one of the 249 seats of the National Assembly, the Wolesi Jirga. Since then, she has emerged as the youngest and most outspoken critic of the country's current leaders and Members of Parliament.

'I will do my best,' she says, 'to stop the warlords and criminals from building any laws that will jeopardize the rights of Afghan people, especially the women.'

Representing the remote province of Farah, 28-year-old Malalai is a women's literacy and health worker. The daughter of a former medical student who lost a foot while fighting the Soviets, Malalai is married to a Kabul-based student of agriculture and she has six sisters and three brothers. Recently she was profiled in a prize-winning documentary film, *Enemies of Happiness*. But her participation in Parliament lasted less than three years.

Many warlords, drug lords and criminals have seats in Parliament, acting with impunity for their (civil) war crimes and misdemeanors. When Malalai publicly denounced them in a television interview, in which she likened the Afghan Parliament to a zoo, she was expelled until the end of her term in 2010. She received many death threats and survived four assassination attempts, partly due to her interrupting the Loya Jirga (Grand Council), which was in special session to ratify the Afghan Constitution (see box below), and criticizing the mujahedin. Although these fighters made their name in opposing the Soviet Union, afterwards they fought among themselves in a bitter civil war that only ended when the Taliban seized power in 1996. But Malalai holds them responsible for Afghanistan's civil war and for many crimes committed since then.

'The warlords are like snakes in the sleeves of the Government,' she says. 'Only if the Government tackles them head on, with great determination and with international support, will we see a brighter future.'

Confronted by a continuous stream of death threats, she says: 'I know that, if not today, then probably tomorrow, I will be physically annihilated. But the voice of protest will continue, because it is the voice of the people of my country.'

Malalai has been used to intimidation by the Taliban since she started working in the country in 1998 after returning from Pakistan and Iran, where her family had emigrated during the civil war. When the people of Farah province elected her as their representative, initially she didn't feel up to the task. But their genuine demands made her gather the courage to bring their suffering to the world's attention. She wanted to let the world know that even though the men and women of Afghanistan have had to live in ignorance and poverty for many years, they don't trust the mujahedin.

Democracy, security, human rights and women's rights only exist on paper. Human rights activists, journalists and other democratic voices in Afghanistan are threatened, suppressed or killed. Even inside Parliament, Malalai herself was beaten and other parliamentarians threw bottles of water at her, shouting: 'Take her and rape her.'

While on a worldwide lecture tour of universities, women's rights and human rights organizations, she gives numerous interviews to newspapers, radio and television stations. Due to her youth and diminutive height, when lecture audiences first set eyes on her she seems like a young girl. But when she starts addressing the audience, she speaks fearlessly and breathlessly like an avalanche, as if there is no tomorrow.

'Why do I do this? Because I can and someone has to do it.'

Malalai Joya
Afghanistan

'A stable or a zoo is better than this Parliament!'

For this statement Malalai Joya (born in 1978) was expelled from the Afghan Parliament. But regardless of death threats and four assassination attempts, she continues to defend Afghanistan's human and women's rights and to speak out against the US-backed warlords and criminals who hold power.

'You can cut the flower, but you cannot stop the coming of spring.'

UNDER THE BANNER of liberating our people, the Americans attacked Afghanistan. But in doing so they sacrificed our security and our freedom. We don't want occupation, we want liberation! Our history shows that. The Americans pushed us from the frying pan into the fire.

I was born only days before the coup of Russian puppets which started decades of war and bloodshed in Afghanistan. My father left our village and joined the resistance against the Russian regime, so my grandfather and uncle took care of us. For years we had no idea whether my father was dead or alive. Eventually we learned that he was alive, but living in Iran.

I was four at the time, when tens of thousands of Afghans were pouring out of the country to escape the brutalities of war. Our family joined this exodus. We emigrated to Iran to join my father in a refugee camp, and my earliest memories come from there. As there was no school for Afghan refugees, we moved to another camp in Pakistan when I was seven. I studied in a school run by the Revolutionary Association of the Women of Afghanistan (RAWA) in the Pakistani city of Quetta. It was the first time I attended school. It was also in that school that I had the honor of meeting Meena, the leader of RAWA (see box on page 224, 'Meena').

Next, our family moved to a refugee camp near Peshawar, where I finished my primary education. I then took up teaching literacy classes for some years. After the fall of the Russian-backed regime in 1992, our family moved back to Afghanistan. But due to the civil war and the crimes committed by fundamentalist groups, we were soon forced to return to Pakistan once again. So by the time I was 15, I was a student in the mornings and teaching literacy courses in the evenings, thanks to my early schooling. It was not easy as I was so young and many of my students were older than me. But I tried my best and members of the Afghan camp committee came along and gave me the courage to continue. I started at such a young age because I was the oldest daughter and my family needed the money.

When I was working like this, day by day my life started to change. I enjoyed the eagerness and love for learning of the students. In Pakistan I had gone to different camps – Akora Khattak, Haripur, Jallozai and Sharwali – to teach, and I enjoyed doing that. At the same time it was very hard. I remember some visiting journalists that described our camp as 'a living graveyard' because many people fell victim to hunger and disease and died. I have many memories of people suffering. I cried with them and laughed with them. And one of our greatest joys in class was when, together with my school friends, we translated English newspaper articles into Dari. After I had finished school in 1998 I returned to Afghanistan. I first stayed in Herat and two years later in Farah. It was the time of the Taliban.

After Grade 12 in school, I had been eager to go to university and continue my formal education, but financially this was impossible in Pakistan and I had to do a job to help my family, so even during school, I was teaching women literacy in the camp and was paid by an NGO that was active there. Then, in 1998, I joined an NGO called Organization of Promoting Afghan Women's Capabilities (OPAWC) to get involved in their projects in Afghanistan and teach girls in their secret classes. In 1998, while the Taliban were in power, our family moved to Herat in western Afghanistan. For years under the Taliban we stayed there and I taught girls in underground classes because women's education was banned.

Clandestine classes

Next I worked as a social worker and literacy teacher for women and girls in Farah and Herat. It was clandestine, so I needed a lot of courage to do it. This time it was for a women's NGO and I was only 19 years old. My family went back to Pakistan. Due to Taliban pressure and drought, life was very hard, so many families took refuge in Iran or Pakistan for a second time and my family was one of them. But the people from the NGO told me about their work and that they needed my support in Afghanistan. They encouraged me: 'You are young and you have experience.' Everyone in the camp knew that I had been a teacher for four years, so I said: 'OK, let's see whether it is possible in Afghanistan!'

I liked this work because it focused on empowering young girls and women. And I especially wanted to help *them*, because most of the time they are the victims of the situation in our country. I had to deal with many family and marriage issues. Many quarrels are about who pays for a woman, who will take care of her, about brothers who control their sisters and about fathers who give away their daughters or refuse to do so. On one occasion an old man wanted to marry a girl of only 13. But she refused and her family didn't want the marriage either. To demonstrate his sincerity, the groom-to-be then 'swore' on a glass of fruit juice that she would not have a miserable life and would not be maltreated. I said: 'But she is threatening to burn herself!' The man: 'In that case I am prepared to pay compensation.'

At the same time I was giving underground literacy courses, even though there were many problems due to the Taliban.

My neighbors warned me: 'It's not wise to do this, it is very risky!' but I was young and didn't listen to their advice. Slowly, slowly they changed their minds and we established a little underground school despite the Taliban. The girls and young women endured many hardships, but they were so full of hope and so eager to learn! To keep the lessons going, we told them not to take up lessons all at once, but only in small groups. The groups were very varied, some younger than me, some older than me. We had different tricks to escape the Taliban's

---

'Blacken your windows!'

List of Prohibitions issued by the Taliban's Ministry for the Promotion of Virtue and Suppression of Vice: 'pork, pig, pig oil, anything made from human hair, satellite dishes, cinematography, and equipment that produces the joy of music, pool tables, chess, masks, alcohol, tapes, computers, VCRs, television, anything that propagates sex and is full of music, wine, lobster, nail polish, firecrackers, statues, sewing catalogues, pictures, Christmas cards'.

The Taliban ruled most of Afghanistan from 1996 until 2001. Their ideology is a mixture of Islamic fundamentalism and Pashtu nationalism. 'Taliban' is an Arabic loanword meaning 'students (of Islam)'. In 2001, they were removed from power by the Afghan Northern Alliance and NATO countries. However, they are still active as guerrillas in the region adjoining the frontier with Pakistan.

They were led by Mullah Mohammed Omar, assisted by commanders and *madrasah* teachers from Islamic schools in Pakistan. Although in control of Kabul and most of Afghanistan for five years, the regime only gained recognition from Pakistan, Saudi Arabia and the United Arab Emirates. While in power, they implemented the strictest interpretation of sharia law ever seen, particularly notorious for the mistreatment of women. Women were forced to wear the *burqa*;

---

attention and to hide our lessons. When I returned home at night I used to be so tired, but at the same time I was very happy! Every day, their desire to learn gave me fresh hope for the future and energy to continue, even though it was very risky. We appointed guards, so that the Taliban should not become aware that we were running an underground school. But sometimes they did find out and then they beat up students and maltreated them. The girls were very afraid and each time we had to find another house in which to gather in secret. But

they were not allowed to work or to be educated after the age of eight. Women seeking an education risked execution if caught. They were not allowed to be treated by male doctors unless accompanied by a male chaperone; they faced flogging and public execution for violations of the Taliban's laws.

The Taliban were overwhelmingly ethnic Pashtuns. Their first major military activity was in 1994 when they captured the city of Kandahar and the surrounding provinces, losing only a few dozen men. Next, they took over 12 of Afghanistan's 34 provinces, gaining control of Kabul in 1996. They replaced most bureaucrats with Pashtuns or Taliban loyalists, whether qualified or not. As a result, most public offices ceased to function. The Taliban could not communicate with the local Afghans (who spoke Dari or other non-Pashtu tongues), so that they appeared to many as an occupying force.

'We want to live a life like the Prophet lived 1,400 years ago,' Omar's aide and spokesman Mullah Wakil said, 'and jihad is our right. We want to recreate the time of the Prophet and we are only carrying out what the Afghan people have wanted for the past 14 years.' The Taliban did not hold elections, as their version of sharia did not allow politics or political parties. Their leader's legitimacy came from an oath of allegiance in imitation of the Prophet and early Muslims. On 4 April 1996, Mullah Omar had the Cloak of the Prophet Muhammad taken from its shrine for the first time in 60 years. Wrapping himself in the they were so happy that at least they got some education!

While still working with the OPAWC in 2001, I was named its director in western Afghanistan, so the circle of my activities got wider. While at first I was only teaching girl refugees how to read and write, now, after the fall of the Taliban, OPAWC started other projects in Farah. We moved there and I became involved in the establishment of Hamoon Health Center and later, with availability of more funds, we also established an orphanage. We had around 50 children in the orphanage, and I was with them almost day and night. It was a great experience for me and I was like a sister to these children, teaching them and trying to make them happy. I have many great memories of the time I spent with the children.

Many people would come to the Health Center, even from far-away villages. Some of them came a long way on their donkey, just to obtain medicine or medical advice. Even though

---

relic, he appeared on the roof of a building in the center of Kandahar while hundreds of Pashtu mullahs below shouted 'Amir al-Mu'minin' (Commander of the Faithful). He became the highest authority.

Without press conferences, policy statements or photography, no-one even knew what the Taliban leaders looked like. Mullahs with a madrasah education had become cabinet ministers. The Ministry of Finance had no budget and no qualified economists. Cash was collected and dispersed by Mullah Omar without book-keeping. The Taliban were criticized for their strictness and prohibitions on clapping during sports events, kite flying, beard trimming or sports for women. Others objected that their 20 per cent tax – *zakat* – on truckloads of opium should be limited to only 2.5 per cent of the zakat-payers' disposable income.

'Religious police' beat offenders with long sticks. Theft was punished by the amputation of a hand, rape and murder by public execution. Married adulterers were stoned to death. In Kabul this was

---

the clinic provided free medicine, it was not enough for so many people and their many needs and I hope that one day we'll be able to improve it. They wanted to close it due to lack of funds, but thanks to help from Italy in 2004 it is still open. I love this clinic, because many people would be hopeless without it and for women and children it is vital. I am happy that sick people can still come, even though we can now only give free medicine to about 40 to 50 people.

The promise of Parliament

Even though conditions under the Taliban were hopeless, I dared to dream that one day I might go to university. But when the Taliban were deposed and the chance came, many people said: 'You have such open communication with people and they trust you. Why don't you become a candidate in the elections?'

'No! I'm too young,' I said. 'I'm only 25!'

---

carried out in front of crowds in the former soccer stadium. They even ordered 'householders to blacken their windows, so women would not be visible from the outside'. 'Of course we realize that people need some entertainment,' Mullah Mohammed Hassan explained. 'But they can go to the parks and see the flowers, and from this they will learn about Islam.'

The worst attack happened in Mazar-i-Sharif. Driving their pickup trucks up and down the streets, the Taliban shot everything that moved – shop owners, cart pullers, women and children who were shopping, and even donkeys and goats. They killed more than 8,000 people. As burials were forbidden, the corpses rotted in the summer heat and were eaten by dogs.

'You either accept to be Muslims or leave Afghanistan,' declared Commander Mullah Niazi from the Central Mosque. 'Wherever you go, we will catch you. If you go up, we will pull you down by your feet; if you hide below, we will pull you up by your hair.'

But they persuaded me, so I finally said: 'Let's try!' And I asked myself: what is more important? To improve my own education or to serve my people? And I decided that serving my people was the best idea. When I talked to the people, they felt that I understood them. They liked what I said, so I became the first candidate in the province. Many people knew me, because I went all over the district to many villages. And I made up my mind that I would represent them, even though some of my colleagues didn't like that idea.

So when I became a candidate for Parliament, people understood me and there was no need to explain. When they introduced me, everyone clapped loudly in support. I was aware that most people knew about me, but also that I was young and had no experience. We laughed about this and I said: 'You have more experience than me!' I promised them: 'I will serve you as you wish and will be honest on your behalf.' I repeated: 'I'm young!' Again they clapped.

I went to the Afghan Parliament in 2003 for the first time in my life. And also for the first time in my life I came face to face with people who had been responsible for destroying my country. In my mind I remembered the people that I had cried with and laughed with – the people in the refugee camps, in the clinic, in the underground school and in the villages I am supposed to represent. So when I saw these cruel and criminal people, I stood up and spoke out. This was during a gathering for drafting the Afghan Constitution. Speaking out publicly so quickly caused international attention. It changed my life.

Mojadedi, the chairman, then said: 'Sit down! Sit down. The sister has crossed the line of what is considered common courtesy. She is banished from this assembly and cannot return. Send her out!' Other parliamentarians called me 'impertinent', 'infidel' and 'out of the frame of humanity'. The chairman said: 'Guards, throw her out! She doesn't deserve to be here.'

Often I think it would be great if the 68 women in the Afghan

Parliament would unite. But more than 80 per cent of the Members of Parliament are warlords, drug lords and criminals and many of the women are not real representatives. They have links to these fundamentalists and warlords and compromise on many things. Many Members of Parliament cheated, they used guns and they used money and illegal ways to find their way into our National House. Therefore, the democratic, freedom-loving men and women are few and far between.

Some say: 'If you continue like this, they will kill you. You stand alone in what you do.'

Always I tell them: 'The silence of good people is worse than

---

My fellow representatives of the people

Malalai Joya's speech in the parliamentary special session (Loya Jirga) on 17 December 2003.

'My name is Malalai Joya from Farah Province. With the permission of the esteemed attendees, and in the name of God and the martyrs of the colored shroud of the path of freedom, I would like to speak for a couple of minutes.

'I wish to criticize my compatriots in this room. Why do you allow the legitimacy and legality of this Loya Jirga to come under question by the presence of those felons who brought our country to this state? I feel very sorry that those who call the Loya Jirga an infidel institution and see it as equivalent to blasphemy, are in some way justified by what is going on here...

'These people turned our country into the nucleus of national and international wars. They were the most anti-women people in society, they brought our country to this state and they intend to do the same again. I believe they should be tried by national and international courts. They may be forgiven by our people, the bare-footed Afghan people, but history will never forgive them.'

---

the actions of bad people.'

But when I was beaten last year, some of the democratic-minded women stood up and defended me. Some of them were even beaten themselves because they had been helping me. But I told them: 'We are only few. Please try to be outspoken like me. Nobody holds this seat in Parliament forever. We are only a few years in power, so we must use it for the benefit of our people. And what is important? Do not compromise with your enemies!'

It is the strong support of the Afghan people – and of freedom-loving people around the world – that gives me the courage to fight the enemies of my people.

Feminist heroines

One of my greatest heroines is Meena Keshwar Kamal. She

Meena

'Afghan women are like sleeping lions. When they wake up, they can play a very important role in society.'

Meena Keshwar Kamal (1956-1987), commonly known as Meena, was an Afghan feminist and women's rights activist. In 1977, she founded the first Afghan women's rights organization, called the Revolutionary Association of the Women of Afghanistan (RAWA), a group organized to promote equality and education for women.

In 1979, she campaigned against what she perceived as a Russian puppet regime controlling Afghanistan, and organized meetings in schools to mobilize support against it. In 1981, she launched *Women's Message*, a bilingual feminist magazine. She also founded special schools to aid refugee children and their mothers, offering both hospitalization and the teaching of practical skills and handicrafts to support them financially.

In 1981, at the invitation of the French Government, Meena

---

was a great Afghan feminist and activist for women's rights and founded the Revolutionary Association of the Women of Afghanistan (RAWA). Unfortunately, she was assassinated in 1987, most likely by agents of the Afghan secret police or fundamentalist mujahedin led by Gulbuddin Hekmatyar. RAWA is one of the oldest Afghan NGOs and over the last 30 years it has been very active. I hope that one day we will have more organizations like RAWA.

I love Meena and respect her as a heroine of Afghanistan, like other heroines such as Naheed and Wajeha, the two brave girls that were killed in an anti-Russian protest in Kabul.

'Malalai, we support you,' one of the members of RAWA assured me. 'Do not think you're alone. You have many sisters.' I joked with her and said: 'You have many members, no need for

---

represented the Afghan resistance movement at the French Socialist Party Congress. Shamed and disgraced, the Soviet delegation headed by Boris Ponamaryev left the hall as participants cheered when Meena started waving a victory sign.

She was assassinated in Quetta, Pakistan in 1987, a year after her husband – the leader of the Afghanistan Liberation Organization – was killed by agents of fundamentalist mujahedin leader Gulbuddin Hekmatyar. Meena left behind three children whose whereabouts are unknown.

RAWA: 'Meena had a strong belief that despite the darkness of illiteracy, ignorance of fundamentalism, and corruption and decadence of sell-outs imposed on our women under the name of freedom and equality, finally half the population will be awoken and cross the path towards freedom, democracy and women's rights. The enemy was rightly shivering with fear at the love and respect that Meena was creating within the hearts of our people. They knew that, within the fire of her fight, all the enemies of freedom, democracy and women would be turned to ashes.'

---

me!' In my view, all of us are in the same boat. But as for myself, I don't like to be associated with any organization, for I prefer to work on my own. I was happy, my heart was happy, when I did things for people as a social activist. Some fundamentalists say I'm a RAWA member, but it is simply not so. And others accuse me of simply wanting to become famous. I told them: 'Who would want to tell the truth and put their life at risk by becoming famous?' Fundamentalists? They have nothing to say.

I don't want to compare myself to the heroines of the past, like my namesake Malalai of Maiwand, who fought the British in 1880. They are in heaven and I am on the earth. And when I look back at what I have done so far – teaching, social work, becoming a Member of Parliament – I know I have made many mistakes. When you work it is impossible not to make mistakes. But when you do, it will improve you. In my opinion, anyone who ever lived trying to make no mistakes must have died. You can't survive that way, for you won't move! Perhaps my biggest mistake ever was at those times in which I felt hopeless. But I thought to myself: 'No, it is not the way forward to be hopeless. It's not good.' Sometimes I think that the tragic condition of Afghanistan is a world of hopelessness. But when I look at the people and their support, there is lots of hope. As a human being you may sometimes feel weak. But it's only because of hope that we're alive and we struggle. Losing hope is the biggest mistake. People come to me crying and share their stories and their suffering. I give them courage as much as I can. For some, even if I cry with them, it gives them hope. I believe that those who struggle may fail. But those who do not struggle have already failed.

Always searching

In my country, many of us grew up as a war generation. We only saw violence, suffering and crying. We hardly knew happiness. You know why I chose my name to be 'Joya'? In Dari it means 'searching'. When I was a social activist, I explained to my friends: 'Searching is what we human beings are doing. We are searching for freedom, searching for democracy, always searching.' Our history of wars impacted a lot on me. So for me, what is most important in a writer, a singer or a political activist is that they are a freedom-loving, democratic person. I travel a lot and learn from those men and women and I even learn a lot from non-educated people. They too are my heroes and heroines! When I was young, the children of Palestine were my heroes. I remember reading how they were fighting against Israel for the freedom of their country simply by throwing stones. And for me, even those who died at the hands of the warlords in Afghanistan are still alive. I especially love those people whose lives represent a message that gives hope to others. In Afghanistan and in other countries there are many hidden heroes and heroines that nobody knows about.

Our country is a Muslim country, at least mostly. And unfortunately, those who are not Muslim endure violence and persecution. But you should understand that our country, our national unity, has been destroyed. Journalists ask me: 'Are you Pashtu or Tajik? Aren't you from Farah province?' But I always answer: 'No, I am Afghan! I am from Afghanistan!' Farah is only a province. And when I am with Muslim people I wish to be a Muslim; when I am with Sikh people, I wish to be a Sikh, to wear their clothes and to be like them, as they wish. But, in essence, I am a secular Muslim. For the future of my country, I think secularism is the only way to bring back happiness. But over the past 25 years, some people have mixed politics with Islam, using it as a weapon against people. Most Muslims have in their hearts and minds clean emotions about Islam and should be respected for that. And others are not very well educated. The enemies of happiness use both of them because it is easy to deceive them. Some simply joined the Taliban because they were brainwashed: 'You're fine if you join us. We will pay you money for your poor family and after this life you will go to heaven.'

But if we had a secular government, it would not be possible to mislead people like that. That is why I believe in secularism and I am happy that many people, even those who are uneducated, agree with me. Many fundamentalists say about me: 'She's an infidel, she's a communist.' But it is important for the future of Afghanistan that they don't use Islam in the wrong way, for political purposes. People of my province tell me: 'If you are secular and an infidel, then we are also infidels. But we agree with you. We want secularism.' That is the right destination, but it is going to be a very prolonged struggle.

Part of how I want to help to create this in the future is by bringing the warlords, drug lords and criminals to an international court of justice, which is why I make many trips abroad. Sometimes I think: 'Even though one day I may not be alive, my heart is with my people and I am sure that one day these criminals will face a court of justice.' I believe that the power of the people is like the power of God. Today I am alive because of the people. Not because of the Government, because many there want to kill me.

At the moment, I am expelled from Parliament until the end of my term in 2010. A majority of my colleagues voted to suspend me for comments I had made during a television interview in May 2007. I had criticized the Parliament for failing to accomplish enough for the Afghan people. I said: 'A stable or a zoo is better than this Parliament; at least there you have a donkey that carries a load and a cow that provides milk. This Parliament is worse than a stable or a zoo.' They found me guilty of violating article 70 of the Afghan Parliament's rules of procedure. My 'crime' was 'insulting the institution of Parliament' and now they may even sue me for contempt in a court of law. Other Members of Parliament regularly criticize each other, but none of them has been suspended.

Because of my suspension, for the coming three years I cannot voice what I have to say in the Afghan Parliament. Some Afghan journalists say: 'Please write as you like! What you say is also in our hearts, but say it in your own words, and then we can distribute it to all people.' Through this they want to show their solidarity. But the newspapers are in the hands of fundamentalists and are censored. In their hands, everything becomes propaganda and democratic parties have stopped publishing their magazines, for lack of money. Even if I did write, it would not get published. Oh, they do write about me, but it is just propaganda to change people's minds. And I should remind journalists that Afghans are not only warlords, drug lords or criminals. Most Afghans are good and I love them.

Manifesto for change

But if I were reinstated, there are many things that I would like to see changed: no foreign forces; empowerment of women; education in schools and universities; respect for human rights and women's rights; a tribunal against warlords, drug lords and criminals; exposure of the wrongdoings of the Afghan Government and of the United States, supported by the European Union and other Western countries...

It would require a whole manifesto to express my dreams for the future. But I must say these things as someone who is always reminding others that the silence of good people is worse than the actions of bad people! And I *must* say that many Members of Parliament are not good people. And I *must* speak out about the wrong policies of the United States and its allies over these last six years. And I *must* say that right under the noses of thousands of United States and ISAF troops, Afghanistan still is one of the biggest producers of opium in the world. Last year the United Nations announced that Afghanistan under US troops could become a narco-state. Well, today no-one has any doubt that it has turned into a mafia state now that Afghanistan produces 93 per cent of the world's supply of opium. Even high-ranking officials and ministers have links to the drugs mafia.

The opium finds its way to the streets of London and New York. And the four major drug lords responsible for the heroin production are senior members of the Afghan Parliament. So the enemies of our people are in power, making the lives of our people like torture. And neighboring countries like Iran, Pakistan, Russia and Uzbekistan take advantage of this. They give arms to the Taliban with one hand and to the Northern Alliance with the other. Also, the Taliban continue their fascism in the eastern part of our country, which everyone was reminded of recently when 23 Koreans were kidnapped. The Government received three million dollars in exchange for their release, which of course went mostly into the pockets of corrupt people like the Taliban, after which they use it again to suppress our people. They simply made a deal, released some Taliban leaders and after that they were freed.

Recently also an Italian journalist and his Afghan translator and driver were kidnapped. Again, the Afghan Government made a deal and released five Taliban leaders. The Italian journalist was freed, but no-one cared about the two innocent Afghans. The Taliban beheaded both of them.

Despite the presence of thousands of NATO, US and ISAF troops since 2001, five times more people have been killed than in the 9/11 tragedy in the United States, where more than 3,000 people lost their lives. Security is still the Afghan people's greatest problem. When we don't have security, how can we talk about democracy, human rights and women's rights? President Karzai and his Westernized intellectuals have joined hands with fundamentalists and are imposing this mafia system on our people. This is the main reason for today's problems in deadlocked Afghanistan. Those who speak for justice are threatened with death. And how can we talk about security and human rights, while so many people still don't have enough food and water? These things are very important for the liberation of our country.

Instead of by the Taliban, we are now terrorized by the Northern Alliance. But it is also true that if the US troops leave Afghanistan, civil war will break out. At the same time, the Americans do not really want security, because they want to stay longer for their own strategic policies. They don't think about the people of Afghanistan. And I offer my condolences for those of you who have lost soldiers who have been killed in Afghanistan. I met some American mothers who had lost their sons. They hugged me and cried. 'We didn't know about the wrong policies of our country in Afghanistan.' In my opinion all of these people are separated from their governments. But we are proud that even in the United States and other nations we have support. It is also *your* responsibility that no more blood of innocent people is shed, including that of your own troops. Your governments' policies are wrong, because they follow in the footsteps of the United States. They support the United States instead of the people of Afghanistan. So please raise your voice against these wrong policies!

Afghan women's options

The people of Afghanistan suffer. Even if I only focus on the situation of the women, it is evident that today's situation is getting worse and worse. Both in the cities and in the provinces, many of them are so desperate that the number of suicides among women has never been higher. According to official accounts, there were about 250 suicides in the first six months of 2007. While the Taliban were in power they kidnapped women and raped them. But the commanders of the Northern Alliance, who are in suits and ties today and sitting in Parliament, do exactly the same. They abduct girls in cars and rape them. Why did those suit-and-tie people come into power after 9/11? It's a big question for our people. They commit many crimes and the situation of Afghan women is desperate. A month ago, 18-year-old Samiya hanged herself by a rope because she was to be sold to a 60-year-old man. Another woman called Bibi Gul locked herself up in the animals' stable and burned herself to death. Later her family found nothing except her bones. Over the past few years there have been very many cases of women burning themselves. According to a UNIFEM survey, 65 per cent of the 50,000 widows in Kabul see suicide as the only option to escape their misery. One in every three Afghan women is beaten, forced into sex or abused.

Before the Russians attacked Afghanistan, however, the women had freedom: they could go outside and they wore Western clothes if they wanted to. The media are saying that it was the United States that brought women's rights to Afghanistan. But it's a lie. The *New York Times* said that 'a new world of freedom has been opened to the women of this Muslim nation after centuries of seclusion'. But for many years before this, the women of Afghanistan had freedom, money and jobs. Every kind of freedom. Six years ago the United States invaded under the guise of liberating the Afghans and the Afghan women. The media were full of women in burqas. But the burqa is not the problem. Most women who wear a burqa today don't do so for religious reasons, but for security, for sheer survival. I wear it myself, even though I am a human rights and women's rights activist, for security reasons.

Especially in far-away provinces the lives of many women are hell on earth. Taliban commanders and Northern Alliance governors kidnap women and girls and gang-rape them. Even a five-year-old child named Farsia was kidnapped in Kabul. She was raped by a warlord, but as if by miracle she survived, though she is not very well. A 22-year-old woman was raped by 15 commanders of Rabbani, a Member of Parliament for the Northern Alliance. And next they peed in the mouths and on the faces of her children. The media say very little about this kind of shocking news.

According to an Oxfam survey, today only one in five girls is in primary education and only one in 20 in secondary school. Around 200,000 children in Taliban-controlled areas are completely deprived of any education. And how important education is! But the Taliban are burning the schools and they warn girls and women not to go to school. Otherwise, it's the commanders of the Northern Alliance that kidnap them.

That's why security and education are the two most important factors in our country. For if there is no security, how can they go to school? Children are even taken from schools and raped, so why would parents still send them to school? People have staged mass protests a number of times but no-one cares about their sorrow and tears. Only a few of the rape cases find their way into the media. One shocking case was that of a poor 11-year-old girl named Sanobar, the only daughter of an unfortunate widow. The girl was abducted and raped by a warlord and then exchanged for a dog! And this vicious rapist still acts as district chief. Yes, in the capital some women may be well-educated and have good jobs. But in the provinces this is the fate of girls and women. And many women journalists and activists have been killed in their own homes.

Photocopy of the Taliban

You know, the international community is making a big mistake by sending soldiers and blindly following in the footsteps of the United States. Their policies are a mockery of democracy and a mockery of the war on terrorism. There is no question that we need international support, but that doesn't mean we want occupation! We need a helping hand, but the helping hand is not one that assists in keeping the enemies of the people in power. So during the past six years the United States troops have been fighting the Taliban, who are anti-US, by supporting another terrorist group that is pro-US, the Northern Alliance. But the Northern Alliance has the same mentality as the Taliban! They are a photocopy of the

Taliban. Even when the Taliban were in power, the Northern Alliance killed more than 5,000 innocent people. So after the 9/11 tragedy, the situation has got worse and worse. That's why most people in Afghanistan do not experience the current situation as liberation at all. Our message to the Americans is: 'Change this policy! You will never succeed!'

The only alternative in this prolonged and risky struggle is

High hopes of Obama?
Malalai's view

'When asked in Berlin by CNN's Candy Crowley [on 25 July 2008] whether he believed the US needed to apologize for anything over the past seven-and-a-half years in terms of foreign policy, Obama said: "No, I don't believe in the US apologizing. As I said, I think the war in Iraq was a mistake…" This is enough for me to know that Obama is no different from Bush. The US Government has betrayed Afghanistan for the past 30 years. If Obama has a genuine concern for the plight of the Afghan people, he must first strongly criticize the past mistakes of the US Government. While Afghans ask for their withdrawal, his first reaction was to send more troops, pressurize NATO countries to do the same, and even start war in the Pakistan border areas. We're afraid even darker and bloodier days are ahead.

'What matters is not whether the President is black or white, but rather his mentality, his ideas. We have seen other powerful black people in the US Government such as Condoleezza Rice and Colin Powell. They did nothing positive or different from the white élites and leaders, and had a big hand in dragging the world towards war and crisis. If Obama follows this pattern, not even the poor black community in the US will benefit from his presidency. Historically, the policies of US governments remain more or less the same; they are preset by the CIA and other institutions. Without war, they have no future. Obama has no control of it. The only thing he can do is to implement it.'

---

for people from around the world to support the democratic-minded and freedom-loving people, parties, human rights and women's rights organizations and NGOs in Afghanistan. They are the future. It's the only alternative. I am well aware of the hardships and prospects of death from anti-democratic forces. But I trust my people and enjoy their full support and encouragement. I am the voice of the voiceless. The enemies of my people have weapons, political power and the support of the US Government to suppress me. But they can never silence my voice and hide the truth.

I feel happy with the many memories of people in my country. Many of them are desperate and tell me straight from their hearts what they think. Sometimes they say: 'Look how simple and humble she is!' Or: 'Her clothes are even cheaper than ours!' Sometimes they cry, they hug and kiss me. The younger generation is often emotional; the older generation often prays. I feel ready to make sacrifices and I am proud to do it for them, for that means everything to me. I always try to show the people that I love them and I want to give them hope. The warlords will never give us human rights, women's rights or liberation. But there are many, many secret heroes in my country. So we must make sacrifices, especially the educated, democratic-minded men and women of Afghanistan. No other nation can give us rights; the ongoing developments in Afghanistan and Iraq prove it. These rights will only be ours if we raise our voices together. Therefore I say: 'Alone I can do nothing. Join hands! Together we will win.'

Our people do not only want the withdrawal of the foreign troops from Afghanistan, they also want the Northern Alliance and the Taliban to be made powerless. The Afghan people are tired and have suffered a lot. After the Taliban and the Northern Alliance they thought: 'Maybe this time the international community will finally help us.' But no. After the 9/11 tragedy, the United States and its allies simply changed from doing business with the Taliban to the Northern Alliance. The United States is not in Afghanistan for our people. As in Iraq, they are here for their own strategic policies. If we did have a really democratic government, no neighboring countries, no superpower countries would dare to abuse our country or do things against our interests. The Northern Alliance people were there before the Taliban and before 1996 they killed 65,000 innocent people in Kabul alone. These people are in the pockets of the CIA and ISAF. They are puppets of foreign and neighboring countries.

The future of Afghanistan depends on its people. But at the moment we have jungle law. The Constitution is a beautiful thing in the hands of President Hamid Karzai and these warlords, but they deceive people around the world. Sometimes we say that President Hamid Karzai is only the 'Mayor of Kabul', because the Government of Afghanistan has no control outside of the capital.

If Parliament is like I described, then you should think to yourself: what is going on in the rest of Afghanistan? I told them: 'One day you might kill me. I am no better than my people, no better than any other democratic-minded person in my country. You killed them in the past and you still kill them today. But you can never hide the truth.'

Our Parliament is full of criminals and at least nine of them have been pointed out by Human Rights Watch as wanted criminals. Today they control Afghanistan and they are fascists like Pinochet, Khomeini, Mussolini and so on. They are a ruthless gang of killers. Many of them are responsible for butchering tens of thousands of innocent people in the past two decades.

These ministers and officials, they are lackeys, drug traffickers, war criminals and murderers. Let me name a few of the key power holders: Vice-President Karim Khalili, Ismael Khan, Izzatullah Wasifi, General Mohammed Daoud, Rashid Dostum, Qasim

Fahim and many others. They should all be removed from power immediately and put on trial for war crimes. How can we talk about democracy when our legislative, judicial and executive bodies are infected with the viruses of fundamentalism and drug mafia?

The abuse of forgiveness

A report by Human Rights Watch about war criminals in Afghanistan and the hanging of Saddam Hussein scared many Afghan criminals. But now they have even blocked any efforts to prosecute them. Under the name of 'national reconciliation' the warlord Members of Parliament have passed a bill based on which no-one can file a case or prosecute anyone for crimes committed in the past 25 years. Criminals forgive themselves! Only the United Nations protested, saying that to forgive is the right of the victims: Do you forgive these criminals or not? But our President signed this disgusting bill. Together with a few other Members of Parliament I raised my voice against it, but as the fundamentalist warlords hold over 80 per cent of the seats, the bill was easily approved. It provides amnesty to all criminals! But Afghan people who have suffered terribly in the past three decades consider this bill an abuse against them and they want to see these criminals prosecuted for their brutalities. That is the only way to experience a sense of justice and build a brighter future in Afghanistan. It offends millions of Afghans who have suffered and lost their loved ones and they are still waiting for the day of justice. Such bills officially sanction further human rights violations against our defenseless people.

Our Constitution says that we have freedom of the press, but even inside Parliament they beat up journalists! When Members of Parliament realized they could not silence me, they suspended me, which is an illegal act and against our right of freedom of speech. It's a good example of how undemocratic our Parliament is. They also demanded that I apologize.

'No, for telling the truth there is no need to apologize,' I said. '*You* should apologize for the many crimes you have committed and that you are still committing!' One Member of Parliament even threatened to kill me, saying: 'If you won't keep silent, I will use a suicide bomb and eliminate you.' Why do I receive these threats? And why do the people who are not in Parliament give me such strong support and so much solidarity?

Freedom of speech in Afghanistan is also a joke. During the passage of the infamous amnesty bill for war criminals, I had an interview with a local TV channel. They had also interviewed some other people including Abdul Rab Rasul Sayyaf, another Member of Parliament. He is one of the people responsible for killing many civilians in Kabul during the civil war. Even though he is a wanted war criminal, he is still very influential. The TV station broadcast an advertisement for the program a number of times in which they showed some parts of my interview. After this, Sayyaf himself called the TV station and threatened that if my interview was broadcast again, there would be serious consequences for the director. So they resorted to censorship and excluded me from the program. And this is not the first time. Many journalists are too afraid to report my comments and my voice is always being silenced.

The Afghan Government is so bad, that even for the four million refugees living in Iran and Pakistan it is unattractive to return and many more are still trying to flee the country. And besides supporting the Northern Alliance, the United States is even making underground efforts to include elements of the Taliban and Gulbuddin Hekmatyar in the Government. Gulbuddin Hekmatyar is one of the most wanted terrorists, yet his party was allowed to have 34 members in the Afghan Parliament. I keep saying that the US Administration has no problem working with pro-American terrorists and opposes only anti-American terrorists. So if any country really wants to be honest to us, first of all they must act independently. They must support the freedom-loving, democratic-minded people to enable them to fight fundamentalism and terrorism.

When I am back in Afghanistan, even in Kabul, it is so risky that I change houses all the time and need a bodyguard. Despite hating guns, I need to live under the protection of armed bodyguards to survive. When I leave my house, I'm not sure I'll make it back. And especially young children must not know that I am there, because you know what children are like. They tell easily to the neighbors, so how can you trust anyone? Sometimes I stay in the house of a supporter and I may be secure for two days, but it is different for each place. There are many threats, so it is very difficult. Now they are even searching my schedule and in Parliament they announced that I cannot go out. For the rest, I cannot tell the media what it is like.

Right from the beginning of my participation in Parliament, whenever I wanted to say things I was silenced. They turned off my microphone and threatened to kill me, because they are afraid to face an international court of justice. But I say: 'You can cut the flower, but you cannot stop the coming of spring.'

They are not happy about the fact that I go on trips outside of the country. I don't compromise, I speak out and don't keep silent and I am a woman. The fundamentalists are counting the days until they kill me, but I believe in and follow the noble saying of the freedom-loving Iranian writer Samad Behrangi: 'Death could very easily come now, but I should not be the one to seek it. Of course if I should meet it and that is inevitable, it would not matter. What matters is whether my living or dying has had any effect on the lives of others...' I love those words. And in Afghanistan there are many Malalais.

9

The Phoenix
Rearranges its Nest

Introduction

IN 1971 THE Persian monarchy celebrated its 2,500th anniversary
with the intention of demonstrating Iran's magnificent history
and its contemporary advances. Shah Muhammad Reza Pahlavi
held a three-day party at historic Persepolis with kings, ministers,
heads of state and dignitaries, sparing no expense. But many
also remember the event for its stark contrast with the poverty,
drought and malnutrition in many parts of the country.

The oil boom of the 1970s generated excessive wealth. For
some. But the benefits for normal citizens never materialized.
Not only that, the former *Iran Novin* (New Iran) party was
transformed into the *Rastakhiz* party, to which the whole adult
population was required to belong and pay dues. Pious Muslims
moreover were angered by the fact that in 1976 the Shah changed
the Islamic calendar to the Iranian solar calendar based on the
ascension to the throne by Cyrus the Great, so that 'Iran jumped
overnight from the Muslim year 1355 to the royalist year 2535'.

Iran was modernizing, women had a legitimate place in society and, although it was still the time of the Cold War, relations with both East and West were quite open. Some, however, saw the Shah as a puppet of the West and pointed out corruption, elitism and disregard for his own population. This was made worse by the activities of his secret police, over-ambitious economic programs and a general neglect of the real needs of the people at the cost of a small group of favored families. In the words of Ayatollah Ruhollah Khomeini, the Shah's greatest critic, he had 'embarked on the destruction of Islam in Iran'. No-one could foresee though, that the upcoming Revolution would plunge Iran into a situation that was incomparably worse.

Under pressure from US President Jimmy Carter, the Shah was reminded of the importance of political rights and freedom. For a while the Red Cross was allowed to visit prisons and 357 political prisoners were granted amnesty. This trend of liberalization however did not last. Opposition emerged from everywhere: constitutional monarchists, liberal secularists, Marxists and Islamists. From outside of Iran, various anti-royalist groups smuggled speeches of their leaders, recorded on audiocassettes, into the country. Many of these took their inspiration from Khomeini, who had been living in exile in France since 1978. Journalists from across the world found their way to him and his words became a regular feature in the media.

'My conscience is clear,' said Farah Pahlavi, the Shah's wife in a later interview. 'The Shah was an honest man without interest in material things.' But at that time, the Shah was seen as too remote from his people to understand their dissatisfaction. Demonstrations increased every day, setting the stage for a seemingly unavoidable change: the Iranian Revolution of 1979. After increasing calls for the downfall of the monarchy, Khomeini returned to Iran on 1 February 1979, only a few weeks after the Shah had left the country.

'What do you feel about returning after so many years?' asked a foreign correspondent during the flight. '*Heech*! (Nothing!)'

Khomeini said, a comment that most Iranians recall. As he descended from the steps of an Air France jumbo he was welcomed by millions of ecstatic Iranians. By the end of the year, Khomeini was Supreme Leader of the country under a new constitution.

A theocratic republic under the leadership of an 80-year-old ayatollah? This turn of events took many by surprise. Even the revolutionaries. The Revolution had been supported by many different groups of people, who were disillusioned from the moment it was a fact. And now they were in grave danger from what 'promised us heaven, but created a hell on earth'. Revolutionary committees in mosques, schools and workplaces became the 'eyes and ears' of the new regime. A time of arbitrary arrests, executions and confiscations of property began, to purge from society elements that opposed 'God's government'. Referenda for the new Islamic Republic and the new theocratic constitution were approved by 98 per cent of the vote.

A common concept was *gharbzadegi* or 'westoxification'. Western culture was seen as a plague or an intoxication that alienated Muslims from their roots and identity, something that needed to be expelled. Khomeini preached that Muslims should reject both Soviet and American influences: 'not eastern, not western – Islamic Republican'. He also developed the ideology of *Islamic Government, Guardianship of the Jurist*, the title of his book. Muslims, in fact everyone, required supervision from the leading Islamic jurists, like Khomeini himself.

When Muslim students took 52 hostages at the American embassy in 1979, no-one initially knew it would lead to a hostage crisis lasting 444 days. 'This action has many benefits,' said Khomeini. 'This has united our people. Our opponents do not dare act against us.' The hostages were eventually released, but the sanctions put in place by the United States are still in force. The hostage crisis was followed by the invasion by Sunni-Muslim Iraq in 1980, attempting to seize the oil-rich province of

Khuzestan and to destroy the (Shi'a) Revolution in its infancy. Thus began the eight-year Iran-Iraq War, one of the most bloody and destructive of the 20th century. Far from destroying the Revolution, it had the opposite effect. Iranians became fierce patriots, united against the external threat. Hundreds of thousands of lives were lost. The major 'result' was that the revolutionary forces solidified their control of Iran.

Among the many groups that had longed for a revolution to topple the Shah's regime were the Marxists. One of these was Monireh Baradaran, a 26-year-old sociology student at the time. But their hopes for freedom and justice were not fulfilled. A reign of terror began and it soon became clear that their demands would not be met. Monireh would find herself in prison for the next nine years.

Monireh Baradaran
Iran

'I wrote my memoir with shaking hands.'

Monireh Baradaran (born in 1955) had just finished her sociology studies when she was arrested for left-wing activism shortly after the Iranian Revolution. She now lives in exile in Germany and her book *The Plain Truth* was translated from Farsi into German and Dutch. Her articles are an exercise 'to give meaning to bad things'.

WHEN I FLED Iran and arrived in Europe, shortly after the fall of the Berlin Wall, I read and heard that the books that had not been allowed in Iran had been mandatory reading in eastern Europe for decades! And the reverse too: books that were easily accessible and widely read everywhere else had been forbidden. I then realized: the problem is not with the books. Whether it's Iran or eastern Europe, the problem is with the system that allows or disallows them. Books don't make revolutions. They're only there to make people think.

I was born in Tabriz, a city in the north of Iran. It's in a region called Azerbaijan, the Iranian side of the independent republic with the same name. My mother tongue is Azeri-Turkish, similar to the language spoken in modern Turkey. Our family lived in a reasonably big house and I had six brothers and sisters. None of us had rooms for ourselves. All my sisters and I slept in one room.

Outside there was a lovely garden where you could be on your own or play with other children. Nobody would disturb us there. And the garden was full of trees and flowers and there was a big pond, surrounded by potted plants. It was not very deep, but we could swim in it and enjoyed splashing around. There were also chickens and cats. It was customary those days that uncles and aunts lived next to each other, often only separated by one door. So there were a lot of children and it was very lively! There was no kindergarten; we just shared our time with other children. I was the youngest. My older sisters did play with me, but it was difficult to keep up as I was still very small. For them I was like a puppet to play with. But they took care to clothe me and to do my hair, something all of us enjoyed a lot.

But tragedy struck our family. My father died of cancer when I was 11. He had been ill for a long time, but I was not old enough to understand. It had a lot of consequences. My father had been the breadwinner, so now we couldn't buy food any more. In Tabriz there were no jobs, so we had to leave for Tehran, where my older brothers and sisters needed to find work. When we arrived at the end of September, schools had already started. I couldn't speak Farsi very well. In Tabriz we had learned Farsi at school, but I had always played with other children in our mother tongue. I spoke with a very strong accent and other children used to ridicule me. It's an experience that I remember to this day and I know how difficult it is for people who cannot express themselves in their own language. And that problem still exists in today's Iran. Farsi is the official language, but there are of course many different languages.

It was a depressing time. My mother, brothers and sisters had to find jobs and instead of a big house we now lived in a very small house. On the other hand, there were also good things. As a child, I picked up new things easily and simply accepted my new situation as it was. Within months my speaking improved. But around me, in our country, there were much bigger changes. At the end of the 1960s a period of modernization started. It began with little things. All kinds of new foods came on the market and the bread we used to bake in Tabriz was no longer available. And many traditional jobs disappeared. Before my father died he had been almost broke while working as a trader in the bazaar. But the pulse of the economy had moved outside the bazaars, where big shops were set up for all kinds of things like carpets, foods, fruits and so on. Most of it was imported from abroad. The bazaars are still there, but now they only exist as a symbol of the past and as something interesting for tourists.

Suddenly a lot of factories appeared and my brothers worked there as guards. There was also a whole wave of migration from rural areas to Tehran. The city grew in record time! And in society there were also big changes. Tabriz had been a very traditional city and women were not allowed to work outside of their homes. Yes, as teachers or nurses, but anything else was hardly possible. But in Tehran, my sisters did find work. This rapid separation from the traditions of the past was hardest for my mother, but she had no choice but to accept it. The younger ones welcomed it, however. What particularly impressed me was the greater freedom that I enjoyed. My mother had preferred me to go to a religious school and wear a chador, but she could not keep her children away from the influences of modern Tehran. Within a few years, the women in Tehran went onto the streets without chadors and without hijab, wearing Western clothes, especially the middle and upper class people. There still are some very traditional quarters in Tehran. But we said goodbye to tradition very quickly.

My underground brother

One of the biggest influences on my life was my elder brother Mehdi, who was killed 26 years ago. When I was a little girl, he was studying electrical engineering and working at an office at the same time. He was politically active, but underground. I had no idea what he was doing. He was in touch with the radical opposition movements and was one of the founders of the *mujahedin*, the Islamic armed resistance against the regime of the Shah. But before all that became clear, he was simply my older brother. He introduced me to many books and gave me newspapers to read. I enjoyed reading novels like Alexander Dumas' *Count of Monte Cristo*. It was so fascinating. I also read Tolstoy, Maxim Gorky and novels about utopian societies. My brother also encouraged me to write critical essays about what I had read. This was not easy for me as a young girl. The comics I skipped and I only read the serious political and literary articles! So his influence on me was very formative. After he had been imprisoned under the Shah, he distanced himself from religion and became active in the Marxist movement. Of course, like any other girl, I was raised in an Islamic society and in an Islamic family and I even fasted. But for me, Islam or no Islam, it played no role of any significance.

During my first years at university my orientation became leftwing, like many of my fellow students. Ever since the Russian Revolution of 1917 there had been Marxist trends in our society. And across the 20th century there had been a lot of Marxist intellectuals in Iran, inspired by the achievements of Marxism. Several Iranian political parties were based on the Soviet, Chinese and eastern European examples. There were simply a lot of Marxist groups, but they were always under a lot of pressure and many of them ended up in prison, whether under the two shahs or under the regime since the Islamic Revolution.

I was admitted to study sociology at Tehran University in 1974. Universities were – and still are – hotbeds of resistance, protests and places for reading and exchanging forbidden books. And as most of my family was politically engaged, I was very keen on these things. But by the time I started my studies, many of my family members were already in prison. Most of them were Marxists, some were religiously oriented and others were against the Shah. But in some cases they were simply in prison for reading a forbidden book! Anything, a book by Maxim Gorky or Lenin or even poetry, sufficed to put you behind bars! We didn't even know the criteria for what was allowed and what not. American novels were still acceptable, but even Iranian writers had gone underground. It made their books even more desirable.

Politically, I was against dictatorship and against fascism, meaning the Shah and the monarchy. Women's issues or feminism were not on the agenda yet. But it wasn't taboo either, because that had already been broken by the women who had gone before and had paved the way for women to study and so on. We also didn't have a clear concept of democracy. We were neither for nor against it. It was just not on our screen. The foremost things on our agenda were: freedom and justice. And, as I was one of the active students, whenever there was a demonstration, I would be in the front lines. I supported the idea of a revolution to bring justice to our society, because my strongest feeling at that time was that our society was characterized by injustice. There was such a big gap between the rich and the poor, it was noticeable everywhere.

During my studies I was also working in factories as a literacy teacher. I felt very motivated because I wanted to get to know the workers and to understand their problems, as they worked very hard for long hours. Later on, I worked as librarian in a public library in the poor city areas in south Tehran, where big families only had one room for everyone. And most of them had no drinking water; entire city areas used only one tap. Together with other students I also organized an independent library. This of course included forbidden books like *Mother* by Maxim Gorky, books by Bertholt Brecht and novels about social issues. We had no permission, so it was an ongoing fight with university authorities. But it was an adventure. And through these jobs I became aware of the fact that injustice was just round the corner. One of my favorite pastimes was mountain climbing, which we did in almost any area in Iran where there are mountains. It was the favorite activity of most of us who wanted to fight in some way, because this sport was such a great way to develop discipline and team spirit and to organize ourselves. It was fascinating to do.

Poor in a rich country

'There are only 40 families that matter in Iran,' we used to say. Those who had any power all had connections with the royal family. That was probably an exaggeration, but that is how it felt for most citizens. And this feeling was very strong, especially because Iran was not a poor country at all! OPEC had just been founded, the oil industry in the entire region was booming and the oil price skyrocketed. And next to oil, there were a lot of other natural resources like natural gas, coal and iron, the profits of which could very well have been used to fight poverty. That was one side of the medal. The other was that the rapid modernization imposed from above didn't include social values like democracy, tolerance or freedom of opinion. None of that. It only focused on technology, road works, and factories – on the economy, not on the culture.

Just eight months before the Revolution, in June 1978, I was arrested for the first time. I had tried to smuggle a pamphlet into jail for my brother. He had already been there several years and had been sentenced to life. At the universities there were a lot of pamphlets against the Shah and other things. This particular one was about a change of position from the organizations that my brother once belonged to. It would have been of interest to him to read it. I had folded the pamphlet into a towel, hoping that it wouldn't get noticed during our family visit. But it was an old trick and the guards soon found out. I was arrested and sentenced to two years.

Before my first interrogation, there was a man from the Red Cross who spoke English. He asked me: 'Do you need a translator?'

'No,' I said, 'I can manage with my broken English.'

He asked: 'Why were you arrested? And were you tortured?'

It was heartening, because it gave me some sense of security. As you can imagine, when going to an interrogation for the very first time in your life, everything is unclear and frightening. Will there be torture? Will they kill me? This time, I was in prison for only six months and then released and even my brother was too. But by the time of my second arrest, during the Iranian Revolution, there were no international observers from the Red Cross or Human Rights Watch. Before the Revolution, there were demonstrations against the Shah all the time. He gradually realized that he was very unpopular, but by then it was already too late. When despots hear they are unpopular, they just get irritated and punish those that speak their minds. For two years I was free, but from the moment the Revolution happened, everything changed for the worse.

From the first day the Revolution began, the motives and demands that had existed before – for freedom and justice – were distorted. That same day, they started doing exactly what they had accused the Shah of: arrests for political opinions, imprisonments, torture. But it was more sinister than before,

God's government

'As a man who, through the Guardianship that I have from the holy lawgiver (the Prophet), I hereby pronounce Bazargan as the ruler, and since I have appointed him, he must be obeyed. The nation must obey him. This is not an ordinary government. It is a government based on the Sharia. Opposing this government means opposing the Sharia of Islam. Revolt against God's government is a revolt against God. Revolt against God is blasphemy.'

Excerpt from a speech of Ayatollah Khomeini, when appointing Mehdi Bazargan as Prime Minister of the Provisional Revolutionary Government (1979-80).

because the new people in power claimed that they were doing God's wishes.

At the same time, many forces had been freed from their chains and they wanted freedom of opinion, freedom to establish political parties and so on. The Revolution simply had very diverse groups of supporters. Many were young people who had dreams, hopes and wishes. Yes, we wanted the Revolution to put an end to the wrongful policies of the Shah. But we *didn't* want to join the religious fanatics that took the Revolution out of our hands! No-one had counted on this happening. Perhaps that was our problem: we knew exactly what we didn't want, but we didn't know well enough what we did want.

Suddenly we found ourselves limited, forbidden and walled in. At first we had been so inspired that we celebrated the Revolution. But within days we were horrified. For two years we still had freedom to demonstrate or to distribute our pamphlets. But the space got smaller and every day we were attacked. First by Hizbullah, the Party of God, that could perhaps best be compared with the fascist period in Germany. They took their orders from the authorities, but the authorities never accepted responsibility. 'These are common people that oppose you,' they said. 'It is your problem, not ours.'

We had no support from above. The first victims were former Shah supporters. But it was so brutal! Every day there were executions, followed by front-page newspaper articles with their names and bloody pictures of their dead bodies. These people were our former political enemies, but we hadn't realized yet that their fate today would be ours tomorrow. It took time, because we had no sympathy for members of SAVAK [the secret police] or ministers that had been so bad for our country. But, regardless of their crimes, they were human beings and had a right to fair treatment and justice.

Islamic Revolutionary courts were established, taking their lead from Islam – from what Islam? The judge and the public prosecutor were one and the same person! These courts were presided over by mullahs from the holy city of Qum. They represent the Islamic wisdom reached in the 14th century, disregarding any achievements of the Enlightenment or afterwards. It was the kind of 'justice' that existed in medieval Europe during the Inquisition. Our space to maneuver diminished until it was our turn.

Mass arrests started happening. I always remember this period when seeing scenes about Chile and the putsch of Pinochet. Cars were stopped, people were searched and arrests could be based on something as innocent as wearing jeans. Even many schoolchildren were arrested. One of the preparatory stages of the Revolution was the Islamic Cultural Revolution, similar to the one in China. First, all universities were closed, enabling authorities to start a new form of education. Most professors and teachers were fired and when universities opened again, only those students were admitted that had 'survived' ideological examinations. Others got arrested, then tortured and executed. And due to censorship, many books disappeared and only those remained of which the contents were correct from an Islamic point of view.

Man hunters at the door

In October 1981, a few minutes before midnight, I had just gone to bed when I heard the bell downstairs. 'I am a friend of your brother!' an unknown male voice said that entered our apartment through the intercom. My eldest sister answered: 'My brother isn't here.' This was followed by a harsh voice: 'Open the door immediately!' We had no doubt: these were man hunters. In those days you would come across them everywhere. In the streets, they would stop innocent people and search their pockets and bags for suspicious objects. They would arrest you even for the smallest reason and immediately deport you. At night they stormed houses and apartments. Schoolchildren, students and intellectuals were their favorite prey. They entered. 'Dress up! You are arrested!' One of the men threw 'forbidden' books in a plastic bag. Another was a boy of only 17, who handled his pistol as if he were playing in a western movie. We were taken outside to a Landrover down the road. One of the men opened the door and said: 'Do you know these people?' I was horrified. My brother, his wife Narges and another family member were inside, blindfolded. The journey was short, after which we were pulled out of the car forcefully. From beneath my blindfold I could see where we were: the detention center of the Eshratabad Committee.

Narges and I were separated from the men. The next morning a guard woke us up and led us to a dark and damp room with another 15 women. I looked around. One of the women read my thoughts: 'There are not enough prison cells for all prisoners. That's why they're now also using bath houses.' I sat down next to them. Most of them were very young. They were schoolchildren and three of them came from the same school. The guard came in again and said: 'You can get your breakfast.' Two women returned with bread, sheep's cheese and a can of tea for the whole group. Next, we were allowed to go to the bathroom facilities. We had to put on our chador, take the slip of the chador of the woman in front of us, and walk like geese, one after the other. There was so much water on the floor that we were in it up to our ankles. But the women who had been imprisoned longer considered their three moments a day in the bathroom facilities as an outing and an opportunity to exchange information about the interrogations.

After our return, I was immediately called in for interrogation. I started to shake all over. A man took me to a cell bordering on a courtyard. First of all, he wanted to know the reason for my arrest during the regime of the Shah. After that he questioned me about a cousin.

'The SAVAK have killed him,' I said.

'Of course not. He has committed suicide.'

'They have never been able to prove that it was suicide. Besides, they tortured him terribly.'

But the man insisted he was right.

'What are you after?' I asked. 'Are you actually trying to justify the behavior of the SAVAK?'

He got angry. 'Get out! I shall come and get you later.'

At the end of the interrogation he put out a pen in my direction that I had to take by the other end. In this way, he was able to return me to my cell without having to touch me. The files that the secret service of the Shah, the SAVAK, had made concerning political prisoners had been taken over by the secret service of the Islamic Republic. They used the same information! But, despite that, many people were being accused of membership of political organizations they had never heard of. Or because they adhered to the Bahá'í faith. Some people even ended up in prison based on mistaken identity. Regardless, the interrogators forced them to make 'confessions'. But what could they possibly 'confess'?

'Your last diploma?' he then asked.

I lied and signed a paper saying 'high school.'

'Filthy liar,' he said. 'Didn't you study at university? For this lie you will get 60 beatings with a stick on the palm of your hand.'

I trembled. At the first hit I felt a burning pain, at the second I withdrew my hand. The interrogator asked for the assistance of a woman. She came in and held my hand in place. After another 10 beatings he said: 'I forgive you. The remaining beatings are acquitted.' It seemed like a farce. But when I looked at my hand, it was swollen and completely purple from the bruises. Sometimes we overheard interrogations or torture of other prisoners. One of the guards used to beat people so mercilessly, that he would get out of breath and literally gasp for air. A woman once fell to the ground moaning and her voice made us cringe. But the guard simply continued kicking and beating her. We had no choice but to listen, without being able to do anything about it.

My cellmate at that time was Manije. When she fervently prayed and read in the Qur'an, her face became radiant and she forgot everything around her. And while she prayed, I did exercises to stay fit. But over the course of three years she completely changed. She had written a 'declaration of remorse' and had become a *tawab*, a prisoner who had publicly denounced her political past and promised to serve Islam. After that, she collaborated with the prison authorities and even felt satisfaction at torturing and interrogating her fellow prisoners. What on earth had they done to her to cause such a change?

'I will tell everything!'

From the detention center we were transferred to Evin Prison. The moment we arrived, we heard a lot of screaming and the sound of whips hitting bodies. The screams came right through the doors. I was absolutely terrified. Evin was famous for its methods of torture and its name struck terror in everyone. This hell was just beyond imagination! I heard a man in the cell opposite, who was being whipped.

'Stop it, stop it! I will speak. I will tell everything!' The whipping stopped. With a broken voice he mentioned an address in Roudaki Street. Later that day I entered the bathroom facilities with other women, where we took off our blindfolds. It was the first time since my arrest that I had seen myself in the mirror. I was shocked. My eyes were deep in their sockets, my hair was disheveled and dirty and my face had sunk in.

After five days of waiting, I was finally sent for another interrogation. In the interrogation room I was pushed onto a table and immediately beaten.

'Why are you beating me? I give answers to your questions, don't I?'

'So that you won't forget where you are.'

What an answer! As if it was possible to forget what I had

seen and heard over these past days!

'Your identity is known to us' said the paper in front of me. 'Give an extensive and complete description of your activities'. When I had finished writing, I put my pen away. After a short pause, during which they read my declaration, they beat me with a stick and with their fists. I was screaming in pain.

An hour later I was brought back to the interrogation room again and told to sit down on a chair. I had to stretch my arm to the back over my shoulder, so that my hand was positioned between my shoulder blades. With my other hand I had to reach, so that the finger tips of my hands touched each other. I felt a terrible pain in my shoulder, but apparently that wasn't enough. I had to put my hands on top of each other and they were tied together. The interrogator took off my watch. This method of torture is called *qapan*. The pain soon traveled through my whole body. It seemed like time stood still. It felt like all the muscles and sinews were being torn apart one by one. I started sweating all over. Occasionally the interrogator would hit my hands and I was tied up like this for hours. It felt like I was on fire. I was thirsty and asked for water. 'Of course, madam, you just ask! I shall soon come with the *aftabe*.' So revolting! This was the water jug used for cleaning the anus after defecating.

At that moment, somebody else entered the room. The interrogator humbly greeted him. The man came to stand right next to me. From underneath my blindfold I could see that he was wearing the robes of a mullah.

'Who is this?' the mullah asked.

'The brother of this woman was our guest yesterday,' the interrogator said.

It was clear. My brother had been tortured by them the day before. Later I found out that he was executed 40 days after his arrest.

'Tell us where you have hidden the weapons. Then your hands will be untied,' said the mullah.

'You probably don't know my file yet,' I said. 'What weapons are you talking about?' I said with a sarcastic smile.

'As long as you don't confess, you will have to remain in this position,' he said and left the room.

Immediately after he had left, more whips lashed on my arms and hands. 'You slut! How dare you laugh in the presence of Hadj Agha? Do you have no shame?'

I don't know for how long we were sitting like this. Now and then he asked a question and one time he wanted to know whether I was prepared for an interview. I answered: 'But I cannot be that important, can I?' Following that, he dragged me off my chair and put me on my stomach on the floor. Another man was called in, who sat with his full weight on my handcuffed arms. That hurt so much that everything they had done before seemed insignificant. They put a filthy, stinking rag in my mouth and started whipping my legs. At every beating, my body jerked. Gurgling sounds emerged from my throat. Because of my intense breathing, the rag fell out of my mouth and suddenly my screams filled the room. Someone then threw a blanket over me. The man that sat on my handcuffed arms held my nose and mouth closed. I was suffocating. From sheer fear of dying I tried anything I could to free my mouth until I lost consciousness.

Scenes from hell

When I regained consciousness, the blanket was gone and the man was no longer sitting on top of me. 'Cover your head, you shameless slut!' I heard a voice from far away. 'Do you have no sense of decency?' I wanted to move my hands, but I couldn't because they were still cuffed. The interrogator then untied them and they fell down to the floor like lead weights. He shouted: 'Cover your head!' One time, when recovering after interrogations, I came past the lower floor of the prison, where there was a place for the sick and the infirm. Everywhere, on the ground, on beds, on stretchers, there were heavily tortured prisoners, blindfolded and with their legs and arms in blood-drenched bandages. Some held up a drip feed by themselves. It was a scene from hell.

When a number of prisoners were to be transferred to the Ghezelhesar prison, there was a farewell party in cell 7. I was also invited. We sang songs and some women recited traditional poems. After that, there was a little play about an interrogation. The cunning answers by which the prisoner outsmarted the interrogator caused hilarious laughter. One of the women present was Nayer, a renegade of Islam. She was sentenced to life. In a voice hardly audible through her tears, she told me: 'Once upon a time they brought me to an interrogation with other women. In the courtyard we had to take off our blindfolds. There were corpses hanging, dangling back and forth. These men had just been hanged. Their faces were blue and their swollen tongues were sticking out of their distorted mouths.' I felt sick at hearing this and we both started to cry. The next day we said goodbye and we all sang 'Kiss me for one last time'. This song has had a symbolic meaning for the Iranian resistance for more than 40 years. It's about a man that says goodbye to his wife before walking towards his inescapable fate.

Kiss me, for one last time

Kiss me, for one last time,
For I am going towards my fate.
The past has passed me by,
I am seeking my destiny today.
Kiss me, for one last time,
For at midnight
I have a rendezvous with my beloved...

Song by Iranian-Armenian singer Vigen Derderian (1929-2003)

The only 'man' on our department was a little one-year-old boy named Ali. People had been looking for his father, but they never found him. That's why they had arrested his mother, who had taken Ali with her into prison, as there was nobody else to take care of him. He was incredibly sweet. We all felt sorry for him, but our excessive attention didn't do him any good. Because of the pressure he became very nervous and difficult to handle. Later I would see many more women who were forced to keep their babies with them in prison. But a child reminded us of good things, which we needed desperately as we felt low and depressed most of the time. Another reason for our exhaustion was related to the great amount of camphor that was added to our food. A high dose of camphor affects the hormonal balances and can even reduce the reproductive hormones. A direct consequence of this was that many of us no longer had our period or only now and then, causing great psychological tensions.

There was only hot water three times a week, between 10 at night and 6 in the morning. To avoid fights during our nightly turns of washing, we had appointed two cellmates as shower co-ordinators. One divided the women of our cell into groups; the other was responsible for the remaining cells. We now had to share showers with four or five of us at a time, which made us expert at doing it in record time. Our movements had become very well orchestrated. While one woman washed her hair, another soaped herself and a third rinsed the shampoo out of her hair and so on. Thus, we profited in an optimal way from the hot water. For an outsider, our hectic movements must have looked like scenes from Charlie Chaplin's *Modern Times*.

In our cells it was always damp and our hand-washed clothes were always hanging in front of the windows to dry, so that it was half dark. On top of that we had lice, a present from the newcomers that had spent a long time, weeks sometimes, in corridors and interrogation rooms without having been able to wash or put on clean clothes. As soon as they arrived, their hair was cut short; they washed and treated their heads with DDT, a very poisonous chemical. But it worked. One woman, who had beautiful long hair reaching down to her waist, refused to sacrifice her hair. It was still full of lice and also kept other women awake, because we slept head to toe. Despite our efforts to convince her, she never gave up. After requesting for a long time for extra DDT, we finally got it. We treated our blankets and the carpet with it. After that, we were allowed to go into the courtyard. It had snowed. We hadn't been outside for months and our joy was indescribable. For the first time we felt happy again. We tumbled around like madmen, held snowball fights, rolled through the snow and enjoyed this unexpected freedom for as long as it lasted.

The 'Ku Klux Klan'

Meanwhile, the number of tawabs kept increasing. Some of them had even started whipping their fellow prisoners. And in our wing there were women who had been arrested, beaten and interrogated by their own daughters. Tawabs had to cut the umbilical cord that connected them with the past; the road back should be hermetically sealed. Some of them became so hardened, that they helped preparing executions and sometimes fired the first shots. Faranak, one of the tawabs, admitted it without shame. 'It is a great honor for us to do this. It is our sacred duty to eliminate atheists and hypocrites and it equals holy war. Islam forbids women to do holy war. That's why, unfortunately, we cannot shoot the convicted prisoners ourselves; the brothers do that. But we can participate in everything else, which makes us feel proud and happy.'

We were speechless. And then there were the 'angels of death' or the 'Ku Klux Klan'. These visiting tawabs didn't want to be recognized, so they wore a black stocking over their heads, covered again by their chador. Whenever they came, we had to line up. And if they recognized someone, they would be transferred, interrogated and executed. There were also male tawabs. They wore cardboard pointy hats with only two holes for their eyes. They too were sent to betray their former comrades.

Among the new prisoners were a mother and her daughter that I enjoyed talking to. The daughter was called Shahrnush Parsipur. She was 38, a writer with a sharp wit and a social democrat. The *hadj* once asked her for her political convictions, but couldn't understand what a 'social-democrat' was. He just scratched his belly with one hand and played with his prayer beads with the other. 'So, so, miss *loyal democat*, aha, miss *loyal democat*,' he said, after which he quickly disappeared.

One day, we heard that an interview would take place in our section. Musawi, a young mullah responsible for ideological re-education, held a microphone and challenged us to a discussion. 'You can be at ease. You may say anything without being punished for it.' But after hearing some of us speak, he lost his temper: 'You Marxists have fished up your conviction from the bottom of a bucket full of shit. You better shut up, because you're nothing but traitors!'

Musawi's 'free discussions' ended in disaster, but he insisted on more. He invited Shahrnush for a discussion about the chador. To our surprise Shahrnush appeared without the mandatory chador. When she passed rows of men, they started whispering. Musawi began: 'Now this woman has declared to be prepared to exchange views about the clothing regulations for Islamic women. Do not be cowardly. Participate in the discussion and make use of the freedom to express your views openly.'

'What kind of freedom are you talking about, if I cannot even decide how I dress?' Shahrnush answered.

'Then talk about wearing the veil.'

Shahrnush spoke about the historic development of women's clothing, the main purpose of which is to hide the shape of the female body from vision. Some 20 minutes passed. Musawi, however, hadn't understood a word of it. Instead, he began a story about sexuality and the arousal men feel at seeing a woman without a veil. He got so carried away by his own 'arousal theory' that he asked: 'If I get aroused because Shahrnush is in my presence without a veil, who is responsible for my arousal?'

Shahrnush refused to answer or lower herself to Musawi's level. We all understood why, but Musawi paid no attention, grabbed the microphone again and poured out another avalanche of nonsense over us. Afterwards, he believed that he had silenced Shahrnush by the excellence of his arguments. Wherever he went, he bragged about his 'accomplishment'.

Occasionally 'doctor' Hosseini came along. He was a tawab, but he behaved more like a guard. He didn't even inspect us and gave his standard diagnosis instantly: 'There's nothing wrong with you. You're completely healthy.' Or: 'Your complaints have no organic cause, but are neurotic in nature.'

We were not treated like human beings. And the words 'political prisoners' were never used. 'Hypocrites' and 'heathens' – that's what they called us. We were 'anti-social, foolish and hysterical troublemakers'. And I was a 'contra-revolutionary hardhead'.

This continuous pressure was hard to resist. 'If you stick to your political convictions,' the interrogator told me, 'you'll be executed. Your execution may be converted into life imprisonment if you take on a more moderate attitude.' After a long and soul-searching inner struggle, I decided to recite the daily prayers. I considered this as a capitulation, but it was the fear of death that kept me alive. When I bent forward during prayer I hated myself and I felt humiliated.

What Mother said

One evening, Abolghasem Sarhadizadeh entered. Under the Shah this man had been in prison because of his political-religious activities. But after the Revolution he was given important public positions and became a member of the committee responsible for the prisons in Iran. After a long speech on the corridor that few women cared for, he came to our wing. He greeted us and sat down on the floor next to my cellmate Gitti, who was, as always, crouched in a corner. We had no idea what the reason for his visit was. Finally he said to Gitti:

'What are your wishes?'

'Personally I have no wishes,' Gitti said.

He hadn't understood her very well and repeated his question. Then a young woman of only 20, who had a life sentence, harshly responded: 'There is no need that you ask us one by one after our wishes and problems. You have been in prison yourself, haven't you? You know what the official rights of prisoners are and how these are dealt with in the Islamic Republic. We demand the same provisions as you got when you were imprisoned during the regime of the Shah, enforced by strikes!'

Sarhadizadeh frowned and looked at the floor.

She continued: 'You chaired the committee for prison affairs and you know more than anyone else about the dismal situation here. What news could we possibly tell you? Would you like us to beg you for elementary rights like having warm water or a bathroom in which things function normally?'

Sarhadizadeh seemed to shrink. Insulted, he mumbled: 'I haven't come here for this kind of talk.' He left.

At times, prisoners were able to defy their oppressors. One of them, a woman we admired and simply called Mother, said to one of the guards: 'I am 50. And I don't feel like having some snot-nosed little bastard like you telling me how I should wear my veil!'

Then came the black summer of 1988. In mid-July we heard on the afternoon news that the Iranian Government had agreed to Resolution 598 of the UN Security Council. We should have been pleased about the end of the war with Iraq, but we waited nervously for what would happen. Ominously, Khomeini had said in a speech that day: 'I have drunk the goblet of poison.' He may have been referring to the Greek philosopher Socrates, but no-one really knows.

Those of us that were sentenced to the hereafter usually got a piece of paper on which they had to write their opinion about the mujahedin, the Islamic Republic and the principle of unlimited power of the clergy over the people. In the middle of the night we started hearing gun salvos. We counted single shots, because that was the number of persons executed. Sometimes a group of *pasdaran* – guards – would march across the courtyard shouting: 'Death to the hypocrites! Death to the unbelievers!' At first they had been volunteers to keep an eye on the resistance to the Islamic Revolution. But now they were engaged in making endless arrests.

Official Friday prayers were broadcasted at a deafening volume so that we couldn't hear each other speak. I recognized the voice of Ali Akbar Rafsanjani. His words hammered through our wing. He spoke about the 'eradication of the hypocrites', referring to the defeat of Iraqi soldiers and other opponents of the regime. 'We have bombarded them from the air and destroyed them all. It was a great victory over our enemies, and we all helped them on their way to hell.' One of the wives of the mujahedin had exploded a hand grenade close to her face. 'She wanted to make her filthy face unrecognizable,' he said. It sounded so aggressive that it made me feel sick.

Black summer nightmare

More and more people disappeared from our prison and other prisons. None of us could imagine the magnitude of the slaughter that was taking place. Was it possible that all those who went missing were being murdered? As we heard later, the authorities only informed family members months later about the fate of their sister or brother. Their standard statement was: 'This prisoner has been executed. You can take his belongings.'

Some people experienced such a state of shock that they never recovered again. Every bit of news about another person that was executed was another blow to us: Leila Hadjian, Ghamar Akzia, Effat Khoi, Mariyam Talebi, Sohaila Rahimi... More than 50 mujahedin from our wing and about 200 women of wings 1 and 2 were executed. We became so paralyzed that we couldn't even cry. Many of us suddenly developed heart conditions. My friend Goli said: 'In Evin Prison, it would be a luxury to die of a heart attack.'

In vain we looked for news about the mass executions of that black summer. Or was it only a nightmare? No-one could tell. Finally, the newspaper *Keyhan* published a reaction of the Ministry of Foreign Affairs in the winter of 1988. It was a reaction to a report of Amnesty International. The Ministry denied everything. The report mentioned the execution of single prisoners, but no mass executions. How was it possible they didn't know? Even though I was in a small cell, I felt connected to people in other parts of the world. I sympathized with the Palestinian people and with the miners in England and with progressive movements like the Sandinistas in Nicaragua, who had decided to take a peaceful road. But I felt as if the rest of the world had forgotten all about us.

Shortly after Khomeini's death on 3 June 1989, a new wind started blowing. In the autumn I was surprised by newspaper articles about eastern Europe. The countries behind the Iron Curtain showed cracks, the Berlin Wall fell and there was an uprising in Romania. All these events happened so unexpectedly that I experienced a lot of inner turmoil. I got hold of the Qur'an and started reading the story of Joseph and Solaycha, becoming engrossed in this love story.

'Aha! So we're reading the Qur'an again!' said the prison director, who had unexpectedly sneaked up on me.

'It was the only book I could find,' I said.

'We always take care that there is one in every cell, so that you may read it in silence.'

'Of course we only read it secretly. Otherwise you might get the wrong impression!'

Then he said he wanted to send us home and asked me for my decision. 'You must be prepared to sign the leave application.'

'Yes,' I said, and gave him my sister's phone number.

I could still not believe it, but on Wednesday 15 October 1990 I signed the papers. With my family I drove home through the empty streets of Tehran.

Only six months after my release I left Iran for good. There was no need for a visa for Turkey, so I flew there and straight on to Germany, where I requested asylum at the airport upon arrival. A new phase in my life began, and since then I have been living in exile. When leaving Iran I only had a few clothes in a small suitcase. But my memory and my thoughts were still intact. *Those* didn't need a suitcase. And that has helped me to find my way in Germany. Very quickly I started writing *The Plain Truth*, a memoir about my prison experiences that was also published in German and Dutch. I had already started doing so in Iran, but I had been censoring myself for fear that my notebooks would be found. That would have been very dangerous both for me and my family. I wrote with shaking hands. Altogether it took four years. Not the writing itself, but I needed many months of breathing space, because it forced me to relive my experiences all over again.

Since then, I have also written a book about the *Psychology of Torture*, which aims to understand the developments in the Iranian Republic from a psychological standpoint. It looks at the phenomenon of psychological reform, which really means brainwashing and deformation of people's minds. How do you create 'other' human beings – if the ones present are not 'right'? It relates to the *tawabs*. It is typical of ideological regimes. I also wrote *Truth Commissions*. And almost every week I write articles such as those about children, art, and women in prison. Studying social sciences again and writing were two dreams come true, because in prison you have no opportunity to train your thoughts.

What gives me hope are the current civil movements in Iran such as the One Million Signatures Campaign that demands equal rights for women. And there is also a very public campaign against the stoning of women. Yes, there are setbacks: arrests, trials, closures of their internet sites and refusal of their right to demonstrate and so on. But they persist. For a society in which women are treated as second-class citizens, these are hopeful signs. Other good signs are that there are workers' unions, student movements and movements of the peoples of Iran: the Azeris, the Kurds, the Baluchis and so on. In the past they tried to seek self-determination by taking up arms, but now they try to accomplish this through democratic means – magazines, internet, cultural centers, language courses and so on. When struggling in this way, they can also obtain more support, not

One Million Signatures Demanding Changes to Discriminatory Laws

'Iran is a signatory to the UN Convention on Civil and Political Rights and, as such, is required to eliminate all forms of discrimination. Based on these commitments, the Government of Iran needs to take specific action in reforming laws that promote discrimination'.
Monireh Baradaran

Iranian women's rights activists have initiated a nationwide campaign demanding an end to legal discrimination against women in Iranian law. The campaign aims to collect one million signatures to demand changes to discriminatory laws, following a peaceful protest that took place in 2006 on Haft-e Tir Square in Tehran.

The campaign aims to serve as a catalyst for social change and the elimination of injustice, ensuring that the needs of women are just from inside Iran, but also from abroad. I believe that every day the Islamic Republic is moving towards its decline and these movements are going in the opposite direction. They become stronger every day.

Why are people in politics so bad? Why do they not understand? When you have experienced many horrible things, you wonder why things are that way. But there are many good people in the world, including those who lost their lives beside me in prison. I'm against the foreign policies of the United States, but when I see how many Americans want peace and actively try to make a difference in human rights issues, there is hope. And in my neighboring country Afghanistan, where they speak the same language, Malalai Joya is doing great work. Such courage inspires me.

I must admit that my brother played a very important role and I still respect him to this day. He gave his life for his belief in

---

addressed at national policy level. 'Legal problems faced by women are not a private matter, but rather symptomatic of larger social problems faced broadly by women. In other words, this campaign is committed to carrying out bottom-up reform and to creating change through grassroots and civil society initiatives, and seeks to strengthen public action and empower women.'

From the start, it was assumed that the struggle for equal rights in Iran would be a 'lengthy, difficult and arduous process'. But through the power of numbers and the sheer energy of their activism, the campaigners hope to achieve their goals. Their demands do not contradict Islamic principles. In fact, Ayatollahs Sanei'i and Bojnourdi also advocate the need for reform. Not to do so would be contradictory to the basic beliefs of Islam. The campaign relies on face-to-face, door-to-door dialogue with individual women, but there are also seminars and group discussions in any public location imaginable.

From: www.change4equality.net

---

humanity and sacrificed his life for his ideals and his principles. I will never forget that. I see him as a phoenix or *simurgh*, the mythological bird in our literary classics. Perhaps Iran can arise again through the movements that are active today. But there won't be peace, unless this period of Iranian history is held to the light by a Truth Commission. Without it, our country cannot rise again like a phoenix.

Walls or Bridges?

---

1 'Investigation may be likened to the long months of pregnancy, and solving a problem to the day of birth. To investigate a problem is, indeed, to solve it.'

2 'We want to act according to the UN Declaration of Human Rights. We want to be free. We want independence in our country. We want freedom.'

3 'We have real enemies in the world. These enemies must be found. They must be pursued and they must be defeated.'

SERIOUS 'INVESTIGATION' went into checking the details of the foregoing chapters. The 'UN Declaration of Human Rights' was the backdrop for ascertaining whether the stories of the contributors merited inclusion. And the 'real enemies' are those that undermine human decency and dignity. There you have the hinge points of this book. But no, words are cheap and writing can be deceptive. Language can obscure just as much as it reveals. My entire first paragraph intentionally sails under false colors.

What were your first impressions when reading the quotations above? You might find one or two, or even all three statements commendable. But actions speak louder than words. Knowing that these statements are from Mao Zedong, Ayatollah

Khomeini and Barack Obama (in that order) might change your view. This highlights the potency of oral history. When telling your life story including all its background noises, it becomes more difficult to mold or manipulate the recipients' perception. Why? The story *is* you.

Ignorance runs faster than intelligence, or, as HG Wells said, 'history is a race between education and catastrophe'. Who will point out that our grasp of the world about us amounts to no more than postcard images? Hungry Africa, Turbulent Balkans, Skiing Switzerland. 'You don't live in a windmill,' an angered man told me. 'You don't wear clogs. You don't smoke marijuana. You don't visit the red light district every fortnight. You must be an impostor.' All right, I'm exaggerating, and people in other countries are perfectly aware that such notions about my country of birth don't correspond to reality. But if we don't try, we will think that some people are born terrorists or that China's Great Leap Forward 50 years ago actually was a great leap forward.

One day I spoke with a man who had been working for years as a trauma counselor in a conflict area with victims from both sides. But not too long into our conversation I had to take a break. I couldn't handle it. He had catalogued – in current terminology – more than 250 'enhanced interrogation techniques' in descriptive detail. One technique masqueraded as 'the submarine'. I leave it to your imagination. Talking with this courageous man was not the same as reading a report. It was like being dragged into a nightmarish world of depravity. He too could not continue. 'After the death of my own brother, it all rushed in. I had to stop.' The resulting article never managed to convey the harm and the personal traumas that last forever.

All right. Those are extremes. But when you are faced with real challenges, there is, as Youk Chhang points out, no refuge in neutrality. There, the consequences are immediate and inescapable. There is no prompter and no-one offers a handbook for the occasion. There is not the oversight of the reporter, the hindsight of the historian. Your 'privilege' of first-hand experience develops in a completely different way. When watching starving people on television, we bear hunger very easily. But the moment it touches us personally, when it is our own child, everything changes.

Often, the truth is slow to catch up with reality. No-one in their right mind supports throwing stones at moving cars without any concern for the lives of their passengers. It's unthinkable and irresponsible. But in East Turkestan, oppressed by China since 1949, Uyghur boys throw stones at Chinese jeeps, just as Palestinian boys do at Israeli patrols. The context changes the meaning of the act. Sometimes the catching up never takes place. But as a matter of principle, it should – remember your child, one paragraph ago. 'Their rights are our rights' said the Introduction. In Bassam Aramin's story it was: 'your child is our child'. The issues of the laogai in China, child prostitution in Thailand or differently-abled people in South Africa do not require intellectual brilliance, but simply following through existing agreements. It is not more words we need. Taking a position on these matters is an ability worth exercising. An ability everyone has.

On the ground, in the middle of real events with real people and all their strengths, weaknesses, oddities and peculiarities, all is not what it seems. In that respect, neatly packaged writing, like the chapters in this book, offers an illusion – or at best a 'reconstruction'. One can only hope that this book faithfully represents the 'construction' underneath, especially as our memories and perceptions are subject to change. We rearrange our mental library all the time. This takes on even more surprising aspects when people from opposing views end up in exile in the same country. As passport holders of their new Australian, Canadian or Norwegian nationality, the preceding context fades and is somehow 'cured' by the host nation. By extension, this means that the ills of the world can be remedied if we ourselves choose to 'host the cure', a deliberate rearrangement of our mental library as exemplified by the agents of change portrayed in this book.

Our conscience and consciousness are not set in stone. What we found reprehensible in the past may appear commendable in the future. But we have been entrusted with the ability to distinguish between morality and perversion, between justice and foul play. 'We need bridges, not walls,' said Rami Elhanan. Building those bridges will take more than *Nine Lives*. Let us act upon our conscience, and not be fooled by words.

Peter Braaksma

Further Reading

Afghanistan; Malalai Joya
www.malalaijoya.com
Coll, Steve, *Ghost Wars* (Penguin Books, 2004)
Gannon, Kathy, *I Is for Infidel* (Public Affairs, 2005)
Kolhaktkar, Sonali & James Ingalls, *Bleeding Afghanistan: Washington, Warlords, and the Propaganda of Silence* (Seven Stories Press, 2006)
Schroen, Gary C, *First In: An Insider's Account of How the CIA Spearheaded the War on Terror in Afghanistan* (Ballantine Books, 2005)
Woodward, Bob, *Bush at War* (Pocket Books, 2003)

Cambodia; Youk Chhang
www.dccam.org
Chandler, David, *Brother Number One* (Silkworm Books, 1999)
Ponchaud, François, *Cambodia Year Zero* (Holt, Rinehart and Winston, 1977)
Power, Samantha, *A Problem from Hell: America and the Age of Genocide* (Harper Perennial, 2003)
Short, Philip, *Pol Pot: The History of a Nightmare* (John Murray, 2004)
Ung, Loung, *First They Killed My Father* (Mainstream Publishing, 2000)

China; Harry Wu
www.cicus.org
www.laogai.org
Bergsten, C Fred, Gill Bates, Nicholas R. Lardy & Derek Mitchell, *China: The Balance Sheet* (Public Affairs, 2006)
Jung Chang, *Wild Swans: Three Daughters of China* (HarperCollins, 1991)
Jung Chang & Jon Halliday, *Mao: The Unknown Story* (Vintage Books, 2005)
Laogai Research Foundation, Laogai Handbook 2005-2006 (2006)
MacFarquhan, Roderick (ed), Timothy Cheek & Eugene Wu, *The Secret Speeches of Mao: From the Hundred Flowers to the Great Leap Forward* (Harvard University Press, 1989)
Mao Zedong, *Quotations from Chairman Mao Tse-Tung* (Foreign Languages Press, 1966)
Wu, Hongda Harry, *Bitter Winds: A Memoir of My Years in China's Gulag* (John Wiley & Sons, 1994)
Wu, Hongda Harry, *Troublemaker: One Man's Crusade against China's Cruelty* (Chatto & Windus, 1996)

Costa Rica; Oscar Arias Sánchez
www.arias.or.cr
www.armstradetreaty.com
www.controlarms.org

Arias Foundation for Peace and Human Progress, *The Arms Trade Treaty (ATT) and Central American Existing Law* (2006)
Arias Foundation for Peace and Human Progress, *Arms Trade Treaty: No More Arms for Atrocities* (2005)
Arias Sánchez, Oscar, *Horizons of Peace* (Arias Foundation for Peace and Human Progress, 1994)
Control Arms Campaign, *AK-47: The World's Favorite Killing Machine* (2006)
Isacson, Adam, *Altered States: Security and Demilitarization in Central America* (Center for International Policy, 1997)

Iran; Monireh Baradaran
www.campaignforequality.info
www.iranrights.org
www.meydaan.com
www.we-change.org
Baradaran, Monireh, *Plain Truth: Surviving in a Women's Prison in Iran* (in Dutch: De Naakte Waarheid; Greber, 2001)
Ebadi, Shirin, *Iran Awakening* (Rider, 1997)
Khomeini, Ayatollah Ruhollah, *Islam and Revolution I – Writings and Declarations of Imam Khomeini* (1941-1980) (Mizan Press, 1981)
Nafisi, Azar, *Reading Lolita in Tehran: A Memoir in Books* (Fourth Estate, 2003)
Nemat, Marina, *Prisoner of Tehran: A Memoir* (Free Press, 2007)

Israel / Palestinian National Authority;
Rami Elhanan / Bassam Aramin
www.combatantsforpeace.org
www.theparentscircle.com
Antonius, George, *The Arab Awakening* (first published 1939; Simon Publications, 2001)
Avnery, Uri, *Truth against Truth* (Resource Center for Nonviolence, 2007)
Fisk, Robert, *The Great War for Civilization* (Fourth Estate, 2005)
Hass, Amira, *Drinking the Sea at Gaza* (Holt Paperbacks, 1996)
Karpf, Anne (ed), Brian Klug, Jacqueline Rose & Barbara Rosenbaum, *A Time to Speak Out: Independent Jewish Voices on Israel, Zionism and Jewish Identity* (Verso, 2008)
Kurzman, Dan, *Soldier of Peace: The Life of Yitzhak Rabin* (HarperCollins, 1998)
Neumann, Michael, *The Case against Israel* (CounterPunch and AK Press, 2005)
Pappe, Ilan, *The Ethnic Cleansing of Palestine* (Oneworld, 2006)
Reinhart, Tanya, *The Road Map to Nowhere* (Verso, 2006)
Sa'di, Ahmad H & Lila Abu-Lughod (ed), *Nakba: Palestine, 1948, and the Claims of Memory* (Columbia University Press, 2007)

South Africa; Chaeli Mycroft
www.chaelicampaign.co.za
Geralis, Elaine (ed), *Children With Cerebral Palsy: A Parents' Guide*
(Woodbine House, 1998)
ICON Health Publications, *The Official Parent's Sourcebook on Cerebral Palsy*
(2002)
Stepanek, Mattie JT, *Just Peace: A Message of Hope* (Andrews McMeel
Publishing, 2006)

Thailand; Sompop Jantraka
www.depdc.org
Gardner, Howard, *Five Minds for the Future* (Harvard Business School Press,
2007)
Sorajjakool, Siroj, *Child Prostitution in Thailand: Listening to Rahab* (The
Haworth Press, 2002)
Steinfatt, Thomas M, *Working at the Bar: Sex Work and Health
Communication in Thailand* (Ablex Publishing, 2002)

Index

About the *New Internationalist*

The **New Internationalist** is an independent not-for-profit publishing co-operative. Our mission is to report on issues of world poverty and inequality; to focus attention on the unjust relationship between the powerful and the powerless worldwide; to debate and campaign for the radical changes necessary if the needs of all are to be met.

We publish informative current affairs titles and popular reference, like the *No-Nonsense Guides* series, complemented by world food, fiction, photography and alternative gift books, as well as calendars and diaries, maps and posters – all with a global justice world view.

We also publish the monthly **New Internationalist** magazine. Each month tackles a range of subjects, such as Afghanistan, Climate Justice, or the Economic Meltdown, exploring each issue in a concise way which is easy to understand. The main articles are packed full of photos, charts and graphs and each magazine also contains music, film and book reviews, country profiles, interviews and news.

To find out more about the **New Internationalist**, subscribe to the magazine, or buy any of our books take a look at: **www.newint.org**

Look out for the other **World Changing** title – *People First Economics*.